The Challenge of Attachment for Caregiving

D1147684

The Challenge of Attachment for Caregiving describes a theoretical model for the development of caregiving that complements and also extends attachment theory. The model highlights the conditions under which adult caregivers can remain in a state of arrested development, impairing their own ability to give care and resulting in attachment problems for those who seek care from them. It shows how insecure attachment in childhood and adolescence impedes the development of caregiving and how, in times of crisis, even securely attached individuals need appropriate support in order to sustain their capacity to give effective care.

Constructing a systemic model of the self, the authors place the instinctive systems for caregiving and careseeking (attachment) within a theory that relates them to other systems of the self, such as the systems for sharing interests, sexuality and for self-defence. The model describes the interplay between these goal-corrected behavioural systems. Because it includes the defensive mechanisms and strategies which an individual values most, it is particularly helpful to the therapist in understanding the interpersonal processes between people who are seeking to influence each other's behaviour. It is presented in a form that enables the therapist to formulate hypotheses about a client's predicament and their way of relating to the therapist and then explore and test these hypotheses in the course of therapy.

Drawing on many years' experience as clinicians and researchers, **Dorothy Heard** and **Brian Lake** explore in depth an aspect of human development which has profound implications for our future survival. Presenting its own challenge to both theory and practice, this book offers students and practitioners a new perspective on attachment.

The Challenge of Attachment for Caregiving

Dorothy Heard and Brian Lake

London and New York

First published 1997
by Routledge
11 New Fetter Lane, London EC4P 4EE

Simultaneously published in the USA and Canada
by Routledge
29 West 35th Street, New York, NY 10001

Typeset in Times by Routledge
Printed and bound in Great Britain by
Hartnolls Ltd, Bodmin, Cornwall

British Library Cataloguing in Publication Data
A catalogue record for this book is available from the British Library

Library of Congress Cataloging in Publication Data
Heard, Dorothy, 1916–
The challenge of attachment for caregiving / Dorothy Heard and Brian
Lake
Includes biographical references and index.
1.Attachment behavior. 2.Caregivers. 3.Psychotherapist and patient.
4.Object relations (Pychoanalysis)
I. Lake, Brian, 1922– . II. Title.
RC455.4.A84H43 1997   96–29387
616.89'14–dc20   CIP

ISBN 0–415–14017–X (hbk)
ISBN 0–415–14018–8 (pbk)

Contents

Part III Principles of therapy guided by an attachment-based theory of caregiving

Acknowledgements

We are both fortunate to have had two such outstanding figures as John Bowlby and Harry Guntrip as our mentors. One of us (D.H.) had the incomparable experience of being supervised by and attending the seminars given by John Bowlby during the early sixties when he was developing the ideas expressed in his trilogy and finding scientific evidence to support them. His ideas resonated with an intuitive sense of how people relate to one another and his conceptualisations made this wordless understanding tangible. A somewhat similar experience took place for the other author (B.L.) during and after a training analysis with Guntrip, which began in the final stage of Guntrip's own analysis with Winnicott which succeeded his earlier one with Fairbairn. The opportunity to be closely in touch with Guntrip's warmth, profound understanding and clarity of thought was an indelible mutative experience. We express our deep gratitude for having had these maturative experiences.

Many people have contributed to the production of this book. Some have borne patiently with us during its production, others have helped us clarify our ideas. We express first our very real gratitude for the support given by members of our families who come into both categories. We particularly wish to thank Barbara Lake who, as someone with long experience in higher education and an author herself, read and advised us on early drafts and gave us invaluable help and time in compiling the index. We owe another considerable debt of gratitude and many thanks to Helen Heard who generously, light-heartedly and consistently gave us invaluable assistance over the presentation and production of the manuscript. We also owe her special thanks for having identified several passages where the meaning was unclear or ambiguous, for whose correction she made appropriate and creative suggestions.

Our friends in Swaledale have also contributed by their willingness to join with us in our particular interests. We are especially grateful to the Reverend Frank Lindars and to the late Colonel Donald Humphries who over a period of two or three years discussed with one of us aspects of the book, including the nature and function of ideals, from their own professional experience in two significant institutions. In a less structured way our farmer friends have educated us in the types of attachments and caregiving commonly seen in sheep and in dogs.

Of the many colleagues who have shown a supportive and constructive interest in our views on attachment and caregiving we give special thanks to Professor Ian Sinclair, Ms Una McCluskey, Dr Celia Downes and Mrs Lisa Millar of the Dept of Social Work and Social Policy of the University of York, to Dr Mary S. Moore of Boulder Colorado, to Dr Jeannette Josse of Cambridge, to Dr Celly Rowe of the Psychotherapy Department, Leeds Community and Mental Health Services, Teaching and NHS Trust, and to Dr Ruth Sims and the team at the Beech House Clinic, Wakefield. All of them in different contexts have questioned our views in supportive and companionable ways. They have inspired us to continue a search for patterns that clarified clinical issues.

We are also greatly in the debt of Mrs Margaret Walker, Librarian of the Tavistock Library, and the library staff for their valuable assistance given freely and generously in helping us chase down references.

We are very appreciative of the opportunity given to us by Mr Gary Burns to quote from and use the study reported in his unpublished MSW thesis.

We are grateful to the Hogarth Press for permission to quote from John Bowlby's publications.

Part I

The conceptual base for a theory of companionable caregiving

Chapter 1

A caregiving focus to an extension of attachment theory

This book is written by practising psychoanalytic psychotherapists with a background in medicine and psychiatry. We are writing for members of the caregiving professions who are interested in exploring the nature of caregiving and the circumstances in which it appears to succeed or fail. It is interesting that among the range of theories centred on the development of human beings and 'the self', the capacity for caregiving has been taken as implicit and until recently has attracted little attention in its own right.

Most therapists are aware that the predicaments brought by patients or clients are often centred on failures of parental caregiving. They are also aware that parents are often ineffective caregivers because their own upbringing had not encouraged the development of caregiving abilities. In the relative paucity of theoretical explanations of how the capacity to give care develops, we have put forward a theoretical model of caregiving that is based on Bowlby's model for instinctive behaviour and is complementary to his model of attachment and attachment behaviour. It draws into one theoretical frame a number of recognised clinical and empirical findings that have a crucial bearing on the development of the capacity to give effective care, to which the phenomenon of attachment in the form of careseeking is a major challenge.

After surveying recent literature on interpersonal phenomena, we continue to hold the view already set out (Heard and Lake 1986) that Bowlby's (1982) theoretical model of instinctive behaviour, of which caregiving is a component, is the most solid theoretical foundation available for understanding how the relationship a child has with his parents can affect his well-being and the unfolding of his developing sense of self. Bowlby's attachment theory of careseeking matched by caregiving has relevance for many species and has generated a flood of research, although his model for instinctive behaviour (Bowlby 1982) has remained virtually unused by therapists, despite it being a response to Freud's (1925a) lament that no adequate theory of instincts existed.

Although Bowlby's model is primarily focused on attachment, it can readily be adapted to explain other aspects of instinctive behaviour. We use it as a foundation on which to construct a theoretical model with a range of psycho-biological systems whose functions enable individuals, within definable environmental limitations, to survive with a range of competencies that enable them to enjoy interests and friendships and to rear children who can in their turn become effective parents.

BOWLBY'S MODEL FOR INSTINCTIVE BEHAVIOUR

Bowlby's model for instinctive behaviour was influenced by psychoanalytic object relations theory, ethological concepts, general systems theory, and control and information theory. He presented a view of psycho-biological systems that defines their functions and their goals. An important part of his theoretical statement is that an individual is motivated by the activation of one or more of his instinctive behavioural systems to reach its goal, when the behaviour is terminated and the motivation is switched off. Many instinctive systems undergo developmental processes that lead them from simple to more complex forms. They are all activated in specifiable circumstances and they revert to a state of quiescence once the goal of the system (which is distinguished from its function) has been reached.

INSTINCTIVE BEHAVIOUR WITHIN RELATIONSHIPS

Bowlby brought relationships into his model for instinctive behaviour with the idea that behavioural systems can be complementary. By this he meant that an individual whose attachment (careseeking) system has been activated is unable to reach the goal of receiving care without the co-operation of a caregiver, and vice versa. When the caregiver fulfils the current needs of the careseeker, both partners feel satisfied, the goals of their respective systems having been reached. At that point the careseeking system of one and the caregiving system of the other become quiescent.

By introducing the concept of complementary goal-corrected

systems, Bowlby implicitly brought into his model the idea that some behavioural systems have goals that we make explicit by referring to them as either interindividual, interpersonal or interdependent. Reaching these goals can be seen as a social act. These systems stand in contrast to other systems whose goals can be described as intra-individual, intrapersonal or independent, that is to say, they can be reached without the help of another person and are associated with personal (individual) competencies rather than those that are social. Both kinds of system are present in our model of a systemic dynamic caregiving self. To avoid discussing whether non-human primates can be described as having a self, we use the terms interpersonal and intrapersonal only when talking about human beings and the human self. We use the terms inter and intra-individual when discussing these systems as they are shared by human and non-human primates. We like the term interdependent goal for systems with complementary goals, but think that its opposite, independent, can give a false impression of being able to do without other people.

To return to interindividual systems, should caregivers fail to meet the needs of careseekers, the latter cannot experience the goal of careseeking, and commonly become frustrated and then depressed. What happens when each partner is failing to reach their goals, and what is happening to their respective caregiving and careseeking systems, is increasingly being researched and understood in both non-human primates and human beings. In human beings, three common behavioural outcomes can be seen:

1 conflict, with each partner attempting in various ways to influence the other to meet his demands for satisfaction;
2 the apparent submission of one to the demands of the other; and
3 negotiations to reach a compromise, so that the loss of what is desired by both partners is minimised if not avoided. It is a common experience that this latter outcome does not come about unless one partner (the parent, when adults and young children are involved) is able to suggest a compromise, or make issues of reality clear, without being drawn into a controlling or compliant pattern of relating.

Bowlby rounded out his model by including in it:

1 the innate ability to construct internal working models of the environment, and of the self interacting with aspects of the

environment and with other people. These models are used for making plans and decisions about future action;

2 the mechanisms of psychological defence by means of which the pain of failure to reach the interpersonal goal of careseeking is mitigated or avoided; and

3 a view of the nature and function of affects, feelings and emotion.

In exploring the field of information processing, Bowlby noted that people discard much of the information to which they are exposed, but are alert to any that refers to themselves. He also noted the stability over time of early working models of self and attachment figures. He gave an explanation of the effects on children when parental figures insist that their account of an event is true, when the parental account contradicts what the child has actually witnessed or experienced. He developed this issue in his lectures 'On knowing what you are not supposed to know and feeling what you are not supposed to feel' and later gave them to a wider audience (Bowlby 1988). He considered that the outcome of this kind of experience can be the formation of multiple working models of the self and attachment figures which can give rise to the formation of multiple personalities. This view is explored by Barach (1991) and Liotti (1992).

In adding these aspects to his description of instinctive systems, Bowlby created an opening for the expansion of his model, and left a number of issues to be developed. For example, despite his acute awareness of the anxiety, anger and despair which is aroused when attempts to achieve the goal of the care-seeking (attachment) system fail, and of the joy, the sense of security and freedom to explore when the attachment bond is maintained or renewed, he did not commit himself to a description of the blend of feelings, thoughts and urges that make up an individual's subjective experience of reaching or failing to reach the goals of careseeking and of caregiving. Nor did he make explicit the ways in which the development and functioning of interpersonal and intrapersonal systems are affected by the values and ideals held by parental figures and by peers, and by the ideals a person develops (once old enough) on their own.

This book marks a second stage of extending Bowlby's ideas by focusing on the concept of supportive companionable caregiving. In the first stage (Heard and Lake 1986 and Chapter 5), we introduced into the concept of an attachment dynamic (Heard 1978), a second pair of goal-corrected interdependent systems – the systems for exploratory interest-sharing between peers. We used findings from the Strange Situation Test (Ainsworth *et al.* 1978) to point to the circumstances in which unmet careseeking needs are most likely to override an individual's exploratory and interest-sharing behaviour. We described the ways in which the experience of reaching, or not reaching, either of the two pairs of interpersonal goals can affect a person's mood, sense of competence, self-esteem and general well-being. We showed how an internal caregiving system can develop through using internalised working models of self and attachment figures, and can reduce the need for proximity to caregivers when attachment behaviour is aroused in older children and adults.

At that stage we had not conceptualised in any detail a model for a self and were aware that our concept of emotive messages (whereby people make others aware, mainly through non-verbal signals, of the relationship they want with others) had not gone far enough. For example, we did not discuss the phenomenon of social referencing (see Chapter 8); nor did we discuss the physical and psychological effects of being shamed and/or overexcited. We had not considered the relations between Bowlby's instinctive systems and how individuals come to construct a hierarchy of passionately held values and ideals some of which are discovered personally, but many of which are transmitted by others. And finally we had not considered important differences between systems that maintain physiological and psychological homeostasis and those that carry forward processes of growth and development.

Since finishing our paper in 1985, we allowed our separate capacities a free rein to search for information that is relevant to these concerns. The new literature that we found the most seminal described research findings that filled conceptual gaps or set out ideas that drew us to explore and clarify our intuitive understanding. They included:

1 Stern's (1985) work on attunement and the studies by Trevarthen (1979) and by Murray and Trevarthen (1985) on intersubjectivity;

2 MacLean's work (1990) on the non-verbal signals by means of which humans and non-human species convey relational intentions to one another, and a clutch of writings on biological psychology, notably the papers on the psycho-biology of attachment and separation edited by Reite and Field (1985); and

3 Sperry's (Sperry 1990, Trevarthen 1990) view that the neural infrastructure of any brain process mediating conscious awareness is composed of elements and forces which give rise to simple–complex systems arranged in a hierarchy of levels of organisation; and that consciousness is an emergent self-regulatory property of neural networks which enables them to reach certain built-in goals. Genetic instructions set adaptive goals which give the organism intricately co-ordinated forms of action and categories of experience. Sperry's mentalistic viewpoint and his concept of hierarchies of simple–complex systems that play a part in expanding subjective consciousness provide individuals with a measure of freedom from reacting to stimulus-bound responses. That is to say, rational thought can influence instinctive behaviour in such a way that innate survival behaviour is influenced by the use of human cognitive capacities.

We also reflected on Gilbert's views (1984, 1989, 1992) on depression and suffering. We kept abreast of the burgeoning attachment literature, especially the work of Mary Main on the disorganised child and her adult attachment interview. We noted Kagen's (1994) views on the self and on temperament, and the views of the authors assembled by Chance (1988). We have also noted recent advances in psychoanalytic thought and current views on moral behaviour. The picture of a self and of instinctive partnerships described in this book reflects the integration of this kind of information. It forms the second stage of an extension of attachment theory which we hope will provide a fuller understanding of the effects of the phenomenon of attachment upon the development and functioning of the caregiving system.

To construct the theory we have focused on interpersonal phenomena that psychotherapists are most frequently called upon to understand and handle in the course of their clinical work. We describe them in concrete terms from a subjective point of view that takes into account 'Who does what, to whom, and when?' and 'What does it make the individual feel?' In developing the theory, we have used a mixture of anecdotal evidence from clinical experience and research findings. However, we rely on research studies to correct and develop this theory's explanatory power through the exploration of theory-based hypotheses. Such findings will either support aspects of the theory or will point to the direction in which it needs to be reconstructed or discarded.

THE PLAN AND CONTENT OF THE BOOK

In order to tell a coherent story, we have divided the book into three parts. In Part I we set out the conceptual base on which we have constructed a theory of companionable caregiving, before showing in Part II how we use this information to construct the theory. Part III describes how the theory can be used as a guide when working with clients.

Following this introductory chapter, we describe the studies of MacLean on the evolution of non-verbal signals, which also point to the evolution of caregiving, and a primate pattern of relating in which dominant/submissive patterns are a prominent feature. We then describe studies (primarily those of Trevarthen, Fernald and Stern on the non-verbal communication of mothers and infants) to suggest the evolution of a uniquely human pattern of relating which is phylogenetically in advance of the patterns of non-human primates. Here caregiving is more supportive and companionable and, when caregiving is on this level, dominant/submissive patterns are not used to a significant degree. From this perspective, we move on to describe Bowlby's model for instinctive behaviour and the extensions which we added in 1986. We end the first part with a chapter on Sperry's views about how brain is related to mind and his concept of high-order systems which enlarge human consciousness and free individuals from impulsive instinctive behaviour.

The second part discusses the construction of the theory of caregiving. It begins with a categorisation of instinctive goal-corrected systems according to their functions. In the course of so doing we distinguish four behavioural systems with interpersonal goals: caregiving, careseeking, interest-sharing and sexual. This chapter is followed by one which reaches a personal level by showing how behavioural systems are represented in relationships between specific people. The part ends with three chapters showing the way in which individuals evaluate the experience of reaching, and not reaching, the goals of the behavioural systems and the part played by aspirations and ideals to develop and maintain their personal and social skills and well-being.

We open Part III with a chapter giving an outline of the various psycho-biological theories of human nature commonly used by therapists, which we consider to be supportive of the integrative attachment-based object-relational theory of caregiving on which our therapy is based. We move then to discuss assessment by presenting a frame of reference which enables the assessor to arrive at a view about: one, the way prospective clients relate to the assessor and talk about their life; two, the number and quality of their affectional relationships; and three, how far they are seeking to reach maturational ideals that help them move on to new stages of development and how far their maturation is impeded by aspirations that can be described as non-maturative defensive idealisations. In the final two chapters we discuss how a therapist can put into effect the principles of professional caregiving we have found to be therapeutic.

THE LANGUAGE IN WHICH THE BOOK IS WRITTEN

Although we inevitably introduce specialised terms, our aim has been to use words as defined in standard dictionaries and avoid language associated with theories that we have not used. Such language (e.g. libido) inevitably carries meanings that are specific to the theories to which it belongs, and which tend to override any other meaning placed on it. We have sought to find terms which will keep the focus on what is happening between each individual person when two or more people interact with one another. This has led to some longwinded terms such as supportive companionable relating and caregiver/careseeker partnerships. In the interests of making the text less cumbersome we have used abbreviations to some extent (e.g. SC relating for the former and CG/CS for the latter) although we find them unattractive and mechanical. For the same reasons, we have, after careful consideration, reverted to the convention of using he, him and himself to refer to unnamed individuals who may be of either gender.

In the interests of brevity we do not argue the merits of one position against another in relation to a phenomenon or a topic that is not as yet adequately understood, such as consciousness, emotion, the regulation of the affective state of one person by another, or attachment. Having indicated that no one really knows, we adopt a well-argued view. Similarly, we have not reviewed the attachment literature but hope that the references we have cited, either in the text or in appendices A, B and C, will open this information to those who wish to follow a particular issue further. In the interests of clarity we generally describe therapy and relationships from the point of view of one therapist and one client seeking to keep the focus on what is happening as each person interacts with the other. The principles we outline apply to threesomes and groups but the inter-actions are more complex and beyond the scope of this book.

We have used the terms caregiver and careseeker as generic appellations applicable across the lifespan and in general talk about parental figures rather than mother or father or attachment figure. We are aware that in so doing, we might be seen as underestimating the importance of the mother and the maternal relationship. We have adopted this terminology for reasons strongly supported by our clinical experience and by Bowlby's observation that infants become attached to a small hierarchy of attachment figures and that the person at the top of the hierarchy is the person who looks after the infant the most, who may not be the biological mother.

We consider it is supremely important for clinicians not to over-look the role of fathers by concentrating too hard on that of moth-ers. Thus when it is uncertain who contributes to the blend of caregiving provisions required by careseekers of any age, we consid-er it safer to use the term parental, or sometimes attachment figures, to refer to those within the hierarchy of attachment figures. Our clinical experience has been that adults of both sexes suffer from not having had sufficiently fatherly persons within their attachment hierarchy.

We also use the term therapist in a generic sense to refer to any-one, of any professional discipline or calling, who has a professional therapeutic relationship, in its broadest sense, with another person or group. We finally decided to use the term client rather than the familiar and more strictly accurate term patient. We have never yet met a client who was not a sufferer. But being called patient has overtones of being a sick person who will be treated by an expert. The image of clients we wish to promote is of currently distressed people, to whom we give respect and the kind of help that can enable them to know themselves better and become more confident and effective in handling the vicissitudes of life.

THE PLACE OF EVOLUTIONARY THEORY IN THE MODEL FOR COMPANIONABLE CAREGIVING

By integrating Bowlby's model and his stance on evolution, with MacLean's work, we have given an evolutionary perspective to our view of human nature. We do not suggest how evolutionary change or genetic mutation may come about, nor how interaction between genes and between genes and their environment can affect the way in which the self functions. We have taken to heart the warning given by Jones (1993), who wrote that Mendel was triumphantly right, but only up to a certain point. When molecular biologists became able to construct genetic maps, Mendel's beautiful story about peas turned into a murkier tale which looks more like pea soup. This theory may well suffer the same fate should research turn up evidence that contradicts the assumptions we have made.

Chapter 2

Caregiving from an evolutionary perspective

The biologists who first studied how animals in their natural habitat fed themselves, found mates and reared their young did more than put a new subject – ethology – on the map. In recognising stable patterns of behaviour, such as nest-building, or the retrieval of wandering young, they advanced the scope of evolutionary thought to include the study of the evolution of behaviour as well as of physical characteristics.

When members of other disciplines began to think about human beings from an evolutionary point of view, they studied the issue from their own perspectives. For example, socio-biologists are concerned with exploring behavioural phenomena to show whether they carry a potential for increasing the chances that individuals will hand on their genes to the next and succeeding generations, defining an increase in the chances of handing down one's genes as 'inclusive fitness'. Their approach is largely statistical, being concerned with probabilities rather than absolutes. Although many interesting findings are coming to light, it is clear, as Gilbert (1992) points out, that the relationship between being successful at a socio-cultural level and at a biological reproductive level is complex.

Gilbert (1992: 119) and Bailey (1987) describe a third line of interest which was introduced by MacLean (1990). He began from the propositions that the primate line evolved from previously evolved species and that all animals, including primates, retain vestiges of earlier designs. Some vestiges appear but then disappear (for example, the human embryo goes through a phase when gill slits appear and disappear); others remain functional.

THE CONCEPT OF THE TRIUNE BRAIN

MacLean considers that an examination of the brains of existing vertebrates and fossil records indicates that the human forebrain has evolved while retaining, in functional forms, features of three evolutionary formations: the reptilian brain (the oldest), the paleomammalian brain and the neomammalian brain. He considers each differs radically from the other two in their chemistry (that is to say in the relative amount of specific neurotransmitters and the effects of hormones) and in their structure, while in an evolutionary sense they are countless generations apart.

At the phylogenetic levels at which all three formations are present, they interact with one another and function as a 'triune brain', each formation receiving a greater amount of information than it would by functioning alone. However, MacLean considers they can also function somewhat independently, which is an issue we take note of in Chapters 3 and 8.

THE AIM OF MACLEAN'S RESEARCH

MacLean's desire was to identify forebrain structures that lie behind the signals that species from reptiles to humans use to communicate their intentions to each other. He studied these signals (which he termed prosematic communication) before and after stimulating or interfering surgically with specific sites in the brain. He searched for structures at each phylogenetic level that could be said to be the neural substrate for stable behavioural patterns of the kind observed and studied by ethologists. In addition he was interested in distinguishing the kind of mentation associated with each of the three formations as well as the relations between emotion and thought.

MacLean distinguishes three forms of mentation: protomentation, which covers rudimentary thinking at the level of the oldest formation or R-complex; paleomentation, governed by the emotional thinking of the paleomammalian brain; and the rational mentation governed by the neomammalian brain (the 'youngest' formation). He considers (1990: 424) that mentation involves self-generating neural replica of events either as they first occurred or in some rearrangement. How the original ordering of the events is preserved, that is to say memorised, or is reordered, that is to say imagined or conceived, remains a mystery. MacLean, concluding that rational and emotional mentation can occur somewhat independently, puts forward the view that – granted that emotion and thought are complementary – there is evidence that the two can occur independently because they are products of different cerebral mechanisms (MacLean 1990: 12).

MacLean takes a Cartesian view of emotion (1990: 425) and reserves the word to refer to the behaviour that conveys the affective state of another person. He sees affects as imparting subjective information to an individual that is instrumental in guiding the behaviour required for self-preservation and the preservation of the species. Affects differ from simple sensations in that they always have the distinction of being subjectively agreeable or disagreeable; they are never neutral.

Given the division of affects into pleasurable and unpleasurable, MacLean looked for a workable classification to use in various investigations, including the identification of brain mechanisms underlying psychological experience. He settled for dividing affects into three classes:

1 basic affects – these derive from signals concerning different kinds of internal states identified with basic bodily needs for food, water, air, sexual outlets, sleep;
2 specific affects – this term applies to perception generated by activity in specific sensory systems (e.g. odours, tastes, sights, sounds and touch). Some are unlearned, others are conditioned; examples are fragrant or foul odours, harmonious or noisy sounds, which include aesthetic affects identified as agreeable, or disagreeable kinds of music and other forms of art; and
3 general affects – these are distinctive feeling states that do not depend on immediate experience, since, owing to mentational processes, they can persist or recur after the fact. General affects apply to feelings aroused by other individuals, situations or things. They are informative of threats to the individual or species, when they are classed as disagreeable, whereas those feeling states that signal the removal of threats and the gratification of needs are agreeable. We consider that this view of affects is compatible with the one subscribed to by Bowlby (see Chapter 4). It is further discussed in Chapter 9.

We now turn to MacLean's studies on signalling. We found that reading them, after we had been excited and intrigued by Stern's views on attunement and tuning and Trevarthen's studies on intersubjectivity (see Chapter 3), gave us new ideas about the non-verbal aspect of the communications we had described as emotive messages (Heard and Lake 1986). MacLean's findings opened vistas for us in how to conceptualise a social self. His work suggested that humans have two patterns in relating to one another which can be used in everyday life. One pattern is derived from functional vestiges of the phylogenetic past. It has been shown in MacLean's description of the signals of the rainbow lizard and those of the squirrel monkey. The second pattern is much more recent. It is introduced in the next chapter by describing evidence from the separate studies inspired by Trevarthen and by Stern. Their findings suggest to us that humans have evolved forms of non-verbal communication that draw people into co-operative contact with one another, while retaining patterns of dominating and submissive behaviour that is inherited from non-human primates and ultimately from reptiles.

SOCIAL COMMUNICATION AT THE LEVEL OF THE R-COMPLEX

The reptilian brain (or the R-complex as MacLean prefers to call it) is a collection of structures, generally known as the striatal complex. It lies just above the mid and the hindbrain. The forebrains of lizards and turtles are little more than the R-complex. Birds, lower mammals, higher mammals, non-human primates and humans have, in that order, increasing quantities of forebrain.

Animals deprived of a forebrain, who survive the operation easily (e.g. frogs, lizards, pigeons, and rabbits), remain able to respond to various forms of sensory stimulation and to move in a co-ordinated fashion. But if left to themselves, undisturbed by an external stimulus, they stay on the same spot and unless artificially fed, die of starvation. What is striking about the loss of the forebrain in any animal is the removal of any kind of spontaneity and any evidence of the capacity to learn from experience. Physiological functions are organised in such a manner that they can be carried out automatically, but only in a highly protected and nurturant environment.

MacLean used the rainbow lizard to study communication at the level of the R-complex. Social encounters between conspecifics are conducted through four displays. These are:

1 two types of assertive display which seem to signal possession and achievement;

2 two varieties of challenge: challenge at a distance which warns intruders that they are trespassing and close-in challenge which may progress to combat;
3 submissive displays that signal compliance and forestall or terminate the punishing and potentially deadly actions of a dominating animal;
4 the displays of courtship and mating. As rainbow lizards are mute, signals are conveyed by body posture, colour and size. These lizards change colour according to temperature, sex, maturity and status and have the ability to puff up certain features which humans consider makes them look more menacing.

Interoperative behaviour sited in the R-complex

MacLean has used the term 'interoperative' to refer to six forms of behaviour, which are seen in several contexts and are not regular characteristics of a recognisable form of social behaviour such as fighting or courtship. MacLean sees it as a form of behaviour that does not actively interoperate with other forms of behaviour. Rather it is the brain itself that is interoperative in this respect. We understand MacLean to be saying that the ability to be (say) repetitious is a capacity of the brain, sited in the R-complex, and used instinctively to potentiate social behaviour. MacLean gives persuasive examples suggesting that interoperative behaviour is a characteristic of all primates. He shows that these capacities do not operate if specific areas in the squirrel monkey's striatal region are ablated. The list of interoperative behaviour includes:

1 The routinisation of behaviour, which seems to regulate in a round-the-clock sequence the order in which actions occur.
2 Isopraxis or performing in a like manner. MacLean uses this term in preference to a word such as imitation to avoid causal overtones. Isopraxis does not imply interaction.
3 Repetitious behaviour refers to the repetitive performance of a specific act. As an example, he cites the compulsive hand washing of Lady Macbeth, adding that unless one is familiar with the play the repetitious hand washing would have little meaning. He notes that, in many circumstances, the animal who makes the largest number of displays wins out.
4 Re-enactment is distinguished from repetitious behaviour. It applies to a repeated performance of a number of acts that are

meaningfully related. A repeated performance of the entire scene in which Lady Macbeth compulsively washes her hands would be a re-enactment.

5 Tropistic behaviour refers to the fixed action pattern response to a specific characteristic of an entity. For example orange coloured objects attract the attention of cock lizards and are often eaten. It seems that only the presence of orange colour makes it possible for a cock lizard to recognise another territorial male.

6 Deceptive behaviour, which needs no description, is considered to be one of the most important for survival.

A picture of the social life of a rainbow lizard

MacLean's gives a racy account of a day in the life of an alpha male rainbow lizard which allows comparisons to be made between the social exchanges of the lizard and those of the squirrel monkey. He describes a drama of a male lizard facing sequences of relentless challenge from a marauding male lizard that, despite counter-challenges, ends with the deposition of an emperor and the defection of his retinue to a new master. All this happens with expressionless faces within a shared feeding area and the confines of a personal territory, in which there are places for the rigidly kept routines of the lizard's daily life: crevices in which to sleep, separate areas in which to warm up or cool off (cold-blooded lizards can be active only after absorbing heat from the sun), to feed, to eliminate, and in which to establish lookout posts. The picture is of a highly defensive creature, bound by stereotyped pre-programmed fixed action pattern responses, whose co-operative social behaviour is so limited that the term, a member of a society, has a hollow ring. None the less, despite the unfriendly messages given in assertive and challenge displays and the way in which individuals with blemishes are harassed and eliminated, some proximity to familiar members of a species is tolerated. Many varieties of lizard live in colonies of about forty, made up of a male 'tyrant' with a retinue of females and juvenile and subdominant males. The alpha male tyrant defends his territory from marauding males, but seldom from one of his own retinue. Colonies stay together when there is enough food and water. Males announce the possession of a territory by giving the signature display. They maintain a dominance hierarchy through threats backed by challenges, which are met either by submissive appeasing signals, by flight or by counter challenge which often become fights. Strangers are not tolerated, males often joining to attack them. Apparent mimicry (isopraxis) occurs regularly, but without evidence of interactions, although lizards sometimes help each other shed their skins. As regards parenting, females occasionally help young emerge from the egg, but that is as far as it goes. Hatchlings give appeasement signals from the start and keep out of sight. If not, they are liable to be devoured. Co-operative activities are limited to courtship and mating, and play is absent.

Although feelings and thinking – as humans know these terms – play no role, lizards are highly responsive to their environment from the moment of hatching. Observations suggest that their repertoire of signals is used with some guile and that experience plays a part. MacLean considers (1990: 216) that since these displays involve conspecific recognition, the R-complex must play a role in this psychological function. Thus the showing of the submissive signal soon after hatching brings up the unanswered question – what is it in the R-complex that makes dominant adults stop in their tracks when they see conspecific submission? Whatever it is, a lizard's unlearned behaviour is organised into responses that enable them to keep enough proximity and prosocial behaviour for their genes to survive. But this is true only so long as the environment does not deviate from narrow definable limits.

THE SECOND FORMATION: THE PALEOMAMMALIAN BRAIN (THE LIMBIC SYSTEM)

Coincident with the evolution of mammals, there was an increase in forebrain material, largely due to the evolution of the great limbic lobe described in 1878 by Broca. The limbic area is considered to be the centre for emotional life, adding sensations to the inbuilt stereopathy of the R-complex. It is involved in some forms of memory and is currently the focus of active investigation. Knowledge of its functions has been enriched by reports gathered from sufferers from psychomotor epilepsy (temporal lobe or limbic epilepsy). No other clinical condition provides such extensive information about the cerebral structures involved in the subjective experience of emotional feelings.

Psychomotor epilepsy is characterised by automatic acts in the form of partial, unremembered seizures rather than generalised convulsions. These are preceded by an aura during which vivid emotional states are experienced which are remembered. The seizure sometimes appears to enact the aura, and the patient may become angry and abusive if the seizure is interrupted. Auras and seizures are associated with abnormal bioelectrical discharges and may be reproduced by stimulation of an appropriate area within the temporal cortex of the limbic system.

A list of auras provides a tantalising catalogue of well-known experiences, without any information about how they are organised to fit everyday life. The commonest auras are those of fear, which are associated with sinking feelings, a sense of loneliness, and impending death. There may be a compulsion to flee, or to seek someone's help. Some of these are associated with paranoid feelings of people saying derogatory things (MacLean 1990: 440). MacLean describes five other kinds of aura:

1 feelings of desire;
2 dejected feelings associated with a sense of homesickness and of sadness;
3 gratulant feelings associated with enhanced awareness, satisfying recognition, achievement, success and discovery (labelled the 'eureka' feeling);
4 feelings of affection described as 'like on a sunny day when your friends are all around you';
5 feelings associated with anger (but not of anger itself) in which the aura can be experienced as 'a funny feeling in my stomach of seeing something dead and disgusting'; but before, and during the aura, the patient acted in an angry and irritable way. Sexual feelings are also mentioned and a free-floating sense of intense conviction can be experienced. But in the records of several hundred case histories, there were no auras suggestive of feelings or sentiments related to parental behaviour, which suggests that parental feelings are not so discreetly localised.

The three divisions of the limbic system

The limbic system has three divisions of which the first two are, phylogenetically, the older, and are connected with the olfactory (smell) apparatus. They are present in reptiles who show some parental propensities. One division contains the amygala, presently the focus of much investigation into its role in the organisation of emotional expression. Primates, who have had this area removed surgically, become docile, more solitary and show less care for young. They pick up and eat objects indiscriminately and are unable to defend themselves. The removal of the second or septal division interferes with sexual efficiency and some forms of parental type behaviour.

The third division of the limbic system and its relation to careseeking, caregiving and play

The third or thalamocingulate division of the limbic system, has no counterpart in true reptiles. It bypasses the older olfactory system, is connected with vision and hearing and has many connections with the neomammalian cortex (the third formation). MacLean considers that it is concerned with behaviour that characterises the evolutionary transition from reptiles to mammals who have young who require care after birth. The 'new' behaviour is concerned with: nursing and other activities that characterise parental care, which also require hormonal input; audio-vocal communication for maintaining contact between mothers and offspring; and with the capacity for play which takes place between the young of non-human species, rather than between adults or parent and child.

Although some workers (Steklis and Kling 1985, Hadley 1989) give other impressions, MacLean has confidence in his conclusion that the third division of the limbic system is involved with the organisation of interindividual feelings, with motivations which are concerned with caregiving, careseeking and play. He considers that all its wide connections to the neomammalian cortex, to the older portion of the limbic system and to the viscera make it possible to integrate information from the private world of personal experience with that from the world at large, thus placing an affective stamp upon every perception. He suggests that emotional thinking, conveyed in the form of psychological information, provokes physiological changes within the organism (MacLean 1990: 23), and that this phenomenon contributes to a sense of self.

Communicative behaviour of the squirrel monkey

MacLean chose the squirrel monkey as an experimental animal because it is a primate whose brain is of a size that allows serial sections for microscopic examination to be cut through the entire brain – a labour-intensive procedure but an immensely powerful tool in brain research.

This monkey shows four basic displays – aggressive, courtship, greeting and submissive. MacLean considers that aggressive displays are comparable to the challenge of the lizard, and at least one form of greeting display is the counterpart of assertive or signature displays of the lizard. The circumstances in which the displays are evoked are similar to those of the lizard, but the actions through which they are expressed differ somewhat. For example, in the greeting display, the male squirrel monkey displays an erect penis which is anatomically impossible for the lizard, and females show genital tumescence. Decourcy and Jenssen (1994) discuss the confusions and difficulties that can arise when a label is assigned to a display on the basis of the social context in which the display appears. None the less, MacLean's work using stimulation and systematic ablation of specific areas of the brain shows that the four displays of the squirrel monkey originate in or are closely associated with the R-complex.

MacLean also discovered that the intensity with which the greeting display is given is associated with the time of year. He found significantly fewer displays in March and more in January (when these monkeys were heaviest and the males were in a spermagenic phase) which suggests that neuroendocrine factors and brain mechanisms (so far unidentified) are involved in the integration of penile erection with a social, and apparently non-sexual, activity.

The outstanding difference between the signals of the lizard and those of the squirrel monkey is the appearance of vocalisations. Six kinds have been identified, of which some are linked to the R-complex displays. MacLean reviews the complicated evidence about the location of the neural substrates responsible for each call in rodents and monkeys.

He is definitive about the siting of the separation cry. Its production appears to depend on a continuous band of limbic cortex contained in the supragenual, pregenual and infragenual cingulate cortex (1990: 405–6). There are close associations with nuclei involved in the perception of pain which gives pointers to the pain of separation. Mothers respond to the cry, which MacLean considers ranks as the earliest and most basic mammalian vocalisation, and maintains maternal–offspring contact. Mothers also have a 'chuck', to which infants respond. It is used when an infant is slow to feed and it alerts the infant to return to the mother. MacLean implies that the site for the maternal chuck (like the site of the calls by which young peers appear to keep in contact) is also in this 'youngest' limbic division. The existence of the 'chuck' implies that the adult squirrel monkey not only has a neural substrate for recognising the separation cry but a behavioural response whose end result is to re-establish contact with the infant.

The place of the R-complex and limbic system in the regulations of proximity and distance between non-human primates

The vocalisations of the squirrel monkey suggest that their main function is to maintain proximity between mother/infant partners, peer playmates, and partners in sexual interactions. Calls such as shrieks and cackles seem to reflect isopraxis between members of the troop and are associated with raised arousal levels and with fear. However some 'cackles' and a 'growl' seem to enhance a coercive process leading to maintaining distance and the state of submission.

There is evidence that the neural substrates responsible for both affiliative behaviour and play have no representation in the R-complex. There is also evidence that play takes place only at times when young, group-living primates are not alarmed and have no physiological needs (e.g. for food or shelter). Although young primates soon begin to work out with one another what dominating and submissive relationships are all about, early engagement in play seems to contribute later in life to the stability of the adult group.

Distancing, which seems to preserve personal space and occurs between adult and adult, and between adult and young who are beyond early infancy, is achieved through threats of challenge and also through rejection by mothers of young, whenever they seek a degree of closeness that is unwelcome to their mothers. Following maternal rejection and after dominating threats, the young will return to the vicinity of mothers (when they will often be accepted). Following threats, adults often return to give attention to a higher-ranking adult (a phenomenon described by Chance (1988) as reverted escape).

Overall, thanks to their limbic-based signals and their degree of mentation, integrated with harsh, ruthlessly observed R-complex rules about respecting the personal space of those with higher status, squirrel monkeys can maintain a balance between closeness and distance. Using these patterns of relating, mothers look after and protect their young, but this decreases as they become able to look after themselves and find companionship in the company of their peers. Adult males do not attack females or immature males – a protective function which in MacLean's view merits investigation. Nulliparous females, who themselves have been mothered, give care to an infant. Young peers can enjoy episodes of play during which they learn the skills that are needed to survive when adult. Individuals of all ages can enjoy periods of affiliative prosocial exchanges.

MACLEAN'S THIRD FORMATION: THE LEVEL OF THE NEOMAMMALIAN CORTEX

The neomammalian cortex is, phylogenetically, by far the 'youngest' formation. In humans it has the same general structure as in other animals, but is unique in terms of weight and surface area relative to weight. It has extensive connections with the limbic system, especially with the third division. And, which we consider is of special import, the neocortex has direct connections to the R-complex and to the viscera. The latter suggests relations between psychosomatic symptoms and neocortical activity. The neomammalian cortex is seen as an executive area which helps mammals adapt to the environment. It is not the source of signals though it certainly affects signalling. We come back to this issue in later chapters.

CAVEATS REGARDING THE NEURAL SUBSTRATE OF SOCIAL BEHAVIOUR IN PRIMATES

MacLean and other neurobiologists investigating social behaviour have voiced caveats about what is safe to conclude from current findings. Steklis and Kling (1985) draw attention to the large range of social conditions within which different kinds of non-human primates live. Many small nocturnal prosimians and the large orangutan have a near solitary existence. There is the highly specialised monogamous gibbon, the siamang, and some small New World species, the comparatively gregarious, large heterosexual bands of the baboons and macaques, as well as the group-living gorillas and chimpanzees. In their view such diversity in social structure opens the possibility of diversity in the underlying neural mechanisms. MacLean supports this idea when he speaks of differences in the findings of neural investigative procedures in primates kept in various kinds of captivity and those who have lived in the wild. And he refers to genetic, physical, neurological and behavioural differences between two varieties of squirrel monkey. He also points out that the counterpart of the reptilian forebrain in mammals is not the same as that in extant reptiles. To think that it is would be equivalent to saying that the modern automobile engine is the same as that of the first car. Nevertheless, the whole thrust of his argument is that across species, while there are many differences, there are well-marked phylogenetic similarities.

The complexities of the field are compounded by the tendency of workers with different interests and different theoretical paradigms to direct their attention more to some data than to others. This tendency allows a variety of pictures and models of what may be happening in particular areas of the brain to be constructed. MacLean has focused on phylogenetic changes in communicative behaviour and on discovering links between the function of the behaviour and locations in which such signals appear to originate. He presents the thalamocingulate gyrus as the site of the behaviours of nursing, careseeking and play although he does not discuss affiliative behaviour as it is defined by Steklis and Kling, nor the phenomenon of attachment. Steklis and Kling (1985) wish to understand the psycho-biology of attachment and separation, which leads them to a different focus and the proposal that the orbital frontal and anterior temporal cortex as well as the amygdala establish and maintain affiliative bonds in non-human primates. Hadley (1989), from another perspective, provides psycho-biological evidence of a general 'motivational' apparatus. She has found correlations between definable subsystems of this apparatus and the five motivational systems proposed by Lichtenberg (1989).

Our own focus is on the meaning, for humans, of the evidence presented in the next chapter showing that there are substantial differences, as well as close similarities, between the non-verbal signalling of human and non-human primates; and also on the effects on the physical and psychological development of individual human beings, of living within partnerships in which supportive companionable caregiving can take precedence over dominating or submissive caregiving. Speaking as psychotherapists, who have not researched in the field of brain physiology – and therefore lack the intimate knowledge of those who have – we realise that MacLean's views on the siting of caregiving in the same region as careseeking and play between peers may have led us to take a conceptual risk. We consider his findings support the idea that, although other areas take part in caregiving, some important organisation of caregiving is carried out in the thalamocingulate division of the limbic system, and that this region is central for three instinctive behavioural systems that all have interpersonal goals.

Chapter 3

Human non-verbal and symbolic communication and two alternative patterns of relating

In the last chapter we mentioned that MacLean's studies considered alongside those of Stern (1985) and of Trevarthen (1979) suggested that humans have two distinct patterns of relating: one carried over from their primate ancestry and one which evolved at the time when the human brain took on human characteristics, and the development to adult status became much slower and required prolonged caregiving. We note that humans have additional limbic-based and neocortically potentiated, non-verbal patterns of relating that non-human primates show in more rudimentary forms. In this chapter we discuss evidence for this hypothesis, beginning with Trevarthen's concept of primary intersubjectivity.

TREVARTHEN'S CONCEPT OF PRIMARY INTERSUBJECTIVITY

A high level of affective mutuality is achieved between mothers and their eight-week-old infants when they are in separate rooms but can see and hear one another through a television circuit (Murray and Trevarthen 1985). There is no opportunity for touch or smell but the infants are in a state in which they have no immediate physiological needs. When asked to talk to their babies in these circumstances, non-depressed mothers use intonations and rhythms that give their voices a pitch contour that is the same across cultures, despite differences in maternal speech. Mothers speak to their babies in 'motherese' (Fernald 1985, Murray and Trevarthen 1985), a form of communication which has a warm, unanxious 'I am interested in what you are doing' quality. Mothers appear to enjoy making sense of what the baby is 'saying' or doing, and enjoy the infant doing something which has not previously been a part of his repertoire. 'Aren't you a clever boy/girl' is one of the commonest remarks made by mothers across cultures. Infants pay attention to their mothers and express themselves with a wide range of facial expressions and gestures and an extensive repertoire of babbles. Both mother and baby smile at each other frequently, each taking turns to 'talk', with matching gestures and facial expressions that bring a conversational element into the exchange of body language, adult speech and infant vocalisation. Anecdotal evidence shows that this kind of interaction is also seen between infants and fathers and other caregivers. Trevarthen (1979) has described these 'motherese' interactions as 'primary intersubjectivity'. Observers enjoy watching them, and have no hesitation in declaring that both partners show a high level of arousal, and delight in the way in which each reciprocates and validates what the other has done. The two could be described as mutually facilitating a sense of shared well-being. It should be emphasised that motherese exchanges are only possible when the infant is not fatigued and has no immediate physiological need.

Two variants of the scene described above have been explored. In one, baby and mother are deceived by being presented on the screen with a repetition of what each had done during an interaction they had enjoyed a few minutes earlier. Both mother and baby become upset, and it would appear that each needs and looks for a response that is directly contingent on the other's previous communication. The second variant arises when a depressed mother is asked to talk to her baby via the television screen. The mother appears unable to use 'motherese', and the baby becomes restless and avoids her gaze. How serious in the long term it is for a baby to experience a lack of primary intersubjectivity awaits further research. The subject of the effect on children of exposure to depressed mothers has been reviewed by Cummings and Davies (1994) and it is a complex issue. While there is evidence that parental depression can interfere with developmental processes in childhood (Murray et al. 1993) it may well do so by increasing the likelihood of familial discord, which is well known to have deleterious effects on child development. As therapists it is difficult to gainsay the effects on clients of being related to in a supportive, companionable and exploratory way.

As the months pass, the to and fro that makes up primary inter-subjectivity becomes more robust, the mother linking the exchanges to nursery rhyme games and both adding variations to a familiar theme. At this stage the emergence of interest-sharing can be seen.

The nursery rhyme game can be seen as an early form of sharing an interest in something that is external to both mother and child thus moving into what Trevarthen (1979) describes as secondary intersubjectivity. Motherese changes, but a tone that conveys the qualities of warm unanxious interest in the other remains. At this point we consider Stern's concept of selective attunements.

STERN'S CONCEPT OF SELECTIVE ATTUNEMENTS

Stern (1985) and three colleagues studied the behaviour of nine-month-old infants playing with their mothers. Their aim was to focus on the degree to which the mother matched the infant's affect. To this end they studied behaviour that signified: that mothers were matching (i.e. were attuned to) the affects displayed by their infants, and how the infants responded; that mothers were not matching the infant's affects, and the response of the infants to various forms of mismatch or misattunements. The researchers did not record when the mother copied the infant's behaviour, but rather how a mother recast and re-presented the feelings expressed by the infant.

Criteria for affect matching (attunement)

Six dimensions of interactional behaviour were identified as criteria of affect matching. These are:

1 Absolute intensity: the level of intensity of the mother's behaviour is the same as that of the infant, irrespective of the mode or form of the behaviour (e.g. the loudness of a mother's vocalisation might match the force of an arm movement by the infant).
2 Intensity contour: the changes in intensity over time are matched (e.g. the intensity of a mother's vocal effort and that of her infant's physical effort, both might show acceleration followed by a sudden quicker phase of deceleration).
3 Temporal beat: a regular pulsation in time is matched (e.g. the nodding of a mother's head and the infant's gesture conform to the same beat).
4 Rhythm: a pattern of pulsations of equal stress is matched.
5 Shape: matching in shape occurs when a spatial feature of a behaviour is abstracted and rendered in a different act. It does not mean imitation. Rather a mother 'borrows' the vertical shape of an infant's up/down arm movement and adapts to it in her head motion.

6 Duration: the time span of the behaviour is matched. This is a subsidiary dimension shown by many misattunements. For a fuller assessment of the degree of affect matching (attunement) and mismatching (misattunement) that had taken place, the record of a ten- to fifteen-minute session of video-taped play between mother and baby was followed by a review of the recording with the mother. The collaboration of the mother was sensitively enlisted in order to establish why she did what she did. Questions included: what did she think her baby was feeling when she did . . . ? Was she aware of her behaviour when she did . . . ? What did she wish to accomplish? Mothers were not always aware of what they were doing when they attuned to their infants, which they did approximately once a minute; the usual reason they gave was to satisfy a desire 'to be with' their infant or 'to join in'; a state which Stern describes as interpersonal communion (which seems to be the same as what we have described in Chapter 5 as psychological closeness or intimacy) in which affects of sadness, joy and vitality are communicated and shared. Of these three affects, the vitality affects occupy a position of special importance for the infant. Stern suggests that infants perceive the actions conveying a vitality affect, before they perceive the formal content of the action – rather as an adult will experience 'vitality' in the action of a dance. Stern considers that, as a result of attuning experiences, infants begin to categorise acts in terms of their vitality affects (see Chapter 8).

The process of attunement can be seen in adult/adult interaction; and Stern also applies it to the feeling tone adults can experience when reflecting upon a work of art and allowing themselves to appreciate the artist's statement of their affective state. Although the phenomenon of attunement can be recognised by observers, and manipulated so that the response of the infant to various kinds of misattunement can be studied, the processes through which it comes about are not understood. In Stern's view, the act of attuning is not the same as being empathic, for which cognition is required – a topic we discuss in Part III. Rather, attuning to an infant is an intuitive affective response that seems to tell infants which of their subjective experiences are within, or beyond, the limits of mutual experience with mother. Evidence for this conclusion lies in the observation that, by and large, attunements by the mother do not interrupt what an infant is doing, whereas misattunements cause infants to stop what they are doing and to look at the mother.

From Stern's descriptions it would appear that adults can attune to adults as much as mothers attune to their infants, and that the sense of being-attuned-to is one aspect of feeling understood. In Part III we discuss additions to feeling understood contributed by empathy and the use of a tone of voice that has similarities to the tone used in motherese and combines affect matching (and appropriate tuning) with an unanxious approach to the other person(s).

Different forms of affective mismatch (misattunements)

Stern distinguishes 'purposeful misattunement' from 'true misattunement'. A mother makes a 'purposeful misattunement' when she 'slips inside of' the baby's feeling state far enough to capture it, but she then mis-expresses it by altering the intensity, timing and 'shape' of her response so that it no longer matches that of the infant. He calls purposive misattunement, 'tuning'. The degree of misattunement is enough to alter the infant's behaviour, but not enough to break the sense of an attunement in process. He states that its purpose is to increase or decrease the baby's level of activity and affect, and so regulate and 'shape' the baby's psychic state as well as behaviour.

True misattunement comes about either when the mother identifies incorrectly the quality and/or quantity of the infant's feeling state, or when she is unable to find in herself the same internal state. He gives a vivid picture of a mentally ill mother who was never seen to attune to her baby but yet treated the infant with extreme care. This situation, if regularly experienced, will affect the child as powerfully, but very differently, as the regulation exerted by tuning.

According to Stern, the young infant, like everyone else, has the capacity to deal with the degree of stimulation from their environment provided they get some help in regulation from the parent. They have 'optimal levels of stimulation', below which stimulation will be sought and above which stimulation will be avoided. Different children and adults have different thresholds of external stimulation, which are characteristically set at higher or lower levels for tolerable amounts of stimulation and for tolerable durations of exposure. He differentiates between expectable and tolerable overstimulation, in which the mother expands or stretches her infant's tolerance of excitement or arousal. Such stretching he calls 'constructive' mismatching and differentiates it from intolerable overstimulation or understimulation.

We consider that constructive mismatching occurs when interacting with the infant in what Chasseguet-Smirgal (1985) calls a place just beyond where they are and where they are developing towards, which in Vygotsky's terms is within the 'zone of proximal development' (Vygotsky 1978: 86). The intolerable form of overstimulation is an insensitive, forcing, intrusive interaction by an excessively controlling parent pushing the child beyond tolerable limits into a need to self-regulate downwards by persistent aversive and avoidant responses. This is one form of the pattern of dominating relating discussed below.

Stern's view is that through the use of selective attunements, parents can shape the development of their children's subjective life, as well as the development of their interpersonal feelings and behaviour. The avoidant behaviour of young infants with depressed mothers suggests that 'shaping' a child's affective state can begin early in life and that a baby at that stage can pick up (attune to) and be affected by the affective state of others.

We now consider the raising of affect vitality by one's own endeavours.

EFFECTANCE PLEASURE

Besides the pleasure derived from the experience of primary intersubjectivity, pleasure is also derived from intra-individual activities in infancy and in later life. Infants appear to be biologically prepared to engage in purposive interactions with objects in the environment, and to express pleasure on discovering their ability to bring about a predictable response as the result of their own endeavours. A most telling observation of Bower reported by Lichtenberg (1989: 126) is of a blind infant who by eight weeks of age had not smiled. On discovering that he could produce a sound of small bells by kicking his legs, the infant began to smile and coo with increasing vigour. Smiling was only seen when he was exercising control over the bells. Prior to the experiment that enables the baby to have contingent control, the sound of the bells had no effect. There are many examples to show that pleasure is derived from the awareness that one's own actions can bring about a predictable effect upon the environment.

Sources of pleasure in infancy and in later life

In summary, it would seem that those infants who have an environment in which they can exercise some contingent control experience pleasure associated with a sense of competence from the ability to maintain a state they evaluate as pleasurable by interacting with people (i.e. Trevarthen's primary and secondary intersubjectivity); and also from the ability to bring about a desired effect on physical aspects of the environment (effectance pleasure). It would seem that in adults, affect vitality is also enhanced and a sense of well-being evoked when either of these two forms of competence is experienced. Support for this view is given by the studies of Hazan and Shaver (1990) (see Appendix C) showing that adults rated as having secure attachments had a higher level of work satisfaction than those whose attachments were insecure.

INNATE RESPONSES OF INFANTS AND YOUNG CHILDREN TO THE DISPLAY OF PARENTAL EMOTION

We now consider the innate affective responses of infants and young children to the display of emotion by their parents. Studies showing the sensitivity of infants to the expression of emotion by their caregivers have been reviewed by Harris (1994). In response to their mother's expressions of happiness, infants look interested, gaze forward at their mother, and spend more time playing with toys; in response to expressions of sadness, infants gaze at the floor and engage in mouth movements of chewing and sucking. Our understanding of these reactions is that infants are programmed to have interest expanded by interaction with a mother showing happiness, unalloyed with sadness, and that infants engage in defensive self-comfort (see Chapter 7) through non-nutritive sucking when their mother is preoccupied by sadness.

It is clear that the expression of parental anger is a disturbing event for all infants and young children (Rutter and Rutter 1992). In response to a mother's anger, the majority of infants avert their gaze, look angry or remain still or 'frozen'. Older children regularly show that they are upset when they see adults quarrelling and this affects their own later behaviour. It frequently elicits a tense, frozen attention that tends to suppress temporarily any other emotional expression or cognitive ability. Later they can behave in an aggressive manner towards playmates, although a range of

responses are observed. The way in which exposure to anger poten-
tiates aggressive responses is not well understood. It is not considered to be simple imitation. The child who has experienced verbally
angry adults, will often proceed to hit playmates. We suggest how
anger of adults can potentiate aggressive responses in children when
we discuss two alternative patterns of relating.

Complementary lines of research (Sorce *et al.* 1985) on social referencing (i.e. seeking emotional signals when experiencing uncertainty) show that if caregivers express fear when their infant
approaches a particular object or location, the infant will be less
likely to approach those objects associated with a caregiver's fearful
response. The expression of happiness has the opposite effect. The
phenomenon of social referencing shows there is an innate propensity to pay attention to what a parent signals as safe or dangerous
by showing approval or disapproval.

Parental responses that facilitate learning by infants and children

Research into the learning of sign language by children with
impaired hearing has been discussed by Trevarthen (1990). When
there is an explicit and helpful input to encourage hand signing as
the alternative to speech, stages similar to those of unimpaired children occur during the deaf child's mastery of language, and at the
same ages. In the first three years the child advances through stages
of one word, to sentences, and on to coherent discourse as observed
in the hearing–speaking child. Between three and six years, the child
gains proficiency in signing grammatical distinctions correctly. In
other words, parallel advances are made by both hearing and deaf
and/or hearing-impaired children. The same progression appears in
the development of reading, provided that written words are presented as a form of play, and are linked in at moments when the
child is interested in the meanings and wants to share in meanings.
In all cases, the meanings are found in persons, objects or events
that greatly interest the child and which occur in spontaneous, natural and playful communication with trusted companions and
teachers. This environment is similar to one described by Heard and
Barrett (1982) that enabled children with specific reading disability
to improve.

It is noteworthy that the quality of the interactions with humans
that enables chimpanzees to learn sign language seems to be similar
to that described by Trevarthen for teaching deaf children. We think

this correspondence is additional evidence showing that human caregiving, which includes empathic understanding of another's affective state and preparedness to share affects and interests, has evolved beyond the protection, nurturance and tension reduction shown by non-human primates in affiliative exchanges. It is certain that exposing chimpanzees to human methods of teaching can extend their affective–cognitive competence to levels that are not observed in the wild.

We consider these findings to support the view that human caregivers can integrate their caregiving system with their interest-sharing component of exploration. They can automatically oscillate between the two systems in response to the needs of a careseeker, but only when their caregiving and exploratory systems have not been overridden by fear or by any other factor that strongly activates the caregiver's own careseeking system.

TWO ALTERNATIVE PATTERNS OF HUMAN RELATING

We have taken the findings of Trevarthen, of Murray, of Stern and of MacLean as evidence that human beings have the capacity to relate to one another through two alternative patterns of behaviour. One we suggest is a more recently evolved pattern of caregiving integrated with interest-sharing described above, which we term supportive companionable (SC) relating. It exemplifies a protective, explanatory and exploratory form of relating which owes as much to non-verbal signals and tone of voice as to communication through verbal symbols. It is a pattern to which people of all ages seem to be innately prepared to attend and to be influenced to adopt an exploratory stance. The tone of voice is related to speaking in motherese. It is warm, unanxious and is accompanied by appropriate constructive misattunements as described above and by an unanxious acknowledgement of ignorance and an interested preparedness to extend knowledge. Conflict, when it arises, is handled by the recognition of the other's points and resolved through negotiation and compromise. Parents, teachers and colleagues treat other adults and children as worthy of respect. They are alert to signs that show when the interest of other people is waning and adapt accordingly, often using humour. Examples of professional SC relating are shown in Stern's description of how he explored a mother's intentions when 'attuning' to her infant. There is strong empirical evidence that close, confiding and emotional exchanges are protective against stress in children and adults (Rutter and Rutter 1993, Hazan and Shaver 1990, Parkes *et al.* 1991).

The other pattern is relating through dominating and submissive forms (hereafter referred to as D/S relating). The dominating form forces others to follow the decisions of a controlling leader. It can appear not to be damaging to others when it carries the stance of a protective and even indulgent dictator. But those who do not accept a submissive and obedient status face coercion in various forms, including being shamed and humiliated.

In Chapter 8 we describe the function of these alternative patterns and in Chapter 11 the value given to each of them by people of different relational experience. In Part III we discuss how D/S patterns can be demonstrated in the therapeutic alliance and in marital conflicts, with comments on how they can be handled in a therapeutic fashion.

Generalising from MacLean's findings from the squirrel monkey, it is likely that in humans D/S patterns of relating are sited in the R-complex and that the range of responses shown by young children and adults to people who are frightening, or who fail to respond as expected, are similar to the R-complex individualistic defensive responses of non-human primates. Depending upon their previous experience, age and temperament, children, and many adults, become dominating to those they assess as likely to become submissive. Or they become subservient to those expected to greet their protest and dominating behaviour by a greater display of anger or coercion.

These two patterns bear a resemblance to Chance's concept of hedonic and agonic modes of relating (Chance 1988, Price *et al.* 1994). They are however distinct through being based in a different theoretical frame.

THE CAPACITY OF HUMANS TO USE SIGNS AND SYMBOLS IN THE COMMUNICATION OF MEANING

In this chapter we include a note on the use of signs and symbols in human communication which extend the meaning of non-verbal signals. In all that has been said about non-verbal communication, a signal signifies (conveys) a specific meaning about the intentions of one individual towards another. However, the meanings conveyed by human communication become increasingly sophisticated and complex as development proceeds. The meaning conveyed by a signal is experienced by a receiver in the light of their developmental status and the length and quality of the relationship with the sender. It gradually becomes a sign about the relationship whose meaning is affected by earlier layers of meaning within a particular relationship. Furthermore many meanings will have been jointly agreed with a caregiver, others may not.

Symbols can be broadly defined as representations that stand for or correspond to something else. They are reminders of, or stand in for, something else. They designate and serve as distinctive marks by which an individual's sensations, ideas, appraisals and evaluations can be recognised and communicated. Symbols in the forms of words convey conventional meanings when they are used to represent things, events or persons that carry a quality of universality. They can be seen as transformations of experience (Langer 1967).

Trevarthen (1990) holds that children learn to speak, then to read and write, as a refinement of an inherent interest they have in sharing experiences, tasks and feelings before they can speak. They express this interest in imaginative and 'pre-representational' play (symbolic and role taking) before ideas about conventions of behaviour and symbolic meaning come to dominate a child's development. He considers that the regular stages observed in the emergence of language, when related to general development and put in the full context of all kinds of co-operative behaviour, provide evidence for a particular strategy of brain development. This can be viewed as a growth in specific interpersonal functions.

Chapter 4

Bowlby's model for instinctive behaviour – based on the concept of goal-corrected behavioural systems

Attachment theory, as commonly understood, holds that the young and vulnerable are drawn to seek care from parental figures by displaying attachment behaviour. Bowlby (1982) considered such behaviour to be instinctive and opened a chapter on a theoretical model for instinctive behaviour with two quotations from Freud. In the first, Freud (1915) expressed his doubts about whether the differentiation and classification of the instincts can be made when considering only psychological material. He considered that assumptions about instinctual life have to be made, and that it would be desirable for them to be taken from some other branch of knowledge and applied to psychology. Despite his own formulations, Freud stated in 1925 that there was no more urgent need in psychology than a securely founded theory of instincts on which it might be possible to build further.

By 1969 Bowlby could state that striking progress had been made during the half century since Freud lamented his inability to find a well-based theory of instinct. He lists three of the many disciplines that have contributed: ethology, experimental psychology and neurophysiology, adding that the latter was Freud's first love. In a comprehensive discussion of how Freud came to his theory, Bowlby (1982) observes that early in his psychoanalytic work, Freud adopted a model which pictured behaviour as the resultant of a hypothetical psychical energy that is seeking discharge; and that although details changed, Freud never considered abandoning it for any other. The origin of this model did not come from clinical work with patients but from ideas widely accepted by the educated and the scientific world of the late nineteenth century.

Bowlby's model has different roots. He drew his understanding of instinctive behaviour from Darwinian principles, ethology, control and information theory, from models suggested by Miller, Gallanter and Pribram (1960) and by Young (1964). As a result he was able to state:

> In the place of psychical energy and its discharge the central concepts are those of behavioural systems and their control, of information, negative feedback, and a behavioural form of homeostasis.
>
> Bowlby (1982: 17–18)

Bowlby saw instinctive behaviour as a sequence of behaviour that is activated by specific signals. It usually runs a predictable course and has a pattern that is recognisable in almost all members of a species (or members of one sex). Certain of its usual consequences are of obvious value in contributing to the preservation of an individual, or the continuity of a species. Examples of it develop when all the ordinary opportunities for learning are absent (1982: 39). He saw some instinctive systems developing through processes of maturation from simple to complex forms; and described how any kind of instinctive system – simple or complex – is only able to function properly within definable environmental limits.

Bowlby's model also brings in a way of conceptualising motivation. The activation of a system provides the motivation to reach the goal of the system. When the system is no longer activated, motivation in relation to that system ceases. On this basis, he put forward the theory of attachment, which he describes as:

> an attempt to explain both attachment behaviour, with its episodic appearance and disappearance, and also the enduring attachments that children and older individuals make to particular figures. In this theory a key concept is that of a behavioural system.
>
> Bowlby (1982: 171–2)

He focused on the attachment (or careseeking) system and the complementary caregiving system. Besides anxiety, factors that activate attachment behaviour, are:

1 the condition of the child, notably fatigue, hunger, cold and malaise;
2 the behaviour of the mother, notably her absence, the perception of her going away, and when she discourages proximity; and
3 other environmental conditions, notably alarming and strange events, and rebuffs by other children (1982: 258).

Bowlby also discusses factors that activate maternal behaviour in several species, noting the dependence of maternal behaviour on hormonal factors and on the age of the child. He concludes:

In the same way that an infant's attachment behaviour comes to be directed towards a particular mother-figure, so does a mother's retrieving behaviour come to be directed towards a particular infant. . . . For a mother to remain in proximity to an infant and to gather him to her in conditions of alarm clearly serves a protective function.

Bowlby (1982: 241)

The parent/child relationship is depicted (Bowlby 1982: 355) as a goal-corrected partnership, the child's careseeking being one half of a dyadic process and maternal caregiving the other. A careseeker cannot achieve the goal of careseeking without the co-operation of a caregiver. Likewise the caregiver cannot achieve the goal of caregiving without the co-operation of the careseeker. To make attachment plans that will achieve their goal, children have to take into account how to maintain proximity and influence a caregiver to provide what they consider they currently require. It is equally true to say that for a mother to make caregiving plans that will achieve her goal, she has to take into account how to maintain proximity to and influence over the child.

Bowlby notes (1982: 355) that since mother and child each have their own continuing set goal to attain, the partnership between them is bought at a price:

In the case of attachment demands, it is evident that during the course of an ordinary day the mother of a two-year-old is likely many times to attempt to change the set-goals of his behaviour. . . . In a complementary fashion a child is intermittently striving to change his mother's behaviour and her proximity to him, and in so doing is almost certain to adopt some, at least, of the methods she herself employs. Therein lies both hope and a warning.

Bowlby (1982: 355–6)

Bretherton pointed out that attachment behaviour can be seen as the output of a safety-regulating system, the activities of which tend to reduce the risk of an individual coming to harm and are experienced as anxiety-allaying responses (Bowlby 1982: 374–5). However it must be emphasised that the child's attachment behaviour is only effective in regulating safety when it is able to activate caregiving.

By means of the concept of a goal-corrected partnership, in which each party contributes to the attainment of the goal of a system that is sited in another person, Bowlby introduced the concept of goals to which we have given the term interindividual or interpersonal.

CHARACTERISTICS OF GOAL-CORRECTED BEHAVIOURAL SYSTEMS

Types of instinctive behavioural systems: simple and complex

Bowlby described goal-corrected behavioural systems as simple or complex. Both are stimulus-bound in the sense that they are unconsciously activated by specific events, unless they are overridden by another system or by other factors discussed below. Simple types are not unlike reflexes. The response to the specific activating information is a fixed-action pattern. Examples include: all the behaviour of the rainbow lizard (see Chapter 2); in human infants, grasping, crying or rooting for a nipple; and in adult humans, sneezing, yawning and some forms of crying (the paroxysms of grief).

The development of goal-corrected systems through processes of maturation

Systems can develop from simple fixed-action patterns to goal-corrected behaviour; and then may progress to patterns of behaviour that are even more highly organised. The attachment system is a good example. During the first year the repertoire of behaviour increases as infants become able to move around under their own steam and as the brain develops and young children become able to plan and to understand the concept of a future. Later still (around four years of age), they become psychologically mature enough to see life from the point of view of another person as well as from their own, and changes in the organisation of instinctive systems take place. After this stage, children are able to share with parents a common set goal and participate in a joint plan to achieve it and so have a sense of common purpose; and they are also likely to identify with one another (Bowlby 1982: 355).

Continuing set goals

Bowlby was careful to clarify his use of the word goal, observing that although it can suggest a temporarily finite end towards which action is directed, the term must also be applicable to conditions that extend over time. He noted that the term is often used to refer to an object in the environment. But he was looking for a term which could be used:

> to refer generically both to a temporarily finite end that is to be brought about through the interaction of an animal with some part of its environment, for example seizure of prey, and to some condition that continues through time, for example a specified relationship of distance between an animal and some part of its environment.
>
> Bowlby (1982: 69)

For these reasons he used the term 'set goal'. The set goal is not an object in the environment, rather it is either a specified motor performance (e.g. singing a song) or the achievement of a specified relation, of short or long duration, between the animal and some component of the environment. Thus the set goal of a peregrine falcon's stoop is not the object (prey) stooped at, but the interception of that prey. In the same way, the set goal of another behavioural system might be the continual maintenance by an animal of a certain distance between itself and an object in the environment (e.g. an alarming object). To refer to behavioural systems that have set goals, he used the term 'goal corrected', which emphasises that the behaviour is constantly corrected to the discrepancy between current performance and the set goal. However, regardless of whether systems are in themselves simple, or simple because they are complex systems at an early stage of development, or are functioning as fully developed complex systems, the behaviour shown is activated by specific factors and ended by others.

How the behaviour of goal-corrected systems is started and stopped

The picture Bowlby gives is that goal-corrected systems are maintained in a state (which we have labelled vigilant quiescence) until activated by the perception of a specific environmental or organismic signal. Once activated, behaviour continues at greater or lesser degrees of intensity, until stopped either by the system reaching its goal or by other means. For example, systems can be placed in a hierarchical order, such that when a higher system and its associated behavioural unit becomes activated, a lower one is overridden. Activation is often influenced by changes in hormonal levels, for example in the predictable sequences of behavioural changes that take place before, during and after giving birth.

In human beings, behaviour related to complex systems seems to be organised according to a plan hierarchy (1982: 77). This idea was introduced by Miller, Gallanter and Pribram (1960) who conceptualised a hierarchy of subordinate structures (termed totes). The distinctive feature of a plan hierarchy is that there is an overall goal-corrected plan, within which sub-plans of any number and kind are integrated. Bowlby illustrates this form of organisation with the example of 'getting to work'. Here the overall plan is made up of subordinate plans such as leaving bed, washing, dressing, having breakfast, each of which can be further specified in greater detail. The set goal of this plan hierarchy is 'arrival at work'. Thus the whole operation can be understood as a master plan to achieve a long-range goal in which sub-plans can be adapted to suit the long-range goal (e.g. if one oversleeps, 'having breakfast' may be skipped).

How behaviour is stopped

Behavioural sequences, however they are organised, do not go on for ever. They stop, or in Bowlby's terminology, are terminated. When this happens the system usually reverts to the state of vigilant quiescence in which it is able to respond to events that can activate it. The factors that cause behaviour to cease are as complex as those that cause it to start. We have selected five significant factors:

1 the subjective experience of reaching the set goal of the system;
2 the effect of hormonal influences;
3 the overriding of one system by another;
4 the appearance of specific environmental cues, the perception of which signifies that the set goal has been reached. To take the example of nest building: a bird ceases to build when the appearance of the nest matches an inbuilt standard of what its nest should look like. Should it cease to come up to standard, and hormonal influences to build a nest are still active, nest building is resumed. Similarly, attachment behaviour is terminated when a

careseeker has received feedback from attachment figures that they are attentive and are being appropriately responsive. It is reactivated when the attention of the attachment figure wanders or they go away before the desired caregiving is attained; and
5 de-activation of the system, which is a complex process during which the individual is temporarily, or more permanently, no longer motivated to reach the set goal of the system. Bowlby discusses de-activation and re-activation in relation to the unwilling separation of a child from attachment figures. It is also discussed in Chapter 7 in relation to defensive self-care and management.

FUNCTION OF INSTINCTIVE BEHAVIOUR

Bowlby (1982: 124–40) devotes a chapter to a discussion of the function of instinctive behaviour, which has to be distinguished from the immediate causes of its activation and from its consequences. To summarise his views: the overall function of the careseeking system is to ensure survival by maintaining protection and contributing to homeostasis. The immediate causes of its activation are illustrated by the events that activate careseeking. The immediate consequences, provided that caregiving has been effective, are that the careseeker experiences a definable subjective state of having been nurtured, protected and no longer having an urge to seek care.

GOAL-CORRECTED SYSTEMS AND THE ENVIRONMENT OF EVOLUTIONARY ADAPTEDNESS

Bowlby considered that the development of behavioural systems is closely affected by environmental experience. Using Waddington's theory of epigenesis (Waddington 1957, Bowlby 1973: Ch. 22), he saw the whole course of development as being shifted into an alternative pathway when the environmental limits within which major systems are best able to function are exceeded. When individuals live beyond these limits, they are outside 'the environment of evolutionary adaptedness', and the organisation of the systems breaks down. He gives two cogent examples:

> So long as the ambient temperature remains within certain upper and lower limits it [the system for maintaining body temperature] operates effectively. But when the ambient temperature stays either above or below these limits for sufficiently long, the system

is unable to achieve its goal. As a result body temperature rises or falls and the organism suffers from either hyper- or hypothermia. The environmental conditions that produce these physiological states are termed stressors, the states themselves states of stress. The personal experience is one of distress.

Bowlby (1980: 42)

The cardiovascular system of the cat will work efficiently within a certain range of oxygen and carbon dioxide tensions and within a certain range of pressures and temperatures; the cardiovascular system of a monkey or a man will work efficiently within ranges of these variables similar to but perhaps not identical with those that are relevant for the cat. In the same way behavioural systems responsible for maternal behaviour in a species will work within certain ranges of social and physical environment and not outside them, and those ranges too will differ from species to species.

Bowlby (1982: 47)

In using these examples Bowlby draws attention to similarities between the organisation of psycho-social and physiological instinctive systems that maintain bodily functioning and homeostasis. And he introduces the concept of an attachment control system maintaining a person's relation to their attachment figures. We return to this theme in Chapter 7, when we discuss the relation between systems that maintain homeostasis and those that carry forward growth and development.

He warns that the environments in which humans live today do not conform to the environments for which the systems for caregiving and careseeking are best adapted, so that definable aspects of the social environment can act as stressors which, if continued for long enough, will result in moving individuals into alternative developmental pathways or even bring about the breakdown of physical and psychological processes. He does not give explicit examples of alternative pathways, but the work of attachment researchers, notably Ainsworth (Ainsworth *et al.* 1978) and Main (Main and Hesse 1990), provides evidence of four alternative pathways. On the basis of Ainsworth's Strange Situation Test (see Appendix A) one-year-old infants and young children can be broadly classed as securely or insecurely attached to a parent. The latter group have been subdivided on the basis of their attachment to mother into avoidant children, resistant ambivalent children and disorganised children. These patterns have been shown to remain constant in children, brought up from infancy to six years by the same caregivers, and to affect their cognitive and social development.

PSYCHOLOGICAL CAPACITIES THAT BACK UP INSTINCTIVE BEHAVIOURAL SYSTEMS

As part of his model Bowlby included what we have defined as 'those capacities of the brain that act as essential adjuncts to instinctive behavioural systems'. One example discussed by Bowlby is the capacity to form representational models. Others are the capacities to use information processing in the service of self-defence and to use feelings as a phase in the intuitive appraisal of one's organismic state or environmental situation.

The construction and function of representational models

To understand the capacity to plan to reach a goal, Bowlby used the concept of the representational or working model. Ideas in this vein have been talked about since the time of Plato. They were developed by Kant, by psychologists such as Bartlett (1932), Craik (1967), Piaget (Piaget and Inhelder 1948), Flavell (1963), Cantril (1950), Lewin (1952), Kelly (1955), by psychoanalysts of the object relations school, notably Fairbairn (1952), and by the biologist J. Z. Young (1964). The common theme is that many species automatically construct internal models or schemata of the world in which they live and of themselves interacting with different aspects of that world. The complexity of the models and the uses to which they may be put varies according to the species, with humans being far ahead of other primates. Of all the variants of the concept, the concept used by Bowlby is closest to the one developed by Young from a study of the brains of octopuses. Young found evidence in the behaviour of neurones following learning which indicated that an animal constructs an imitation world in its brain, which helps an animal respond to the real world in which it lives.

Bowlby regarded working or representational models as essential components of planning. At one stage he saw the two as synonymous but later preferred working models, which he saw as a more appropriate term in dynamic psychology. He considered that the concept of a working model of an attachment figure could in many respects replace the psychoanalytic concept of internal object

(Bowlby 1988: 120). And Bowlby's concept of working models places Freud's concept of transference in another conceptual field.

The imitation world constructed by humans was envisaged by Bowlby as sets of dynamic working models of the world, and of the self living and interacting in the world it knows or can imagine. In the ordinary course of events, these models are kept up to date in the light of new experiences. Bowlby (1982: 80) considered that their function was to transmit, store and manipulate information that helps in making predictions as to how set goals can be achieved. Using models of their attachment relationships, children, once old enough, are able to make predictions about the likely reactions of an attachment figure in particular contexts, and hence to make plans that are likely to be successful in reaching their careseeking set goal:

> Within the framework of these working models he [a child] evaluates his situation and makes his plans. And within the framework of the working models of his mother and himself he evaluates special aspects of his situation and makes his attachment plans.
>
> Bowlby (1982: 354)

Bowlby sums up the significance of working models by making it clear that every situation is construed in terms of the working models we have of the world about us and of ourselves. He sees the role of therapists as helping clients review their working models.

> Our task [as therapists], in fact, is to help him [the client] review the representational models of attachment figures that without his realising it are governing his perceptions, predictions and actions.
>
> Bowlby (1973: 148)

Attachment researchers have given their own preferred slant to the concept of working models and representations. The picture of working models given in Chapter 8 highlights the aspects that we find useful to explore during therapy.

Self-regulatory mechanisms that buffer individuals from the impact of the environment

Although people are vulnerable to the impact of the environment, they have capacities that act, to some extent, as buffers to maintain them on a developmental pathway. Waddington (1957) referred to this self-regulatory capacity as 'homeorhesis'. Bowlby (1973: 369) saw it 'as among those long known in the psychoanalytic tradition of theorising as "defensive"'. He introduced a way of conceptualising defence which is derived from information processing. We use it in Chapter 7 as an essential component in a system for defensive self-care.

Bowlby considered that because the data from which a working model is constructed are derived from multiple sources, there is always the possibility of data being incompatible. For some individuals the incompatibility may be regular and consistent (Bowlby 1980: 230). He gives examples of children whose parents insist that they love the child when his or her first-hand experience of the parents' actions suggests the reverse. He considers children are then in a dilemma about whether to accept the picture as they see it, or to accept the one their parents insist is true.

Bowlby (1988) suggests several outcomes, one of which is a compromise whereby a child gives some credence to both sets of data and oscillates uneasily between incompatible pairs of models, each pair consisting of a model of the parent and a complementary one of himself. This dilemma can be resolved by accepting the parental (or the establishment) view and excluding one's own perception from conscious recall. But this resolution gives rise to feelings about the self that have to be handled in therapy (see Part III). However, information incompatible with an existing model can simply be discounted or neglected. As an example he cites hearing evidence that is in conflict with cherished theory: 'When new information clashes with established models, it is the models that win the day – in the short run almost always, in the long run very often' (Bowlby 1980: 230).

Another kind of information liable to be excluded is that which is so appalling that the recognition of its very existence evokes dread. The evaluation of its true nature is postponed and individuals fail to make effective plans to handle the situation in which they find themselves. Bowlby considered that postponement of evaluation is especially probable whenever a situation is irreversible:

> For, should it prove so, we should be faced with the task of replacing existing models with new ones in circumstances in which the change is wholly unwelcome. Small wonder, therefore, that loss of a loved person should create great psychological difficulties in addition to deep distress.
>
> Bowlby (1980: 231)

We consider that everyone defensively excludes some information but many exclude a great deal. In Part III we discuss how defensively excluded information can be recognised and, when necessary, be recovered in the course of therapy and reprocessed by updating the relevant models.

Evidence for the occurrence of selective segregation of information

Bowlby explores the ways in which selected information is segregated from conscious recall by considering the question 'How can a person selectively exclude a particular stimulus unless he first perceives the stimulus which he wishes to exclude?' He cites the work of Erdelyi (1974) and Norman (1976) showing that before a person is aware of seeing or hearing something, the sensory inflow has been interpreted and appraised and a proportion excluded so as not to overload channels responsible for the most advanced processing. Bowlby (1980, 1988) quotes the results of experiments on listening, when different messages are transmitted simultaneously, one to the right ear and the other to the left. Subjects are asked to attend to one message and repeat it word for word and do not find this task difficult. They disregard the second message, with interesting exceptions. They tend to recall the mention of their name, or a personally significant word. From work on dichotic listening and that of Dixon (1971) on subliminal perception it is apparent that a large proportion of all the information reaching an individual is discarded, but only after it has undergone sufficient automatic processing for its personal relevance to be assessed.

Bowlby's view of affects, feelings and emotion

Bowlby (1982: 104–23) presents the thesis that most of what are termed (in his view rather indiscriminately) affects, feelings and emotions are phases in the intuitive appraisal of organismic states, of urges to act, and of the environmental situations in which individuals find themselves. In so far as an individual is aware of these processes, feelings associated with them provide a monitoring service in regard to one's personal state, urges and situations. At the same time because they are usually accompanied by distinctive facial expressions, bodily postures and incipient movements, they can provide valuable information to other people. He is of the opinion that affects, feelings and emotion should not be treated as though they were entities. He regards feeling as a property that processes connected with behaviour sometimes possess and that it is inadmissible to use a phrase that reifies feelings or emotion. In support of this definitive statement he refers to Langer's (1967) view that feeling is a phase in a process.

Bowlby does not discuss in greater detail the processes for which feelings act as a monitoring service and a communicative channel. We consider that processes monitored by feelings are connected both with reaching (and not reaching) the goals of instinctive systems; and also with monitoring the balance being kept between Bowlbian homeostatic systems and those behavioural systems that carry forward growth and development (see Chapter 7). With this understanding of feelings we have compared Bowlby's view on feeling with those of MacLean (1990) and with more recent work (Ortony et al. 1988, Ortony and Turner 1990, Turner and Ortony 1992, Izard 1993 and LeDoux 1994). We note that the field is far from understood and that our view follows the lines taken by MacLean and by Ortony et al.

Although Bowlby does not agree with Arnold's (1960) conceptualisation of instinctive behaviour, he notes her observation that very frequently appraised input from the environment or from the organism is experienced in terms of value as pleasant or unpleasant, nice or nasty. He considers that the rough and ready sorting of input into pleasurable and painful, nice and nasty is the result of comparing input with internal set points or standards. Some of these standards may remain unchanged throughout life; more often they vary in a regular way to reflect the current state of the organism (for example, olfactory input sorted as nice when hungry can be sorted as unpleasant when replete). In Chapter 9 we discuss the translation of feelings into values which monitor the discrepancy between where the self is now and where it aspires to be. In our view values are placed on a hierarchical scale related to the degree to which the goals of the behavioural systems described in Chapter 7 are reached.

ATTACHMENT PARTNERSHIPS AND THE PROCESS OF MOURNING

The situation which Bowlby studied empirically was the unwilling separation of children from their mothers. He found that the event not only produces distress, but that the way in which a young child behaves when placed in a strange environment and is cared for by a succession of strangers follows a regular sequence:

At first he [a young child] protests vigorously and tries by all the means available to him to recover his mother. Later he seems to despair of finding her but none the less remains preoccupied with her and vigilant for her return. Later still he seems to become emotionally detached from her. Nevertheless, provided the period of separation is not too long, a child does not remain detached indefinitely. Sooner or later after being reunited with his mother his attachment to her emerges afresh. Thenceforward, for days or weeks and sometimes much longer, he insists on staying close to her. Furthermore, whenever he suspects he will lose her again he exhibits acute anxiety.

Bowlby (1980: 26)

It was his aim to find patterns of response to separation in early childhood and thence to trace out whether similar patterns of response are to be discerned in later life (Bowlby 1980: 26). Following the recognition of the behavioural sequences of childhood mourning, adults were found to follow very similar patterns after any significant loss, especially separation by death from a spouse or any other person with whom there had been a close relationship (Parkes 1986).

On the theoretical side Bowlby found that he could relate the three phases of childhood mourning to three central issues of psychoanalytic theory that have usually been considered piecemeal. He considered that these can be seen as phases of a single process by relating Freud's concepts of:

1 separation anxiety to the phase of protest;
2 grief and mourning to the phase of despair; and
3 defence to that of detachment.

Bowlby (1973: 27–8) discusses how it was that Freud did not come until late in his career to the view that missing someone who is loved and longed for is the key to the understanding of anxiety. He concludes:

Not until his seventieth year did he [Freud] clearly perceive separation and loss as a principal source of the processes to which he had devoted half a lifetime of study. But by then others of his ideas were already firmly established.

Bowlby (1973: 28)

He goes on to point out how Freud (1925b) outlines a new route in the concluding pages of 'Inhibitions, symptoms and anxiety'. This has anxiety as the reaction to the danger of losing the object, the pain of mourning equivalent to the actual loss of the object, and defence as a mode of dealing with anxiety and loss.

Throughout his writings Bowlby shows that he sees the main function of caregiving to be protection, although he also mentions parents being companionable in relating to children. However, he does not make clear whether he saw being companionable as a further function of the caregiving system, or an adjunct to caregiving associated with a different system. In the next chapter we describe the first extensions to attachment theory in which we take peer relationships into account by postulating an interest-sharing system in which peers can explore shared interests, treating each other with the respect given to an equal, and adults can be exploratory with infants and children who are seen as potential peers. Later we use Bowlby's ideas, highlighted in this chapter, as the foundations for a systemic structure for a person's self. People are dependent on the quality of the social environment in which they are brought up for the development of their caregiving system on which their offspring will rely.

Chapter 5

Extensions to Bowlby's model of instinctive behaviour

While Ainsworth was working on the Strange Situation Test (see Appendix A), Bowlby was speaking in teaching seminars of the importance of her observation that the exploratory behaviour of infants was reduced during brief separations from their mothers in strange surroundings. This finding led Heard to compare Ainsworth's observations with those of Winnicott (1971) who had described the way in which a child's play, which seemed equivalent to exploration, can be overridden by anxiety or any strong emotion, but re-established when a mother 'holds the situation'. She postulated that there is a dynamic interaction between the systems for parental caregiving, for careseeking by a child or adult, and for intra-individual (see Chapter 1) exploration (Winnicottean play), which she named the attachment dynamic (Heard 1978 and 1982).

FIRST STEPS TO USING THE CONCEPT OF THE ATTACHMENT DYNAMIC WITH ADULTS.

Lake (1985) translated the concept of ego strength into that of personal competence (i.e. competence in activities in which one engages single-handed such as riding a bicycle) and social competence (activities in which one engages with other people). Ego strength is associated with a sense of having both personal and social competence in a variety of contexts, ego weakness with relative incompetence in personal and social activities. When we began to discuss personal and social competence in the light of the attachment dynamic, we saw ways in which a sense of competence (or incompetence) could affect attachment and peer relationships in adult life.

The first idea to emerge was that the pursuit of interests by peers (people of broadly similar intelligence, stamina, capacity to handle fear and panic, and competence in the pursuit of interests) is the equivalent of mutual play (mentioned but not discussed by Winnicott). This led to the idea that there is another pair of complementary instinctive behavioural systems with interindividual goals – the exploratory interest-sharing systems. We saw them as the social component of the intra-individual exploratory system and affected in the same way (in that they are likely to be overridden by the arousal of careseeking). When the exploratory interest-sharing system is able to be active, initially with supportive interest-sharing parents, then with peers, the skills that further the understanding and enjoyment of a joint interest are extended and new competencies discovered. We described exploratory interest-sharing partners as companions, who interact on terms of co-operation, mutual respect and equality which we now see as SC relating. We then defined the conditions under which the interest-sharing system is activated and the feelings associated with reaching the goals of the caregiving, careseeking and the companionable interest-sharing systems.

An individual's interest-sharing system is activated by reaching new levels of understanding in regard to an interest or new achievements in an associated skill and by seeing other individual(s) doing likewise. Mutual interest-sharing between peers (and with it mutual exploration) can begin at the point of communication of one individual's 'eureka' experience (see Chapter 2), which evokes in interested companions a wish to find out more about it.

The goal of interest-sharing is reached during interactions which take place momentarily or may last much longer. Peers show in their body language, and in expressive vocalisations, not always supplemented by speech, their pleasure in an achievement that marks either a new understanding about the interest shared or a development of the skills associated with it. They share delight in the achievement and in and for the person(s) who brought it about. In this context, we introduced the concept of reaching states of comfortable (or uncomfortable) psychological proximity, akin to feeling in rapport (or not in rapport) with someone. At that time we labelled these two states those of assuagement and alternatively disassuagement.

The experience just described contrasts with reaching the goals of either the careseeking or caregiving systems. Here the main sensation is one of satisfaction and relief. Careseekers feel that the caregiving partner understands their predicament and is prepared to be protective, hopefully (and this aspect depends upon past experience) until the environment or the internal organismic state no longer evokes careseeking or, alternately, until the careseeker knows that they have acquired the skills necessary to cope with the predicament. The goal of the caregiver, in which a state of satisfaction is also experienced, is reached when the caregiver considers the careseeker is now able to cope without endangering themselves or desiring a careseeking interaction. Comfortable psychological proximity or rapport is associated with reaching caregiving/careseeking interpersonal goals but without the heightened sense of vitality and intimacy associated with reaching the goal of interest-sharing. Uncomfortable psychological proximity, which is often felt at times of physical proximity, we described as states of disassuagement.

We considered that all interpersonal goals are reached after the exchange of information carried in 'emotive messages'. This concept was derived from Bateson's (1968) idea that every utterance carries a 'command' about the kind of relationship 'speakers' desire with whomsoever they are interacting. We saw each participant conveying, by means of non-verbal signals as much as by speech, the feelings that each has about the behaviour and status of the other(s) and their intentions. To discover the kind of information conveyed non-verbally about reaching or not reaching the goals of careseeking and caregiving, we used experience gained from working with families in which a child suffered specific reading disability (Heard and Barrett 1982), to which we have since added MacLean's findings on signalling and the studies of Trevarthen and of Stern.

At that stage, we differentiated between the experience of reaching the goals of the careseeking and caregiving systems and that of the interest-sharing system. We used the word assuagement to cover the latter experience. Unfortunately this led to confusion and was taken to mean relief and a sense of comfort following caregiving rather than the experience of achievement in exploratory activities. We now restrict the word assuagement to the experience of reaching the goals of careseeking and use the word well-being to describe the experience associated with reaching the goals of companionable interest-sharing, which cannot be fully experienced while unmet careseeking needs are present. We retain the term disassuagement for the experience of loss of well-being, low self-esteem and self-worth, and the anxiety, depression and despair that is associated with failing to meet intra- and interindividual goals.

It was at this stage we learnt of the work of Trevarthen and of

Stern and began to elaborate the concept of psychological closeness we introduced in 1986. We discuss our current understanding of this concept in the last part of this chapter.

THE ELABORATION OF TWO OTHER ASPECTS OF BOWLBY'S MODEL

The conceptualisation of a second pair of interindividual systems led us to elaborate other aspects of Bowlby's model:

1   We found that by conceptualising an internal supportive system derived from internal working models of self and others, and also a personally constructed environment within which the individual could feel supported, the gap could be bridged between the more autonomous adult and the infant who requires a great deal of protection and nurture from others;

2   Bowlby's views on psychological defence were extended to include the development of learnt strategies (in which one can be competent or incompetent) that supplement the psychological mechanisms proposed by Bowlby. These defensive strategies often induce caregivers (or peer companions) to show caregiving (or interest-sharing) behaviour that brings the insecure individual as near as possible to the goals of careseeking (or interest-sharing).

We had not elaborated in 1986 the concept of working models to clarify the crucial part some of them play in the life of an individual. Although we had introduced the term Internal Models of Experiences in Relationships (IMERs), we did not underline their difference from other working models of self and environment. They have a specific function within a person's internal supportive system. The picture given in Chapter 8 highlights the three functions of working models we find it useful to keep in mind in therapy.

THE CURRENT MEANING GIVEN TO TERMS USED IN 1986

We have now updated and refined the meanings we assigned to a number of terms we used in our 1986 paper.

Attachment

After introducing the interest-sharing system as a social component of the capacity to explore, we suggested that the word 'attachment' might be extended to refer to any relationship whose loss is followed by mourning, whether it be the relationship between parent and child or between peer companions with a shared interest. Introducing this extension of meaning led to some confusion. To minimise misunderstandings, we now use the term attachment to refer to two kinds of caregiving/careseeking partnerships, primary attachments between children and a hierarchy of parental figures, and secondary attachments between peers, which usually have a romantic sexual and more, or less, mutually supportive and interest-sharing basis. These are discussed in Chapter 8. We use the term 'bond' to refer to the relationship that parents form with their children and to the relationship that develops between friends. We describe attachments and bonds as being more, or less, enduring, predictable and stable.

Assuagement, disassuagement and well-being

As discussed on page 54 we chose the word assuagement to define the experience of reaching the goal of companionable interaction. We found that nevertheless most readers understood the term to mean the experience of reaching the goal of careseeking together with the relief from the experience of disassuagement. For this reason we now restrict the use of the word assuagement to reaching the goals of careseeking and refer to the experience of the goal of companionable interaction as an experience of well-being. We have retained the word disassuagement to mean the experience of distress and demoralisation with loss of a sense of confidence and competence following failures to achieve the goal of careseeking (for a full definition, see Heard and Lake 1986).

Affiliative and companionable

We have eschewed the use of the term affiliative in favour of companionable in view of the multiplicity of definitions given to it. In psycho-biological circles, affiliative is often used to describe positive forms of behaviour, including the friendly behaviour seen between young peers. It has been defined as those positive behaviours that promote the development of, and serve to maintain, social bonds within primate society (Steklis and Kling 1985). To measure affiliative behaviour (in non-human primates), Steklis and Kling (1985) refer to the amount of reciprocal grooming and physical proximity sought and apparently enjoyed by non-human primates. The behaviour as a whole is considered to provide comfort and to relieve the tension that follows exposure to threats of attack from conspecifics. So defined, affiliative behaviour is somewhat similar to our definition of caregiving behaviour and also seems to cover the hedonic behaviour described by Chance (1988). It does not appear to include an exploratory interest-sharing component which we had postulated as affiliative in our earlier paper.

The term affiliative is also used to refer to the prosocial behaviour seen between young peers as they engage in 'play'. Play in non-human species is commonly thought to have the function of developing skills which are used for survival in adult life. For a human child, play as described by Winnicott (1971) has the additional function of being an exploratory activity in which reality and the meaning of things are discovered. Winnicottean play helps to develop an understanding about what is encountered in the environment and the skills needed to express and enhance that understanding. In addition affiliative is used by Weiss (1986) to describe a bond which is different from the bond of attachment, and is based on the recognition of shared interests which can develop through beliefs about situations, their challenges, or their aims and leads to mutual respect, loyalty and affection.

Since 1986 we have updated our definition of the word companionable, which was introduced to describe relationships between peers as they shared an exploration of an interest. The term is now used to refer to three kinds of interpersonal exchange:

1 to forms of caregiving in which caregivers keep an exploratory collaborative stance in relation to careseekers of any age;
2 to adult careseeking in which careseekers keep an exploratory cooperative stance in regard to the caregiver they approach;
3 to interest-sharing peers in which the interactors maintain a cooperative caregiving stance which we describe as being supportive towards one another during the sharing of the interest with a commitment to attaining a common aspiration. The common factor carried by the word companionable is that exploration and caregiving are both active and have not been affected by care-

seeking aroused to a level of intensity that renders caregiving and interest-sharing defensive (see Chapters 7 and 8).

Support

In 1986 we used the term support to describe caregiving to adults in contrast to the care given to children. In our subsequent thinking we decided this dichotomy could be confusing both for the concept of social support and the concept of caregiving. In 1978 Brown and Harris examined how the social network and social support were related to psychological well-being and to neurotic symptoms. In the subsequent decade there was a great deal of research on social support which Vaux (1988) considered centred around three issues: the range of social ties that are relevant to support; the contrast between objective features and subjective appraisal of social relationships and support; and the different forms that support might take. Attachment theory came into the literature on social support with the development by Henderson *et al.* (1981)of the Interview Schedule for Social Interaction (ISSI) which measures the quality of a person's social integration and suggests that the essential features of support lie in the quality of the social interactions as they are appraised by those to whom support is given. The questions regarding quality of interaction were derived from Weiss's (1974) list of the provisions required for satisfying relationships. These were all pertinent to attachment. Henderson *et al.*(1981) showed that there was a link between the perception of social relationships as inadequate for one's needs and subsequent onset of neurotic symptoms.

Psychological closeness now related to intimacy

In 1986 we described the sense of comfortable psychological closeness as a feeling of rapport with one or more individuals. In this state there is a sense that another person shares feelings and/or beliefs and values in relation to someone or something. The more an individual values and enjoys what is shared with another person or people, the more he feels at one with them on that issue. The wider and deeper the range of issues shared the closer the relationship. Sharing can be expressed in speech but more powerfully by non-verbal vocalisations, signals and touch. Speech backed by whole-hearted non-verbal messages is the most powerful communication. This concept of comfortable psychological closeness and the findings of Stern and of Trevarthen suggest that it is useful to differentiate affect-sharing centred on secondary intersubjectivity from that centred on primary intersubjective closeness. We now consider that these two express different forms of intimacy, which can be experienced singly or conjointly. This conceptualisation leads us to see primary intersubjectivity between infant and primary attachment figure as the forerunner of affectional sexual intimacy in adult life (see Chapter 7) between an individual and a secondary attachment figure. This form of intimacy we consider differs from intimacy based solely on commitments to shared interests that are always external to the participants in the relationship. This means that it is not infrequent to have an intimate friendship that does not have a sexual component. This view of intimacy is of importance when undertaking therapy. Primary intersubjectivity is not in our view a feature of the therapeutic alliance whereas the intimate sharing of an interest in the predicaments of the client is an essential aspect of this alliance. We consider that our view of intimacy complements that of Hinde and Stevenson-Hinde (1986) and supports their final statement that work still needs to be done in defining intimacy in children and in tracing its developing importance in different contexts. Uncomfortable psychological closeness we still consider refers to the state an individual experiences whenever the behaviour of another person or other people is antithetical to the goals of the particular interaction. In this state there is no experience of intimacy.

Chapter 6

The emergence of high-order systems of the self

So far we have talked about the brain but have said nothing about the mind and the relations between mind and brain. To fill this conceptual gap we have used ideas taken from Sperry. Following his intensive neurological studies, which in his early days were focused on discovering the laws that fitted nerves into functional networks and progressed to his seminal work on the different functions of the two hemispheres, Sperry (Sperry 1987, Trevarthen 1990: xxxiii) proposed a mentalistic theory of mind that gave subjective experience a prime controlling role in brain function. Sperry proposed a new mentalistic theory of mind that gives subjective experience a controlling role in brain function and behaviour. The brain model he advanced postulated that the causal potency of an idea, or an ideal, becomes just as real as a molecule, cell or nerve impulse. In his view ideas are causal and help evolve new ideas. They interact with each other and with other mental forces which include the electrochemical and biophysical aspects of the brain. These mental forces direct and govern the inner impulse traffic and they put the mind back into objective science and into a position of top command.

This portrayal presents self-consciousness as a process emerging from cerebral networks and generated by neuronal activity from which it is different and yet inseparable. In his view (Sperry 1987: 164–6, Sperry 1990: 381–5) the conscious self is normally single and unified, mediated through brain processes that typically involve and span both hemispheres through the commissures. Conscious meaning is acquired by virtue of the way the processes operate in the context of brain dynamics, rather than operating as a neural copy or topological representation of an imagined object. Although he fully recognises that the phenomenon of consciousness is far from understood, he sees consciousness as a holistic systemic property and an active dynamic part of high-order brain processing. In his scheme subjective phenomena have a place and use in brain function and a reason for having evolved in a physical system. In other words, conscious phenomena are viewed as dynamic emergent properties of brain activity.

In exploring the concept of the acquisition of conscious meaning, Sperry includes the use of inner conscious representations and inner mental models of the outside world in time and space (cf. the use of working models in Chapters 4, 5 and 8). These allow trial-and-error responses, which he considers free behaviour from its primitive stimulus-bound state and provide increasing degrees of freedom of choice, and of what we understand to be original forms of central processing. On the input side of the conscious system a great deal of sensory processing is completed automatically and unconsciously. On the output side most or all of the complex processing needed to translate conscious aims, percepts and volitional intentions into appropriate behaviour patterns also takes place automatically and unconsciously. He adds in a caveat that the intricate arrays of muscle-contraction patterns require a degree of complexity that goes well beyond the ability of the conscious mind to understand or direct. Nevertheless, although conscious properties represent only a fraction of the brain's total activity, their organisational capacities are indispensable. These include cataloguing, storing and some aspects of memory retrieval.

This is an antireductionist view of the human brain, in which most of its high-order processing is directed towards generating, maintaining and expressing conscious awareness of oneself and one's world. It means that the world of human inner experience with its range of qualities and values need no longer be reduced to neurophysiology or excluded from science.

A summary by Sperry (1987) on consciousness and causality enlarges his view of how the neural infrastructure of brain processes mediates conscious awareness. He suggests that it is composed of elements and forces ranging from subnuclear and subatomic particles at the lower level, upwards, through molecular, cellular, and simple-to-complex neural systems at higher levels. At each level of the hierarchy, elements are bound and controlled by the enveloping organisational properties of the larger systems in which they are embedded. Holistic system properties at each level of organisation have their own causal, regulatory role and also exert downward control over their components, as well as determining the properties of the system in which they are embedded. Thus, brain physiology determines mental effects and at the same time is reciprocally governed by the higher subjective properties of the enveloping mental events. Subjective properties are also determined by spacing and timing properties and the mass-energy elements of the neural components. Consciousness exerts top-level causal influences in the direction and regulation of behaviour. It can supervene rather than intervene in physiological processes and determines choice of action; while neurophysiological mechanisms sustain and help in the process of determining the causes of action.

Sperry's mind–brain model emphasises the primacy of emergent top-down control without minimising bottom-up influences, and helps to reconcile entrenched positions of determinism versus free choice. In contrast with mind–brain identity and parallelism models, individuals in Sperry's view are able to make willed choices of what they subjectively value, desire and wish to do.

In order to conceptualise the simple-to-complex neural systems postulated by Sperry and relate them to the instinctive systems postulated by Bowlby, we have understood Sperry's reference to ideas and ideals having a causal potency to mean that the simple-to-complex neural systems sited in the neocortex and contributing to consciousness are goal corrected. We feel that this view is supported by the commonplace observation that individuals appear to be as (or sometimes even more) strongly motivated to reach an ideal as they are to reach the goal of an instinctive system. However, although we think that the two kinds of system are organised differently, we feel it would enter the realms of speculative imagining to suggest in any detail how they might differ. We finally resolved this dilemma by deciding that high-order systems are reflected in the functioning of neocortical capacities. The five we have selected as most relevant to understanding the predicaments of clients are either absent in non-human primates or are present in forms that are rudimentary compared to humans.

We note and recognise the importance of logical and categorical differences between the mental concept of experience and the physical concept of behaviour. These are pointed out by Goodman (1991) when he revisits the body–mind problem and its implications for psychiatry and psychotherapy.

In the next chapter, in the course of presenting a categorisation of instinctive systems, we describe the five neocortical capacities that we consider contribute to the expansion of consciousness and give them a place alongside the instinctive systems in a model of the self.

Part II

The construction of a theory of companionable caregiving

Chapter 7

Categorising the functions of instinctive systems of the self with comments on their development

Conceptualising the self is probably the most difficult task faced by theoreticians interested in human nature. We do not claim that this attempt is either complete or correct, but we find it is useful as a guide to understanding many interpersonal predicaments that are complained of by clients. The model is based upon Bowlby's theory of complementary goal-corrected instinctive systems and the extensions described in Chapter 5. It includes the evolutionary perspective set out in the first two chapters and Sperry's ideas in Chapter 6 that touch on the relations between mind, brain and goal-corrected systems.

We have taken an unconventional view in describing the systems of the self from the point of view of their functions and the circumstances in which the function of one system may override that of another. From this perspective, we see a systemic self functioning through two types of systems: instinctive goal-corrected behavioural systems and potentiating systems that act as essential adjuncts to the behavioural systems.

One of Bowlby's postulates was the importance of development on the functioning of behavioural systems: an issue brought to the fore by Cicchetti and other developmental theorists (Cicchetti 1989). Looking at development from the standpoint of therapists working largely with adult clients, we have decided to mention only the outstanding phases that have major effects on the functioning of the behavioural systems. For example, the capacity to plan cannot become functional until children have reached the age at which they are able to appreciate a future and are thus equipped to move beyond an existence in a world of the present and the past. We therefore pay considerable attention to the huge developmental shift, often referred to as the period of the child's development of a theory of mind (Astington *et al.* 1988), that takes place between the ages of three and six years. After this age we take the view that cognitive development, other things being equal, progresses in line with Piaget's views, and that physical development progresses in well-known stages.

TWO TYPES OF SYSTEM IN A MODEL OF THE SELF

The two types of system we distinguish are instinctive goal-corrected behavioural systems and what we call potentiating systems. The goal-corrected behavioural systems, of which there are five, are all components of a supraordinate system for self-care and management. They comprise:

1 the system for caregiving to others which is wholly interpersonal;
2 the interpersonal careseeking system;
3 the intrapersonal system for self-defence;
4 the exploratory system, manifest in the intrapersonal exploratory self and in the interpersonal interest-sharing self; and
5 the sexual system which has both intra- and interpersonal components.

The idea that people have an attachment or careseeking system which has an interpersonal goal and separate systems for intrapersonal exploration and defence indicates that a person is not constructed to be either completely interdependent or independent. But they can feel and behave as though they were independent when an effective caregiving relationship is repeatedly unavailable.

The second type of system comprises the potentiating systems which function as essential adjuncts to the behavioural systems. They are of two kinds. First, high-order systems, as proposed by Sperry, whose main function is to enlarge human consciousness. We consider that these systems are expressed through a number of psychological capacities sited in the neocortex. Second, lower-order systems, which are assumed to underlie psychological capacities such as MacLean's interoperative functions of the brain (see Chapter 2). We regard lower-order systems as originating in places other than the neocortex and as shared with non-human primates. In non-human primates, high-level systems are represented only to a limited degree compared with those found in humans, or they are absent (e.g. systems involved with speech).

The division of behavioural systems into two groups

Behavioural and potentiating systems are organised to function as an integrated whole, interacting with one another in such a way that individuals can adapt, within definable limits, to changes in their internal and external environments. To fulfil this adaptive function the behavioural systems are seen as falling into two groups. There is a group responsible for carrying forward the processes of growth and development (the developmental group); and another for regulating both physical and psychological homeostasis and for consolidating newly acquired information (the homeostatic group).

THE GROUP OF BEHAVIOURAL SYSTEMS RESPONSIBLE FOR REGULATING HOMEOSTASIS

The group of systems responsible for regulating and maintaining homeostasis has the primary function of maintaining the physical and psychological milieu that enables growth and development to proceed. It can be described as an infrastructure for the developmental group and for all the potentiating systems. Before itemising the systems within the homeostatic group we outline our understanding of the concepts of physiological and psychological homeostasis.

The concepts of physiological and psychological homeostasis

It has been established for well over a century that the biochemical systems that maintain an individual's bodily metabolism can, within limits, regulate each other in order to keep physiological processes within the quite narrow physical parameters in which each metabolic system can function effectively. Later it was recognised, from a psychosomatic perspective, that the body's biochemical systems are called on to respond to psychological inputs derived from the individual's feelings, thoughts and desires, which themselves are responses to inputs from the individual's external and internal environments.

There is now a growing literature which supports the view that social exchanges play a significant part in regulating an individual's state of mind. Bowlby touched on interdependent regulation (1973: 148); Hofer (1987) reviews it from a phylogenetic perspective; while Schore (1994) and others discuss it from a psycho-biological, psychological and psychoanalytic viewpoint. Stern's concept of selective attunement and tuning (see Chapter 3) covers one kind of interindividual regulation; work on shaming (Nathanson 1987) illustrates how an individual's levels of arousal and sense of well-being can be reduced; Trevarthen's studies on primary intersubjectivity show how an infant and a mother (who is not depressed) can reciprocally raise each other's levels of arousal and vitality; while Main's (1991) studies with the adult attachment interview (see Appendix B) and its relation to infant security show that some care-seeker/caregiver partnerships can lead to disorganising experiences for the careseeker.

All this information supports the concept that social factors have a significant part to play in the maintenance of both psychological and biochemical homeostasis and the maintenance of levels of arousal that are personally optimal. It also supports the view that the caregiver who most completely and consistently supplies the individual with the care that maintains their homeostatic infrastructure (of food, shelter, protection and comfort) is the most preferred attachment figure to whom the careseeker turns first.

Itemising the systems within the regulatory homeostatic group

The systems within the homeostatic group include:

1 all the physiological systems, which we do not discuss further;
2 the interpersonal system of caregiving to others;
3 the interpersonal careseeking component of a system for self-care and management described below;
4 an intrapersonal defensive component of that system; and
5 an intrapersonal defensive component of the sexual system.

All these systems are organised and undergo development on the lines described in Chapter 4. They are repeatedly activated to reach their unchanging goals, and then become quiescent. In so doing they maintain the relatively restricted physical and psychological conditions within which the apparently linear processes of growth and development of the individual can be carried forward.

There are substantial grounds for considering that the functioning of the developmental group of systems and the potentiating systems are impeded when the systems belonging to the regulatory homeostatic group fail to maintain the psychological limits set biologically for them. Dramatic evidence was provided by Harlow and

Harlow (1965) in their studies of the developmental fate of rhesus monkeys when reared on wire or terry towelling surrogate 'mothers'. In our language, these infant monkeys never experienced the goal of their careseeking systems as a result of their failure to experience effective caregiving. In all instances the development and ultimate functioning of their systems for caregiving to others and their sexual systems was gravely impaired.

THE GROUP OF SYSTEMS THAT CARRY FORWARD PROCESSES OF DEVELOPMENT

The developmental group of behavioural systems are responsible for processes that take individuals along recognisable developmental pathways (see Chapter 4). Once on a particular pathway, an individual moves to new stages of development that can be attained only by the emergence of new levels of skills and competencies (like talking and walking rather than babbling and crawling). Old skills remain available to be used in particular contexts. We consider that the developmental pathway along which individuals finally move – and it is possible to change pathways – depends as much on the regulation by social factors of their homeostatic systems as on their genetic endowment and their opportunity to exercise it. By social factors we mean the operation of systems with interpersonal goals. The group of developmental systems functions alongside the group of homeostatic systems, with activation moving from systems in one group to those in the other, for the most part unconsciously, as it becomes necessary to maintain the homeostatic infrastructure. At first this process takes place wholly unconsciously. Later in life, through the influence of high-order potentiating systems and the experience of caregiving/careseeking partnerships encoded within working models of self interacting with caregivers, it becomes possible to exercise a degree of conscious control over the necessary swings between the two groups of systems.

We have included in the developmental group of systems the system for intrapersonal exploration with its interpersonal social component – interest-sharing – and two of the components of the sexual system described below. Exploratory functions include: finding explanations for events, and the degree of control that can be exerted over them. In this sense exploration is concerned with finding answers to questions such as those that five-year-old children appeared to be asking when confronted with a novel object (Hutt

1966): what might it be? what can it do? and then, for some children, what can it do for me? (i.e. will it play the role I imagine for it in my game?). From anecdotal sources it appears that other questions such as 'why does it happen?' can also be asked.

Bowlby (1982: 370) reports the study of Bretherton and Beeghly-Smith where they showed that children as young as two years are interested in causation. The study of causal attributional statements in natural discourse demonstrates that people frequently attribute causes for what happens in everyday events (Stratton *et al.* 1986). We consider that such 'causes' are encoded in the appropriate 'Internal Models of Experience in Relationships with people' (IMERs) (see Chapter 8) where they act as beliefs about the ability and power of oneself, other people and environmental events, to bring about consequences which have to be coped with and suffered or enjoyed. In this sense causal attributional statements uttered in natural discourse that refer to self and others can be regarded as fragments of working models.

We also see exploration as enhancing vitality. The example of the blind baby, given in Chapter 3, suggests that his zest for life was diminished in the absence of an opportunity to exert his capacity to have a repeatable and pleasurable influence on his environment.

The expansion of personal and social competences that are appropriate at each stage of development raises self-confidence and vitality but does not maintain homeostasis. Their achievement can arouse, at any age, high levels of overexcitement, anxiety, fatigue and other physiological needs. The evidence given in Chapter 3 shows that intrapersonal exploration is demonstrable early in infancy, but appears only when physiological needs have been satisfied and anxiety relieved by caregivers.

The development of the components of the exploratory system

In contrast to the intrapersonal component of the exploratory system, which is functional within days of birth and develops as new skills become available, the interest-sharing component of exploration, with its interpersonal goal, comes into the picture from about the middle of the first year. During the first and second years, a child's potential for sharing interests is developed through the experience of comfortable psychological closeness (see Chapter 5) with parental figures interacting, first through primary intersubjectivity, and later through secondary intersubjectivity (Trevarthen

1979), which we equate with interest-sharing. By about the third year interest-sharing is sufficiently developed to engage in parallel and later mutual play with peers. From then on children show a need for company with peers, and for conversation as a form of 'mental play' (Suttie 1935). An important function of interest-sharing is to recognise and approach potential interest-sharers and so expand the circle of companions with whom shared interests can be enjoyed. It also prepares for the movement to a level of development when attachment figures are drawn from one's own generation rather than the earlier one.

THE POTENTIATING SYSTEMS AND THEIR DEVELOPMENT

We consider that lower-order potentiating capacities cover: the construction of internal working models (see Chapter 8), mechanisms of psychological defence, MacLean's interoperative capacities and the capacities for social referencing, watching and copying attachment figures and affective attunement.

The high-order systems are expressed in a number of neocortical psychological capacities that we think reflect Sperry's concept of high-order systems which enlarge human consciousness. These we regard as essential for the development of supportive companionable relating. The most important are the capacities:

1 to create symbols and to use them to signify personal meanings, conveyed through speech, drawings, models or music;
2 to plan, organise and to rehearse in one's mind the possible outcomes of various plans to reach the goals of behavioural systems, and so to take medium- and long-term views;
3 to appraise and evaluate one's feelings, thoughts and actions from a subjective point of view and at the same time to evaluate those of others. This capacity covers our understanding of metacognition and empathy;
4 to appreciate moral, aesthetic and religious values; and
5 to envisage ideals and aspire to reach them. In this way, the future can be made more tangible (e.g. I can see what I want to be and do).

The capacity to plan to reach a goal and to aspire to reach ideals introduces the idea that human beings have an orientation towards the future and to predicting what might happen in it. They also have the ability to share expectations, aspirations and musings about the future, to the extent of thinking what might happen after death and forming groups on the basis of shared beliefs.

Our understanding of Sperry's ideas suggests that an individual's high-level systems can exert top-down influences that go some way to free him from some stimulus-bound bottom-up responses. We suggest that the behavioural systems, when expressed through dominating/submissive (D/S) patterns of relating (see Chapter 3) exert bottom-up influences. In contrast instinctive systems expressed through supportive companionable (SC) patterns of relating are influenced by high-level systems. The top-down effect of the high-level systems on the behavioural systems can inhibit D/S patterns of relating but only when the homeostatic infrastructure is sufficiently maintained (by caregiving and/or self-care and management) to release exploratory activity.

We have briefly outlined the communicative function of the capacity to form and use symbols in Chapter 3. We discuss the function of representational models in Chapters 4 and 8, what is meant by the term metacognition and its use in appraising and evaluating the feelings of self and others in Chapter 13, and the function of ideals in Chapter 11.

A comment on the development of an individual's potentiating capacities and the conditions under which they are functional

We cannot discuss the development of an individual's lower-order and high-order potentiating capacities, but we note the consequences of what seems to be a major difference between them. It would appear that the rate of development of high-order systems is much slower than that of the lower-order systems. This suggests that early in life the behavioural systems will only have the lower-order auxiliary capacities as essential adjuncts. The pace at which an individual's consciousness can be expanded is set by the pace at which high-order capacities develop.

It is a commonplace observation that high-order capacities are not always functional. High levels of emotional arousal and fear can render one speechless, can make it difficult to see affairs from the point of view of others, and difficult to make effective plans to handle the long term as well as the present. We regard caregiving from others and the representation of earlier caregiving (in the form of the internal supportive system and the personal supportive environment) as regulating factors that enable individuals to maintain (or not maintain) the effectiveness of their high-level capacities.

OUTLINE OF THE SUPRAORDINATE SYSTEM FOR SELF-CARE AND MANAGEMENT AND ITS DEVELOPMENT

Bowlby's model of instinctive behaviour focuses on careseeking as an interpersonal phenomenon, although he also discusses self-reliance and mechanisms of psychological defence which have an intrapersonal connotation. To resolve these apparently antithetical concepts we have supposed that each human being is an individual in their own right, and innately programmed:

1 to regulate their own states of psychological arousal and to take over as much of their physical management as they can (e.g. most infants, in the latter part of their first year, show signs that they want to have a say in feeding and dressing); but
2 to rely on a relationship with preferred caregiving (attachment) figures who provide protection and support in satisfying physical needs, in regulating levels of affect vitality and in moving towards the next stage of development.

Self-care and management involve high-order capacities, especially the capacity for long-term planning, for metacognition, and to aspire to reach ideals. It does not begin to be shown until around three to four years of age. It appears in two forms depending on the quality of the interactions represented in IMERs that take part in the internal supportive system. One form is interdependent self-care and management, the other is a defensive form of self-care and management which can be overly dependent or independent. When the quality of the caregiving/careseeking (CG/CS) interactions that make up the internal supportive system are, on the whole, support-ive and companionable, then the development of the interdependent form of self-management is promoted. The individual develops the ability to negotiate with caregivers to have careseeking needs met and to have mutually supportive give-and-take partnerships in regard to each of the interpersonal systems, as well as the ability to initiate and sustain supportive/companionable (SC) patterns of relating. The more interactions with caregivers represented in IMERs are disassuaging, by being conducted by caregivers using coercive patterns of relating, the less an individual develops the co-operative abilities listed above and the less they can sustain a movement towards interdependent self-management. Instead either of the two forms of defensive self-care and management develops. When the CG/CS interactions within the internal supportive system are disorganising as well as disassuaging, and there is a virtual absence of SC relating by caregivers, the movement towards self-care and management is retarded. The individual is then reliant on an independent form of self-care for survival.

Until both interdependent and independent forms of defensive self-management are well established, they are easily disrupted by any situation that evokes high levels of excitement, frustration and disassuagement that are not regulated by caregiving.

In summary, parental caregiving, consistently mediated through SC patterns of relating, provides offspring (of all ages) with an accepting, sensitive, interested, co-operative and developmentally appropriate pattern of relating. It is a pattern that enables offspring to feel increasingly capable of caring for themselves, managing their own affairs, and seeking help from others whom they have reason to trust, in situations which they find are beyond their competence to handle.

Alternatively, when parental figures use patterns of relating that fit descriptions of D/S relating, the child's systems for careseeking, for caregiving to others, for intrapersonal exploration and co-operative interest-sharing relationships (with peers in recreation and work), for mutually affectionate sexual relationships and for overall self-management are reduced. Each of these partnerships is affected by anxiety and frustration so that the functioning of the relevant systems becomes disturbed to the point of disorder. The disorder can then be exacerbated by defensive processes of avoidance or aggressive assertion which are used to mitigate the pain and distress of failing to reach inter- or intrapersonal goals. Our understanding of these complicated defensive processes is unfolded in the remaining chapters of this Part and the therapeutic handling of them in Chapters 14 and 15.

The development of careseeking and defensive self-management

The development of the careseeking system has already been outlined in Chapter 4. The system for defensive self-management similarly operates at different levels of development. The earliest level is that of automatic fixed-action patterns (e.g. the blink reflex and other simple avoidant responses); later, a level of straightforward experiential learning is achieved (e.g. the avoidance of nettles), or still later strategic levels of defence that involve planning and the use of rules which have been laid down in the appropriate IMER (see Chapters 5 and 8). The set goal of this intrapersonal system is for an individual to re-establish through his own endeavours the highest degree of safety and sense of security that he can attain. This system is discussed in Chapter 11 in relation to defensive non-maturative idealisations.

THE FUNCTIONS AND DEVELOPMENT OF THE INTERPERSONAL CAREGIVING SYSTEM

The system for caregiving to others occupies a position of special importance not only for the maintenance of physical and psychological homeostasis in others but also for the development of the self. The system is activated by signals from careseekers, and by the perception of their absence when they are expected (zero signals discussed in Chapter 8). Its function is to provide infants, children and adults – especially those with whom a bond of caregiving exists – with the blend of protection, physical and emotional comfort and educative explanation (Chapter 5, Heard and Lake 1986) that is currently required by the careseeker. The caregiving system thus straddles the homeostatic group of systems and the exploratory group. But as the maintenance of the homeostatic infrastructure is essential for survival these take precedence over attention to the exploratory group of systems.

We see the caregiving system as nascent in infancy and consider that although homeostatic caregiving to others is shown in a fragmentary fashion from quite early childhood, the system is not fully functional; that is to say a person is not able to look after an infant, child or adolescent effectively until early adulthood. The ability to give care requires, to begin with, the innate ability to recognise and respond to an infant's careseeking signals. As the infant and then child becomes older and more venturesome, an exploratory empathic stance is increasingly required by the caregiver, as well as the capacity for long-term planning. As we discuss in Chapter 13, the capacity for empathy requires a capacity for metacognition as well as other high-level capacities. The development of an individual's caregiving system also depends profoundly on the nature of caregiving/careseeking partnerships that an individual has had with their own caregivers.

THE SEXUAL SYSTEM AND ITS DEVELOPMENT

Conceptualising the functions of a human sexual system within the theoretical frame we have presented has led us to conclusions that differ in some respects from those suggested by currently accepted psychoanalytic theory. We see the sexual system as part of the supraordinate system for self-management, and think of it as having three components, two interpersonal and one intrapersonal and as straddling both the homeostatic and the developmental group of systems. In maintaining the continuity of the family and the human race, the interpersonal reproductive component of the sexual system is directly involved in carrying forward the development of that person by leading them to parenthood. The second component in our view is also in the developmental group, and makes lovemaking in adults into a sexualised form of primary intersubjectivity which augments affect vitality. The level of arousal can be higher than that which can be sustained long term by any other behavioural system. This comes about because the goal of the sexual system is experienced climactically and arousal is automatically regulated by the experience of orgasm, although the sense of pleasurable closeness from enjoying a shared desire lingers.

The third component is primarily homeostatic and defensive. It is active when intercourse takes place without an affectional accompaniment, or alternatively when an individual indulges in masturbatory activities. Such sexual activity acts as a distraction from experiencing separation anxiety, loneliness and internal conflict. Affectionless intercourse and/or masturbation usually evokes relief of tension often accompanied by a temporary feeling of vitality, but the experience of intersubjectivity and intimacy is absent.

The development of the sexual system

Like the caregiving system, the sexual system is nascent at birth. Views on its development are still controversial as are explanations relating to homosexuality and the feeling of being of the wrong gender when genetic investigations are unequivocal. We do not discuss its development but have found in therapy that it is useful to bear in mind the following observations:

1 The sexual system from early childhood has the capacity, through masturbation, to relieve tension and temporarily enliven and soothe.
2 Children are intensely curious about adult sexual activities, and engage in fragments of sexual activity with one another.
3 Until they experience the hormone-induced surges of romantic sexual desire in adolescence, children are very resistant to engage with adults in any penetrative sexual act, and often react with fear, and distress when witnessing adults having intercourse.
4 Paradoxically children can be drawn to respond sexually to adults of the opposite sex (and occasionally to one of the same sex) whom they like and who are gentle, and do not hurt or disgust.
5 Children are regularly extremely upset by being used by an adult as a sexual partner and confused by the threats they make should the child tell anyone.

PARTNERSHIPS FORMED ON THE BASIS OF INTERDEPENDENT SYSTEMS

The categorisation of behavioural systems described in this chapter draws attention to the degree to which individuals are reliant upon the relationships they have with others to carry forward their physical and psychological development and maintain the physical and psychological milieu within which such development can take place. It proposes four instinctive behavioural systems that have interdependent goals, which allow for three pairs of instinctive behavioural partnerships: caregiving/careseeking (CG/CS), interest-sharing (IS/IS) and sexual partnerships (S/S). However, in order to understand how individuals are affected when interpersonal goals have not been sufficiently well met, a conceptual bridge is required between the concept of goal-corrected behavioural systems and the relationships within which these systems are expressed. We use the concept of partnerships, introduced by Bowlby (see Chapter 4) when he talked of the situation that arises frequently and inevitably between a mother and her child when, as CG/CS partners, each wants to change the set goal of the other to fit their personal desires *vis-à-vis* the other.

Each close relationship established between two, three or a small group of people is expressed through one, two or all three partnerships. In the next chapter we show that the extent to which the interpersonal goals of the relevant partnerships are met affects the quality of that relationship for the individuals concerned and their sense of who they are.

THE SYSTEMS OF THE SELF IN RELATION TO THE DEGREE TO WHICH THEIR REPRESENTATIONS ARE OPEN OR CLOSED

One of the ways in which systems were originally categorised was to divide them into open or closed systems (von Bertalanffy 1968). In a presentation of family systems in the light of the attachment dynamic, Heard (1982) defined a family as behaving as a more open system when the goals of careseeking and caregiving are being met and family members 'are free to be exploratory and creative'. Alternatively when the family behaves as a less open system the members are largely engaged in trying to reach the goals of careseeking.

In our current presentation we have elaborated the 1982 view. We no longer use the idea of more open and more closed systems but refer to the degree to which internal representations are more closed or open to being updated by the introduction of new information. Thus we see aspects of IMERs as more open, or more closed, to further updating. We discuss the recognition of more closed aspects of IMERs in Chapter 14. We now view a family as an extremely complex system of relationships between people of different generations, with the IMERs of each family member, being more, or less, open to further updating in the atmosphere of everyday living in the family. In this book we pay more attention to dyadic and triadic partnerships than to whole families and discuss how the instinctive partnerships people try to set up when they join a group reflects the CG/CS partnerships they experienced within their families of origin. The whole issue of disordered systems is discussed further in relation to ideals and defensive idealisation in Chapter 11.

Chapter 8

From behavioural systems to adult relationships by way of internal working models

There is a considerable gap between the concept of goal-corrected behavioural systems and the everyday relationships people have with one another. The gap narrows when behavioural systems are discussed in terms of the three partnerships – caregiving/careseeking (CG/CS), interest-sharing/interest-sharing (IS/IS), and sexual – described at the end of Chapter 7. It becomes smaller when these partnerships are seen as integral aspects of attachment relationships or other bonds that are often referred to as close, intimate or affectional.

A bond in adult life can be expressed through any combination of partnerships. It can for example be based primarily on a CG/CS partnership and secondarily on one that is sexual; or primarily on a sexual or an IS/IS partnership with little sign of a CG/CS component. Our clinical and social experience supports the view that most adults, when meeting new people, are open to the possibility of making a relationship that includes the formation of a bond within which various kinds of satisfaction will be found. A new relationship can move quickly or slowly to the formation of a bond when we refer to it as an affectional relationship, which is maintained or can become attenuated to a vanishing point. Alternatively, the relationship can remain unbonded. In unbonded relationships people relate to each other using culturally based contracts (e.g. buying bus tickets and any other commodity) or rituals such as christenings, other rites of passage, celebrations and remembrances. They share interests as opera goers or football fans who keep cultural rules of behaviour enforced by laws which define how a person is expected to behave towards another. A potent source of group conflict lies in the emergence of a subculture with different attitudes, values and rules of behaviour. Such rules and rituals can undergo marked change within a decade or endure unchanged for centuries. Participants in unbonded relationships are referred to as acquaintances or colleagues and partners without further description. People in bonded relationships we speak of as friends, companions, companionable colleagues, parental figures and careseekers, or lovers, depending on the nature of the partnerships within the affectional relationship.

We have used this approach to nomenclature because it avoids using the ugly and possibly misleading term bonded relationships. It does however leave enduring relationships in which any affection is so diluted by painful interactions that the participants feel little, if any, affection for each other still being described as affectional.

There is a steady progress towards the formation of an affectional relationship when the mixture of possible partnerships offered by one of the participants fits the expectations of the other(s) sufficiently well. This is impeded when one person wants one kind of bond and the other(s) have expectations of forming a different kind of bond or no bond at all.

Sometimes all participants give an observer the impression of having fairly regular meetings with no apparent bond being formed. These people can be referred to as long-term acquaintances.

Temperament and other genetic endowments contribute to the nature of an affectional relationship. But although we acknowledge their considerable influence, we do not discuss their nature.

Functional and dysfunctional affectional partnerships

Bowlby discussed disturbances in CG/CS partnerships in terms of the de-activation of the attachment system. We find it more useful in clinical settings to talk about systems as functional and as more, or less, dysfunctional or disordered. A functional partnership is one in which each partner is able to reach the interdependent set goals of their partnerships well enough. They become dysfunctional to an increasing degree as each partner fails to reach their set goals, and as the systems for intrapersonal defensive self-care and management are increasingly activated to mitigate the personal pain of the failure of the partnership. Dysfunctional CG/CS partnerships have widespread adverse effects on all the activities and lifestyle of an individual through their effects on the functioning of IS/IS and sexual partnerships and that of the intrapersonal system of exploration. We recognise that genetically based failures in the careseeking system may occur, and maybe in the caregiving system too, but consider them to be relatively rare. What seems to be commoner is either a mismatch in temperament between caregiver and careseeker (an active outgoing careseeker and a less active more reflective caregiver or vice versa) or, as we discuss in Chapter 11, a clash of values in respect of proximity keeping and patterns of relating. Should an individual's system for intrapersonal self-management not be sufficiently complemented by their system for seeking care (from one or more caregivers) then an individual is having to maintain their homeostatic infrastructure without sufficient help from a CG/CS partnership. When the manner in which that individual defensively maintains his homeostatic infrastructure arouses high degrees of intrapersonal self-defence in the other partner(s), then that partnership can be considered seriously dysfunctional. Unless the process is halted, the partnership is near the point of ending by the partners separating, or approaching the point of being brought to an end by murder, suicide or a fatal exacerbation of a psychosomatic disorder.

Primary and secondary attachment partnerships

Bonds are formed at all ages between people with different experiences within instinctive partnerships, and differences in the degree to which each partner's system for independent defensive self-management has been affected in the past by experiences of abandonment, rejection or impinging overcontrol by caregivers. A child's first bonds (which we refer to as primary attachments) are inevitably made to people of the parental generation, or to siblings or others old enough to give some measure of appropriate care. By early adolescence, individuals are established in looking for support from peers (often in preference to parental figures) and are beginning to make attachment partnerships with their peers (defined as people of broadly similar intelligence, stamina, capacity to handle fear and panic) which can take the form of romantic attachments (Hazan and Shaver 1987) (see Appendix C). We refer to attachment bonds between peers as secondary attachments. In old age, as secondary attachments diminish through death or disability, individuals tend to turn to offspring for care, which we regard as reversed attachments. Sometimes, for a variety of defensive reasons touched on in Chapter 11, reversed attachments are formed much earlier.

A consequence of an individual's recognition of information by the automatic referral of incoming information to their working models is that the individual inevitably approaches secondary and reversed attachments primed by the history of their experiences in their primary attachments and by well-established defensive habits formed by their activation of the system for intrapersonal defence. People therefore tend to behave in secondary and reversed attachments in accordance with what has been learnt from primary attachments.

The function of a hierarchy of primary attachment figures

It is well accepted that infants make attachments to a small hierarchy of primary attachment figures and that they can be securely attached to one parent but not to the other. Our own clinical experience of working with clients who as infants had regular access to a small group of attachment figures and whose mothers were chronically ill, or unable to give sufficient attention to their child for other reasons, is that these clients had learnt that there is safety in numbers. That is to say some attachment figures within the hierarchy could satisfy some components of careseeking much better than others and the clients used each of these figures as far as they could. These clients suffered a considerable loss, often unrecognised by others, when a valued member of this personal group (not always a relative) was no longer available. We have found that the same principle was operating in working with children who were opposed to the divorce of their parents, and with adults who indicated that as children they could only manage if both parents were around. This issue is noted by Ainsworth and Eichberg (1991) when writing on the effects on infant–mother attachment of the mother's unresolved loss of an attachment figure.

AN UNDERSTANDING OF WORKING MODELS

In 1986 we described Bowlby's concept of working models and presented a broad outline of how those working models of self and others with whom an attachment or other kind of bond had been formed provided the basis of an internal supportive system and were also used to construct an individual's personal supportive environment. These special working models we gave the term Internal Models of Experience in Relationships (IMERs). We now describe our current understanding of all working models, which is expressed with a somewhat different emphasis than the pictures of working models given by others, for example Collins and Read (1994) and Crittenden (1990).

We consider that working models hold the history of the relations an individual has with any entity or event in their environment. We follow Craik (1967: 52–3) in seeing representational models as a fundamental feature of neural mechanisms. Their power is to parallel or model external events. He makes the crucial point that the term working model should be considered as an analogy and therefore bound to break down at some point, for example, when it shows properties not found in the process it imitates, or by not possessing properties possessed by the process it imitates.

With this caveat and the dynamic picture of the self described in Chapter 7 in mind, we work on the assumptions that when sensory information from a familiar event is received, an appropriate internal working model is activated, and that should no working model be activated, which means that the situation is not recognised, it is either ignored, actively avoided or actively explored. A new model can then be constructed, provided that the exploratory system is not overridden and there is an opportunity to give the task the necessary attention. In linking this view of working models to the way attachment phenomena may function, we assume that there are separate innate representations of the situation of reaching the goals of the behavioural systems. The representation of careseeking is activated when a caregiver provides the blend of caregiving the careseeker requires in an attentive manner. This includes the behaviour described by Stern as tuning (see Chapter 3) and the tone of voice derived from motherese (see Chapter 3). The combination of these behaviours produces the external situation that when recognised by a careseeker activates their innate representation of the situation of reaching the goal of careseeking. At this point feelings of satisfaction arise and the motivation to seek care is switched off. The analogous representation of the goal of interest-sharing, which is associated with exploratory behaviour, cannot be activated while careseeking behaviour is aroused to more than a critical degree.

We now turn to considering working models that include the individual interacting with various aspects of the environment that have a variety of personal meanings for the individual.

Working models of relationships (IMERs)

As noted earlier, we have placed working models of relationships with people in a special category and call them IMERs. We take Hinde's (1979) view that the nature of a relationship is revealed in the history of the content and quality of the interactions exchanged between the participants. This definition fits the way in which clients talk about their relationships, and it has led us to see an IMER as representing all the interactions that have taken place between the self and other(s) in a particular relationship in chronological order. The model of each interaction includes an affective and cognitive evaluation of the event itself, the context in which the interaction took place, and its consequences in terms of reaching or not reaching the goals of any behavioural system already activated or activated by the interaction itself. The integration over time of all the interactions generates a history of the relationship.

The appraisal of incoming information that awakens a personal meaning

When incoming information activates a representation (say of a car), the individual responds in different ways according to their interest in cars and how much cars in general, or this particular car, activate their working models of cars and IMERs. For example, the car might have been recognised not as just 'a car' but as 'an old round-nosed Morris in remarkably good shape – and I wonder who owns it'. The observer's interest in cars would have been sufficient to transform it into a symbol of an interest and the observer would have moved to being a potential interest-sharer and the IMERs of 'sharers of my interest in cars' would have been awakened. Should the car have been recognised as 'an old banger, blocking the entrance to my driveway' the meaning of the information would awaken other IMERs. The context (where the car is parked) has alerted the individual to the fact that the car is parked on territory regarded as 'closely to do with me' and he is reminded of IMERs associated with how his space was regarded by other people (especially a relationship with a person with whom an attachment or other bond has been formed), how he felt about that, and what he now feels ought to be done about it.

The relationships that are most important for the development and well-being of the self are those in which individuals are relating to people with whom they have affectional partnerships. In relationships with a long history, the other(s) and oneself can sequentially occupy different roles within a particular IMER, which are derived from different partnerships. For example within the IMER of self and a parent, the self initially is in the role of a careseeker, later in life the role can switch from careseeker to that of caregiver with perhaps the addition of an interest-sharing partnership. The IMER of self with spouse can be based primarily on the experiences of sharing of mutual interests and a sexual partnership and secondarily on caregiving and careseeking. Circumstances can intervene so that the experience of sharing interests and a sexual partnership are minimised and a CG/CS partnership predominates.

Since 1986 we have become clearer about how to handle the complexity inherent in having many IMERs, some of which carry incompatible information about oneself, what one values and devalues, and predictions about the future, all of which can affect an individual's sense of identity. We currently take the view that children know of differences within the IMER of me–and–X quite early. However from studies on metacognition, often referred to as theory of mind (Astington *et al.* 1988, Main 1991), we think individuals, until they are about four years, are not able to generalise within each IMER and across IMERs, in order to reach conscious feelings about their own identity, compared with the identity of other people. When models of the self within different IMERs (e.g. the IMERs of self–with–mother, self–with–father, self–with–mates) are too discrepant, they cannot be generalised into one overall coherent model of the self. This leads to individuals feeling themselves one kind of person in some relationships and contexts, and another in other relationships and contexts. Overall such individuals often remain unsure of who they 'really' are. More serious uncertainties about identity often arise when the IMER of the relationship with one person contains major discrepancies. For example: myself with a cheerful, responsive and competent parent in some contexts, and myself and the same parent in very angry or depressed moods insisting on the validity of their catastrophic predictions.

Although IMERs can be reappraised at any stage after a sense of identity has become conscious, such reappraisal may be blocked, especially when the individual has come to accept another image of himself which has been emphatically expressed by valued caregivers. Identity predicaments have been discussed in the literature on dissociation and multiple personality. Some writers (Barach 1991, Liotti 1992) use

Bowlby's ideas of the development of multiple models of the self associated with the segregation of painful information. Sands (1994) uses much the same concepts but does not link them to attachment theory.

Working models and the internal supportive system

In 1986 we discussed how incoming information that evokes careseeking is automatically matched against the IMERs of self with attachment figures, and how reminders (Schank 1982) evoke feelings about, and often memories of:

1   the way in which situations similar to the current situation were handled in the past;
2   their consequences for the self; and
3   how the self felt and was regarded by the relevant caregivers. In this way all the caregivers represented in IMERs can be seen to act as inescapable internalised caregivers and the IMERs as functioning as an internal supportive system. The system can range from being highly supportive in most contexts to being highly unsupportive in many.

The concept of an internalised supportive system is similar in many respects to Fairbairn's concept of internal object relations, and to a lesser degree to Freud's concept of the super-ego.

Working models and the personal supportive environment

IMERs and models of the world in which an individual lives and imagines play a central part in the construction of a 'personal supportive environment' which we proposed in 1986 as the representation of all the contexts in which the goals of instinctive systems have been best met. It is made up of the recreations, personal routines, pace of life, disposition of belongings, kind of terrain and house found to be congenial; the degree of light, colour, warmth and physical comfort one enjoys; and the spatial and psychological distance from and closeness to companions, caregivers and careseekers found comfortable. An individual is constantly constructing this environment through the integration of information derived from memories:

1   of contexts in which well-matched CG/CS and IS/IS and sexual partnerships have occurred;

2 of natural phenomena and human artefacts which evoke a sense of wonder, delight or awe; and

3 religious experience.

This environment has affinities with Lewin's (1952) life space and with the concept of transitional and attachment phenomena (Winnicott 1971, Boniface and Graham 1979). It is discussed further in Chapter 11.

Access to representational models

So far we have emphasised the automatic unconscious activity of representational models. The question now arises, how conscious can one be of the working models that are in use, especially of IMERs? The question is still not answered. Bowlby touched on this topic and the part played by different forms of memory. It is possible for reminders (Schank 1982) to trigger recall of a particular event and all its emotive overtones. For example, reminders often come in the form of an anniversary, a particular scent, sound or scene, or a particular mode of behaviour and emotive message. The reminder may, or may not, be valued and welcomed and will involve different kinds of long-term memory (Tulving 1985). It can evoke the memory of an episode, but it also can symbolise a whole relationship and the general rules associated with it, thus involving semantic memory. Or memory may be in a form that is implicit rather than explicit in that it represents learnt-but-never-verbalised ways of behaving. These have been discussed by Emde (Emde *et al.* 1991). One can also consciously try to recall a relationship. But that process will leave out all interactions traumatic enough to have been segregated from conscious recall. These may be completely 'forgotten' but reminders will evoke the emotive overtones of segregated and dissociated events in the form of free-floating anxiety, unexplainable fear or sense of depression, or a tendency to dislike or to avoid a particular person, scene, time of year or a date.

THE FUNCTIONS AND DEVELOPMENT OF THE TWO ALTERNATIVE FORMS OF RELATING

We now return to two alternative patterns of human relating (supportive companionable (SC) and dominating/submissive (D/S) first described in Chapter 3 and fit them into the theoretical model we have proposed for relationships. These patterns have similarities with Birtchnell's (1993) framework of motives relating to both humans and animals. We present SC and D/S patterns of relating as alternative means by which caregiving/careseeking (CG/CS), interest-sharing/interest-sharing (IS/IS) and sexual partnerships are conducted. SC relating expresses empathic caregiving integrated with exploratory interest-sharing. Consequently careseekers are related to in a caregiving and interest-sharing manner, which has been shown to enhance learning and also using sensitive 'tuning' (Stern 1985) regulates overarousal or underarousal. We regard the descriptions of SC relating given in Chapter 3 as being close to the caregiving behaviour Kunce and Shaver (1994) have associated with secure infant attachment styles; and the caregivers using D/S patterns behaviour we see as similar to caregivers they associate with ambivalent and avoidant attachment styles. In a similar way we regard the way Kobak and Duemmler (1994) have used conversations as a tool by which to study attachment relations over the life span as yielding findings that are compatible with the theoretical model we present.

The functions of SC relating

We point to the functions of SC relating through three examples. The mother who greets her infant, after their separation during the Strange Situation Test, with the kind of comforting that enables the infant to return to play is, in our view, using SC relating, and the infant's behaviour after reunion labels him as secure in that relationship. The descriptions in Chapter 3 show the value of SC patterns in educational settings. Accumulated knowledge about how to make and maintain psychotherapeutic relationships points to the use of SC patterns by therapists as being the most effective in helping clients develop their personal and social competencies (ego strength) and gain a sense of well-being.

SC relating with its caregiving component, maintains peer interest-sharing by ensuring that partners, whose careseeking systems have been activated in the course of pursuing an interest, will be supported. Consequently they are able to return to the interest with minimal interruption. The two-way communication fostered by SC relating furthers co-operation and the settlement of conflict through discussion, compromise and the testing of hypotheses.

Competition between a dyad or members of a group or two teams using SC relating is a different phenomenon than that seen during D/S relating. In SC relating, the aim of competition is to increase abilities and skills relative to a shared interest, rather than defensively maintaining the status and power of competitors as it is in D/S relating.

The development of SC patterns of relating

Although infants, who are not showing a physiological need, are predisposed to respond to SC relating with interest and enjoyment, their ability to maintain it when other people are unresponsive or using D/S patterns is negligible. The maintenance of SC relating seems to require a reasonable level of development of high-level capacities, coupled with a history of a good-enough level of SC relating within primary attachment partnerships. When SC relating is the predominant pattern within IMERs, of self and parental figures over early childhood, in a wide enough range of contexts, it can become established, with the help of the internal supportive system, to be the preferred pattern of relating to others.

There are two items of infant behaviour which we consider show that children are innately geared to look for and accept guidance from parental figures who show SC relating. These are social referencing and the responses of infants to parental attunement (and tuning). The imitation of adult behaviour appears to be related as much to D/S patterns as to SC patterns.

An explanation for the phenomena of primary and secondary intersubjectivity and parental responses to social referencing is suggested by Emde (1988a). It would appear from Main's findings that dysfunctional and disordered parental responses to social referencing that confuse a child can lead children to turn away from guidance by that parent.

The functions of D/S patterns of relating

As indicated in Chapter 3, D/S patterns are primarily defensive. We regard them as expressions of the arousal of the system for intrapersonal defensive self-care and management. They are used by individuals who having suffered a loss of SC relating, or of other valued resources, cannot trust caregivers to be interested in their plight and treat them with respect.

Depending upon previous experience, age and temperament, individuals who have been made fearful of coming under the control of others tend to be controlling to those they assess as likely to become compliant; or they become compliant to those they expect to greet protest and controlling behaviour by a greater display of anger or coercion. The function of these patterns is to secure what has been threatened or to restore what has been lost, with a minimum of further loss and distress. Individuals using the controlling pattern aim to safeguard themselves by influencing others, in one way or another, to become compliant and thus under their control.

The use of compliance aims to minimise further loss by signalling the acceptance of control by the other. The cost is the suppression of anger and protest, and the curtailing of exploratory moves. It has profound effects on the sense of self-worth and effectiveness and the degree to which one values oneself.

Caregiving and D/S relating

Caregivers who are most likely to show D/S patterns are those whose internal supportive systems undermine their attempts to be competent, whose personal supportive environment cannot be maintained and who have no effective external support available. When faced with too many careseekers, or ones that are uncooperative, such caregivers feel incompetent and powerless. To regain a sense of control and competence, there is a marked tendency for them to fall back on coercive controlling or avoidant patterns of relating. Furthermore, adult to adult CG/CS partnerships are also affected. Should defensive strategies, which were successful with primary attachment figures, fail when used in relationships with secondary attachment figures by serving to evoke D/S patterns of relating from the secondary attachment figure, then the careseeker tends to escalate their D/S patterns, in order to induce the secondary attachment figure to relate using the SC pattern. In these circumstances, the use of controlling patterns by either partner are doomed to failure. Commonly, bitter controlling/controlling conflicts ensue until someone submits, or withdraws, or mutual fatigue or arbitration ends the conflict. Many marital conflicts are of this type.

Clinical experience has led us to the view that the risk of D/S patterns of caregiving becoming the predominant pattern depends on the caregiver's own childhood experience of caregiving from their parental figures represented in their IMERs together with the degree of threatened or actual loss the caregiver is currently experiencing from sources external to the particular CG/CS partnership (e.g. losses of other relationships, at home or at work, the recognition of loss of competence in one's own eyes or in those of others, or losses relating to money and other resources). SC patterns of relating can be maintained by individuals only so long as they handle their fears about losing competence and/or resources well enough to maintain a caregiving and exploratory stance towards careseekers, other people and their environment. Unless high-level capacities are able to act continuously as top-down influences on instinctive behaviour, individuals who feel themselves to be without support, fall back on D/S relating.

RELATIONSHIPS AND SCALES OF VALUE

In this chapter we have shown the relations between instinctive partnerships and relationships, and their expression through SC and D/S patterns of relating. We have also shown the extent to which internal working models of early CG/CS partnerships affect those formed later. That is not the whole story. Individuals value some relationships and some patterns of relating (SC or D/S) more than others, either overall or in particular contexts. Moreover people are seldom contented with an unchanging standard of performance. There seem to be deep-seated, we would say innate, desires to reach new levels of ability, skill and competence in what one undertakes, and to eschew failures and distress. These issues are taken up in the remaining chapters of this part. We begin with a short chapter on how personal scales of value can develop. We continue with an outline of the development of the concept of the ego/self ideal which shows how the concept of ego and self ideals has been widely associated with the process of caregiving and with the concept of maturation. We end Part II with a discussion on human ideals defined as the highest conception of what is personally valued, showing that the ideals to which one aspires can either lead towards a further stage of development or be associated with defensively maintaining the homeostatic infrastructure on which the sense of well-being and life itself depends.

Chapter 9

How values are acquired and assigned to oneself, people and other entities

Bowlby made two forays into the processes, still far from under-stood, whereby individuals sift and identify incoming sensory infor-mation so that events that matter for their survival and well-being are recognised, and the behavioural responses that are likely to be helpful are selected. He discusses the appraisal of incoming sensory information and its relation to feelings, affects and emotion in a chapter (Bowlby 1969, 1982) written some years before he discussed information processing in relation to the mechanisms of psychologi-cal defence (Bowlby 1980, Chapter 4).

In Chapter 4 we summarised Bowlby's understanding of feelings as a 'being felt' phase of an individual's intuitive and often uncon-scious appraisal, either of their own organismic states and urges to act or of the succession of environmental situations in which they find themselves. He sees appraisal as a complex process in which two main steps can be distinguished: the comparison of sensory input with standards that act as comparators and have developed within the lifetime of the organism; and the selection of certain gen-eral forms of behaviour in preference to other forms in accordance with the results of previously made comparisons. We would distin-guish a preliminary stage (see Chapter 8) which is concerned with identifying the information by the activation of internal working models. Information is recognised as either known and familiar or as something strange. It can also be defensively not perceived or recognised.

In Bowlby's view the experiencing of feelings is the phase in which people are made aware of their appraising processes. Feelings therefore in his view provide a monitoring service concerning an individual's states, urges and situations. He makes the point that appraisal can be conducted at various levels. For example, fixed-action patterns once begun may proceed without further appraisal, whereas, if behaviour is organised in a more discriminating and differentiating way, which is the kind of behaviour therapists usually have to understand, appraisal is also more differentiated.

Although he does not make a functional distinction between appraisal and assigning a value to different kinds of sensory input, he associates himself with Arnold's (1960) view that interpreted and appraised input, whether from the environment or from the organism, is experienced inherently in terms of value, as pleasant or unpleasant, nice or nasty, likeable or unlikeable. He regards these value categories as a rough and ready, comparatively crude categorisation when compared with the more refined sorting of input into categories that signal the activation of behavioural systems. However, he considers that sensory input, appraised as nice or nasty, is accompanied by behaviour that tends to be predictable. Something appraised as nice is likely to be kept and sought after, while the opposite applies when it is appraised as nasty. Furthermore he considers that when sensory input is sorted into categories that relate to the activation of an instinctive system, a person is likely to experience feelings associated with whichever instinctive system is activated. Bowlby keeps an open mind about the exact point in the sequence at which emotion associated with an activated system is aroused. He is clear that this can happen after behaviour has begun and that progress in reaching the goal is appraised and experienced as smooth, halting or stopped. The reaching or not reaching a set goal and its consequences are also appraised, the latter often being experienced in terms of pleasurable/painful, liked/disliked, good/bad. He adds that learning takes place through the process of regular appraisal and monitoring: the more keenly appraisal processes are felt and the more the consequences of some behaviour are experienced as painful or pleasurable the quicker and more persistent the ensuing learning (Bowlby 1982: 115).

Bowlby also takes up the question of whether feeling or emotion is causative of behaviour. In considering this question he sets feelings alongside the appraisal processes in which they are a phase. For example, he considers that in the causation of a behavioural sequence such as comforting a crying baby, appraising the baby as something to be comforted is a necessary step, and that alternative appraisals (such as the baby is something to be ignored) would lead to different behaviour on the part of the mother. This line of reasoning leads him to conclude that the processes of interpreting and appraising information must be assigned a causal role in producing whatever behaviour emerges.

In discussing the communicative role of feeling from a therapeutic standpoint, Bowlby observes that attributing feeling to someone may be making a prediction about their subsequent behaviour, or it describes what they are supposed to be feeling. But he points out that as feeling is usually accompanied by distinctive facial expressions, bodily postures, and incipient movements, it provides valuable information to others. This means that the experience of feeling can provide a monitoring service, for therapist and client alike, of behavioural and physiological states. Bowlby regards it as dangerous for therapists or clients to suppose that recognition of a feeling state such as anger or sadness is enough. The danger lies in the failure to determine the situation clients are appraising that is associated with their feelings and what they are consequently disposed to do. How a client is appraising themselves, the world, the particular situation they are experiencing, and what kinds of behaviour are consequently being activated, can be judged from the observation of specific non-verbal activities such as a person's intentional movements, displacement activities, physiological changes, or signals like smiling or crying; and also their use of words, which denote feelings, like being 'afraid', or 'hungry' which imply types of predictions, and others that denote moods like 'hopeless' or 'confident'.

We share the general tenor of Bowlby's views of appraisal and note with respect the arguments on the nature of emotions (Izard 1993, Ortony *et al.* 1988, Ortony and Turner 1990, Turner and Ortony 1992, and LeDoux 1994).

ASSIGNING VALUES TO INCOMING INFORMATION

In order to understand the source of one's values, we begin by differentiating between the process of the general appraisal of information, which can include the appraisal of sensations, and the evaluation of that information in terms of feelings such as nice/nasty or pleasurable/unpleasurable, and moral evaluations of good/bad, praiseworthy/unworthy. We consider that what one values most or least can ultimately be linked back to experiences of reaching or not reaching the goals of the behavioural systems, the ways in which those goals are achieved and the influences exerted on them by the use of high-order systems. Support for this view comes from Emde (1988a, 1988b) who argues that both the affective core of the self and early moral motives (Emde *et al.* 1991) are biologically prepared and grow out of the basic motive of social fittedness, which includes the tendency for turn-taking and co-operation. These social behaviours are supplemented as development proceeds by empathy, rules of social interaction, social referencing and lead from the development of a sense of 'I' and 'thou' to the sense of 'we'. He suggests that a broader understanding of these early motives for social turn-taking comes from realising that all systems of morality have a sense of reciprocity at their centre and are versions of the Golden Rule: 'Do unto others as you would have them do to you.'

Taking Bowlby's view that appraisal of incoming information includes its comparison against particular standards, we suggest that there are scales of value associated with each of the instinctive behavioural systems; and that the experience an individual values most highly is that of achieving the goal of a system. The first experiences of achieving these goals act as comparators for those that come later, until that experience is surpassed by one that is valued even more highly, which then becomes the comparator. But that is only the first step.

In our understanding, the goal of an instinctive system is reached when there is no discrepancy between an innately given standard and the experience of reaching it. The greater the discrepancy the more one is made aware, through feelings of disappointment or dissatisfaction, that the goal has not been reached. Although an individual's experience of reaching the goals of the inter- and intrapersonal behavioural systems is unchanging, the degree of completeness with which the goal is achieved and the ease with which it is reached can differ, as will experiences of the consequences.

The journey between the activation of the system and the achievement of the goal can be smooth and easy, frustrating and difficult, or blocked by what are appraised as insurmountable obstacles. Each of these experiences will be evaluated differently, with the smooth achievement of the most complete attainment of the goal yet experienced by an individual acting as one of the comparators by which its value is assessed. An individual's experience of the best consequences following the reaching of the goal acts as a further comparator.

However, the evaluation story is complicated by negative evaluations. The absence of an anticipated (and positively valued) interaction is discussed by Hamilton (1985: 10) as a zero message which may evoke strong feelings. She gives Bateson's (1973: 427) illustration pointing out that the letter you do not write can get an angry reply. Zero messages include those associated with a lost transitional object, whether by children or adults. The ones that evoke the most intense degree of dissatisfaction act as a negative comparator, as also does an individual's experience of the worst consequences. Every final evaluation will therefore be a statement of a computation of the probability of reaching the highest and the most negative evaluations and can thus be a source of intra- and interpersonal conflict. For example: Peter values his mother's warm comforting responses when he is hungry, cold or sick but puts a negative value on her lack of protection whenever his small brother interferes with his belongings. The negative evaluation is amplified by his mother's angry responses to his attempts to protect his own possessions. In this regularly repeated commonplace situation, Peter has conflicting views about the value he gives to his mother's caregiving, to himself as a careseeker, and to the relationship he has with his brother.

The view that the process of evaluation takes into account conflicting evaluations means that all evaluations are personal. They are based on an immensely complex matrix of past and present experiences and future hopes regarding one's relationships and oneself which will not change until a new stage of development is reached by oneself or by other people or until circumstances themselves change in a felicitous direction, or until the various partnerships can be renegotiated. The situation seems to be that while two or more people can share the fact that they each value something highly, or very little, the basis for their several evaluations will be different and, without a willingness to undertake respectful exploration, is unknowable. It is within this area that therapist and client meet and work.

The metacognitive appraisal of the supra-ordinate system of the self

Focusing on relations between phenomena of attachment and the self in early childhood, Cassidy (1990) notes the key role of self-related beliefs and self-related feelings in the child's developmental process. She divides them into two major groupings: (1) those beliefs and self-related feelings relating to self-cognition which suggest a descriptive reference to the self without necessarily being evaluative; these include self-concept (e.g., female, biologist), self-image, self-schema and self-understanding; (2) those relating to self-affect which describe 'the value a person places on him or herself' include self-esteem, self-worth, self-evaluation and self-feeling.

Cassidy (1990) implies that self-esteem is a personal overall judgement. Individuals feel themselves to be liked, appreciated and enjoyed by most others, are confident in their way of relating in work, at play, and in their thoughts and feelings about the future. It suggests a belief in one's capacity to act competently and effectively in a wide range of circumstances in the present and the future. Low self-esteem is associated with a sense of demoralisation and depression.

However a difficulty remains in identifying why it is that some individuals feel themselves to be an integrated person (either confident or not) while other people know they swing uneasily between different views of themselves and are sometimes not sure who they really are. The latter suffer considerable conflicts of values. The relationships in which such clashes of value first arise and which set the scene for later conflicts are those between careseeker and caregiver. These are internalised in IMERs and influence an individual's predictions about how people will value him and how he will value and feel about others.

The effect on the careseeker of the caregiver's standards of value and vice-versa

It is apparent that the effects on careseekers of the caregiver's standards of value lie in their responsiveness to the needs of the careseeker. We define a caregiver's responsiveness in terms of their availability and their sensitivity to the blend of needs expressed, the degree of effort made to satisfy the careseeker and their ability to remain within a supportive/companionable (SC) pattern of relating. This includes the introduction of negotiation and explanation over needs the caregiver cannot, or considers it unsafe to, meet. In either anxious or depressed moods, caregivers can convey attitudes of unwillingness, impatience, inflexibility or overprotectiveness. It is clear from studies on depressed mothers that infants are alert to the affective state of their caregivers. From clinical experience there are substantial reasons for thinking that interacting with anxious, depressed or disinterested caregivers has a profound effect on the value children and adults give (in terms of like and dislike) to such interactions. Nevertheless even when a low value is given to a caregiver's responses, approaches are still made to obtain what is available. It is here that the careseeker's innate and learnt defensive strategies come into action, which represent attempts to cope with the pain of loss of what is considered expectable. The defensive attempts that are most successful are established as highly valued ways of thinking, feeling and behaving. This issue is discussed in Chapter 11.

The effects on caregivers of a careseeker's response to what is offered can frequently lead to changes in the way the caregiver values either the careseeker and/or themselves. The value given to a particular caregiving/careseeking (CG/CS) partnership by either careseeker or giver need not remain constant. Quite apart from episodes of physical separation, it can alter because of variations in factors such as health, the stability of a marriage, and the caregiver's or careseeker's supportive network and employment. It can also change when new phases of development are reached and when children become aware that aspects of their parental caregiving fail to match what others obtain and express their need and aspirations for a new standard that is rarely obtainable.

The effect of the standards of values of each partner during companionable interest-sharing

The degree and quality of responsiveness of one interest-sharer to another over a particular interest is relevant to the value given to the pursuit of that interest and to the value they give to each other. The more there is an attunement to, and wholehearted affirmation of the worthwhileness of their interest-sharing partnerships, the more the goals of interest-sharing will be enjoyed, and the higher the value each individual will give to that partnership. Conflicts in the value given to the interest by partners can arise when the contributions of partners are unequal. Inequality can arise in relations to the degree of planning, skill, time and interest necessary to evoke satisfaction and mutual appreciation.

The value given to intrapersonal exploratory activities

Although intrapersonal exploratory activities (based in leisure activities or work) are the basis for interest-sharing, they can be valued by an individual, in their own right, as a visible tangible expression of their own particular blend of talent and skills. They often have an added value when caregivers provide the opportunity for inter-esting tuition and the sharing of the interest with true peers, and when they validate progress and also ensure that homeostatic needs are met. An individual's exploratory activities can be inhibited and given a negative valuation when fears and self-doubt are aroused by caregivers or companions who are disinterested and fail to notice or value a natural talent, or those who are overanxious, or overcritical and perfectionist forcing the expression of talents far ahead of the individual's zone of proximal development. Such experiences evoke intrapersonal forms of defensive self-care and management, which can often add to a devaluation of the individual's self-esteem and the interest itself.

The effect of the standards of value of each partner in a sexual relationship

An individual's sexual system is seen as having three functions: reproductive, an affirmation of mutual affection through the adult form of primary intersubjectivity and its contribution to the regula-tion of affect vitality. Each of these functions has its own standards of value through which each experience of the activity is evaluated. Sexual partnerships can therefore be valued because they express and affirm the intimacies of affection, the arousal of affect vitality and/or the procreation of children, which can be associated with either of the other functions.

The degree to which caregivers have respected and valued the developmental importance of a careseeker's sexual curiosity or mas-turbatory activities affects the degree of respect and value individu-als give to their own sexual feelings and those of their partners. Affectionate sexual partnerships are given value according to the responsiveness of the partner in terms of attunement, empathy and vitality, leading to the enjoyment of the sexual climax. The value given to a sexual relationship which is entered into by an individual for self-gratification only will depend upon the responsiveness of the other to their needs and demands.

The value given to the ways in which individuals cope when instinctive goals cannot be met

The intrapersonal component of self-care and management is evoked when individuals find that in specific situations they cannot depend upon the responsiveness of caregivers, interest-sharers and sexual partners to meet their needs and desires. Any behaviour and way of relating that is found to be effective in avoiding and mitigating the pain of loss is used habitually. It can be recognised as a strategy and consciously valued or its value is recognised only when circumstances arise in which its use provokes distress and even loss. We consider that D/S patterns of relating illustrate the ways in which intrapersonal defensive self-care is expressed.

In this chapter we have presented our understanding of the psychological processes by which degrees of value are, or are not, assigned to reaching the goals of the instinctive behavioural systems and the ways in which these can be reached. In so doing we discuss who or what tends to be positively valued or alternatively gives rise to conflicts of values. We move in Chapter 11 to regarding what is valued in terms of the ideals to which people aspire and the idealisations to which they often defensively cling. Ideals have tended to have a bad press usually by being identified with defensive idealisations. In Chapter 10 we outline the history of the concept of ego or self ideals before discussing in Chapter 11 the distinctions we have made between the functions of maturative ideals and idealisations that are defensively non-maturative.

Implicit concepts of caregiving in the development of the concept of self/ego ideals

Many people have tended to think of ideals as abstract, usually unattainable, and the domain of metaphysicians and preachers. The lack of an explicit recognition of their significance is intriguing in the light of human aspirations and longings to reach ideals, many of which have found their expression in songs and literature. Could it be that many have succumbed to the belief described (but not subscribed to) by Kant, that ideals refer to a completely unreal world and can therefore be thrown aside as useless or impracticable?

The complexity of the concept and function of ideals at an individual, group or community level and the absence of any developed classification have left ideals to the consideration of the few. Assumptions, on which theories of the ego/self ideal have been explored, are understandably weighted in clinical literature towards defensive and pathological idealisations rather than the development of maturative ideals. Despite this, there are suggestions in the psychoanalytic literature that an individual's maturational ideals are associated with ego strength, which is a significant predictor of his personal and social competence, and of outcome for psychotherapy. Hence, it has been our impression that self and community ideals require a more empirically grounded psychology and taxonomy than is presently available. This led to a paper laying the foundations for such a project which was presented at a meeting celebrating Bowlby's eightieth birthday in 1987 and subsequently at a Royal College of Psychiatrists meeting. It is developed in Chapter 11.

In this chapter a survey is made of the emergence of the concept of self/ego ideals in psychoanalytic and psychological literature, which highlights, inasmuch as parents and children are mentioned: first, the implicit attention given by influential psychoanalysts and psychologists to a major caregiving/careseeking dimension within

the concept; second, the difficulties early psychoanalysts experienced in resolving issues of value which are concerned with domi-
nating/submissive (D/S) and supportive companionable (SC)
relating and implicitly noted within these relationships; and finally,
the significance given by earlier theorists to parents, families and
wider social and cultural groups as transmitters of ideals is discussed in the light of SC and D/S relating.

A CAREGIVER/CARESEEKER PERCEPTION IN EARLY PSYCHOANALYTIC CONCEPTS OF SELF/EGO IDEAL(S)

Adler's perception of self ideals

Adler in 1912 was the first in the psychoanalytic tradition to explore
the nature and function of human ideals (Ansbacher and
Ansbacher 1964). In 1911 he became deeply impressed by the
philosopher Vaihinger's concepts of fictions, which Adler conceived
to be the basis of a largely unconscious and uniquely self-created
ideal of a concrete goal for the future. He initially saw the function
of this self ideal as compensating the self for a sense of loss and
inferiority and for being without advice, guidance and comfort. He
saw this ideal as an imaginative construction for bridging a present
and future state. The purpose of the self ideal was to guide and
shape what we do and how we act, and so create positive feelings for
the future. In his view the capacity to form a guiding fiction (later
called self ideal) was not developed until five years of age.

'Counter-fictive forces' was Adler's name for family, social and
ethical rules, based presumably on ideals, that acted as correcting factors on an individual's guiding ideal. Provided both the corrective
factors and the individual's own ideals were mutually compatible, the
child's guiding ideal could lead to mental health. When they were
incongruent, the parental corrective ideal was devalued, and a high
level of overcompensation took place. Grandiose fantasies of god-
like and immutable supremacy could emerge and with them the development of extreme personality traits and psychological disorders.

In later work, Adler moves from his earlier self ideal, which was
associated with an idealisation of and striving for superiority, an
implicit D/S self ideal, to his later conceptualisation of it as co-
operative, friendly relationships based on interpersonal equality.
This distinction became visible in his development of the concept of
a style of life, which could be neurotic or healthy, and comprised

not only a person's fictive goal or self ideal but his plans and schemes to achieve it. This formulation appears to be a forerunner of the presently more sophisticated conceptualisation of a working model.

Adler also writes of human ideals in more particular and universal terms, not only in the progressive strengthening of ties between the caregiving mother and her child, but in the bonds of marriage – and of family – and in the art of living with companions. Such a life included co-operative endeavours in groups, in working towards harmonious relationships in the community, and in the exalted ideal of love thy neighbour. Perhaps one of Adler's most important perceptions of the self ideal was its integrative function as a unifying principle of personality.

Adler's son, the psychiatrist K. A. Adler, introduced a broadly based formulation of the development of the self ideal (Ansbacher and Ansbacher 1964: 154–8). The ideal, or subsets of it, develops within the child's social bonds in situations which he termed social embeddedness such as family relationships, friendships, school, marriage and work. A development of a misguided form of the ideal is described for individuals who are in error; who, instead of confronting difficulties, distance themselves from them and develop self ideals which lead them to strive towards a goal of personal superiority, false heroism and an appearance of perfection.

Freud's perception of the ego ideal

In 1914 Freud (1914 *SE* 14: 99) introduced the concept of the ego ideal. His concept focused on parents who ascribe perfection to their child and see it as their ideal, concealing from themselves and forgetting all the child's shortcomings. The child is thus perceived as the centre and core of creation with every wish supplied. Parents, it seems, induce in the child a state of narcissistic perfection, as someone who is able to attract, give pleasure and be loved by them. However, through later parental admonitions and those of others, the child's earlier ideal state is lost. The child is left to love what he once was and seeks to recover it by displacing this love on to a new ego ideal. The child does this by identifying with his superior parents whom he admires and fears, and wishes and fantasises himself to be. The new ego ideal provides the child with a sense of satisfaction which is gained by fulfilling this ideal and it is this he measures himself by. The ego ideal thus consists of certain excellences that the ego requires or lacks for constructing an ideal that can be loved.

Freud's concepts of ego ideal and the super-ego

In revising his earlier instinct theory within which his first concept of the ego ideal was constructed, Freud's new theory features the concept of the super-ego, in which the initial ego ideal appears to lose its original meaning of wished-for ideals and reflects more of the child's representations of critical and restrictive parents and their views of how an ideal child ought to behave. This can now be seen as an internalised parental caregiving model which has some equivalence to Adler's external corrective forces, although Freud's super-ego seems more fear-based, conditional, coercive and hence dominating/submissive.

About ten years later, Freud (1930 *SE* 21: 122) goes some way towards enlarging the earlier view of the ego ideal when he describes the aim of the life or Eros instinct, as reflecting an ego ideal that strives to make bonds of unity at every level of relationships to family, race and mankind. This ego ideal bears a similarity to Adler's later self ideal and comes to be the standard and measure of a less fear-based, more co-operative, companionable and unifying mode of human interaction.

Jung's conceptualisation of the function of ideals

Jung (1954: 168–78) considered that most of the major reasons for children's psychological difficulties were the way their parents lived or did not live, the aspirations they fulfilled or neglected, the predominant family atmosphere they created and the methods of education they used. He recognised that parents and others can impose their lofty ideals on children, and burden them with their own unfulfilled ambitions. He saw parents as ordinary incompetent people, some of whom claim to live for their children and yet burden them with their own unfulfilled ambitions. He recognises that it may not be so much the parent as the grandparents and great-grandparents. Even teachers, he thinks, by and large, suffer from the same defective education as the unfortunate children they are supposed to instruct. Finally, he openly admits that we are ourselves children in many respects and still need a vast amount of educating.

Jung thought that what was usually meant by the well-rounded whole personality is the ideal of an adult not a child and saw this optimal development as an innate human need to be at one with oneself and with humanity. He saw it as being measurable, not in terms of conventionalities but of how far the self has progressed to its own completion. The unattainability of this ideal is, in his view, not an argument against it. His reason being that ideals were more in the nature of signposts which pointed towards the goal. They were not the goal itself. Jung supports his thesis by pointing to cults of personality and the enormous value that human beings place on leading personalities and hero figures.

POST-FREUDIAN PERCEPTIONS OF THE SELF OR EGO IDEAL

It can be seen from early conceptualisations of the ego ideal and super-ego that the ideal was implicitly based on a parental caregiver and a careseeking child, although Freud's earlier concept of ego ideal tended to be submerged in his later concept of the super ego. It was resuscitated by Nunberg (1932) who points to the difference between the ego's fearful submission to the super-ego and the submission which is made out of love for the ego ideal. A further point of difference is described by Reich (1954) who thought that the difference was represented by what people feel they ought to be and what they wish to be.

This early confusion between two types of response, one out of fear, the other out of love, is mirrored in Adler's initial view of the self ideal in the dominating mode of forcing, rather than supporting and encouraging, our mind to perfect itself.

Bibring (1964) helpfully saw the function of the ego ideal as holding forth a promised future which engendered hope and provided an incentive. Jacobson (1954) described it as both a pilot and guide and observed that in practice, the more the ideal is kept within reach, the more it stimulates the child to live up to it and to enhance his self-esteem. Her observation, that the function of the ideal is likely to be more realistic when the functions of the self's critical ego are more mature, points to a need to discriminate between reality-based and defensively idealised forms of self-esteem. Piers and Singer (1953) appear to be the first to make the observation that harmony between the ego and ego ideal is vitally related to the image of ourselves that peers reflect back to us.

Post-Freudian views on the maturation and development of the ego ideal

Later Freudian theorists provide a more detailed perception of the way in which the child's ego ideal changes throughout maturational development, and the differences noted between male and female ideals. Erikson (1965: 250) notes the eagerness of the child to learn and to co-operate, using teachers and other adults whom they value as ideal models for work, which can often be inferred from the roles and the dress the child adopts. The new model can replace earlier heroes of story books. In early adolescence (Blos 1962,1979), the ego ideal of young people moves from identification with parents to a search for and identification with the ideals and social values of their own generation and this is manifested in crushes, infatuations, and in the idealisation of particular teachers of both sexes and the heroes of the entertainment world. In late adolescence, the ego ideal moves towards finding and adaptively valuing a loved and sexually attractive person in a less exploitative, more caring way. It leads to a newly emerging experience of affectionate and tender love without a defensively idealised self or idealised object. This maturative view of the ego ideal can be contrasted with the use of a non-maturative ego ideal to attain certain inappropriate goals in order to protect the ego from anxiety. The presence of normal as against primitive idealisation in adolescent romantic love is further discussed by Chasseguet-Smirgal (1985), Kernberg (1980) and by Dicks (1967) in discussing the vicissitudes of the ego ideal in marriage.

The ego ideal as a maturational or a perverse incentive

Chasseguet-Smirgal (1985: 30) conceives the individual's ego ideal moving on one of two developmental routes; one which follows the long and often difficult route of maturation or a short, non-maturational route which evades obstacles. The latter path usually evokes feelings of helplessness, inferiority and at times despair. She sees it to be the mother's task to support her child by integrating his developmental aspirations and ideals. It means offering sufficient incentive for the child to look forward to the next stage of maturation but not too much. The ego ideal of love, in her view, is one of approximation and of tolerance, and yet observing and seeking to make good any defects. It provides the incentive to master the environment, to live up to the example of parents and others who pursue a whole range of maturative, erotic, aesthetic, educational or religious ideals of devotion and self-sacrifice. By contrast, an individual's perverted ideal follows a non-maturative route, aided by a perverse knowledge that is rooted in defensive strategies for maintaining false standards and narcissistic creations and illusions, in personal relationship, religion, science, aesthetics, etc.

Chasseguet-Smirgal draws her illustrations from therapy and literature, and writes of the mother who seductively encourages her small son to believe that he, with his infantile sexuality, is a perfect partner for her, the father being excluded, and supports the belief that one day he could possess her. She comments on the way in which this brings a halt to the child's development and how the mother's deceptive idealisation of her son may be relived in the transference expressed by him as an adult in analytical treatment. We note the mother's seductive dominating pattern of relating which is disguised in a supportive companionable form.

An implicit caregiver/careseeker structure for the ego and self ideal

A structure for the ego ideal in contradistinction from the ideal self is provided by Sandler, Holder and Meers (1963). Stated in terms of the child, it contains the child's ideal object, a loved and admired parent, the image conveyed by parents of how the ideal child would behave, and the child's ideal self – the child's own ideal for itself. The source of the content of each of these components is centred on the child's identification with the loved ideal objects, with the parents' ideal image of an ideal child and with ideals that they have constructed for themselves, based on their previously experienced aspirations.

The integration of the concepts of the ego ideal and ego strength leading to maturation and individuation

Piers and Singer (1953) were the first in the post-Freudian group to make explicit the ego strengthening and maturative function of the ego ideal throughout the whole of life. Guilt and fear are associated with the super-ego which is linked with the goal of talion, that is to say the exacting of equivalent retribution. Shame indicates a real shortcoming and failure in reaching the goal of the ego ideal. Their portrayal of the ego ideal as a maturational drive and the representation of all maturation and individuation processes in human beings, together with the goal of an instinct of mastery, has similarities with and can be integrated with Adlerian and Jungian perceptions. Chasseguet-Smirgal (1985) underlines this view by stating that the ego ideal encourages an individual to integrate all the developmental phases of his development.

The ego ideal and cultural implications

Horney's (1946: 241) therapy for the resolution of neurotic conflict is frequently cast in terms of the gradual analysis of her patient's defensive idealisation and attitudes which were acquired in childhood and involved the patient's parents. The aim of therapy is for patients to acquire the capacity to assume respect and responsibility for themselves and for the individuality and rights of others which becomes a basis for real mutuality and truly democratic ideals. The most comprehensive aims and goals of therapy do not simply coincide with the ideals that wise persons of all time have followed, but they are the elements on which our psychological health is based. Horney clearly defines modes of relating that fit a description of supportive companionable relating as an ideal of relating.

PSYCHOANALYTIC OBJECT RELATION'S THEORY AND SELF/EGO IDEALS

Ego ideals of caregiving seen by Suttie, Klein and Fairbairn

The concepts ego ideal and defensive idealisation are important in object relations theories. Suttie (1935), whose early work provides the anlage of most of the central concepts of British object relations theorists (Bacal and Newman 1990: 17), writes of the importance of the mother in the formation of the very first idealisms, but also in building up the child's first idea-of-itself, its ambitions and purposes. His example of a gang of boys, whose ego ideal is manliness, aggressiveness and hardness, demonstrates a taboo on the ideal of tenderness. They are, he asserts, as much fascinated by power, cunning and violence as those in Fleet Street.

In a recent interpretation of the ego ideal in Kleinian theory (Schneider 1988), an infant's life instinct represents an unconscious preconception of a need-satisfying object and in purest form it is represented as a good/ideal breast or early ego ideal. When the infant's ego is supported by the loving care of the primary object (mother), the infant is helped to live through his persecutory states. These can be evoked by the unavailability of the primary object and be derivative of an assumed death instinct. Defensive splitting initially separates the good, idealised, and the bad experiences which are later tolerated in the ambivalence of the depressive position. Serious problems arise in the establishment of an early ego ideal should the need-satisfying object be inadequate, and more particularly so if the constitutional endowment of the infant favours a predominance of the death instinct which, in its purest form, is seen as a primary form of envy.

Fairbairn was first to present a systemic form of object relational theory in which the internalised representations of the child's ego interacting with parental figures in the super-ego was split into two components. The first is an open ego system which has incorporated the child's experiences of accepting and supportive parents who function as an ego ideal (Fairbairn 1952: 159). The second component, a closed (repressed) ego system, incorporates the child and his bad relational experiences with exciting and deserting, rejecting and neglecting parents. Fairbairn suggests that the good relationship aspect of the super-ego should be designated the ego ideal (Fairbairn 1952: 136). He also acutely perceived a reversal of values in those with a withdrawn schizoid tendency. As the ideal and enjoyment of loving feels to be hopelessly blocked, the individual comes to enjoy the power of hating and in effect makes a pact with the devil. Here, the ideal and pleasure of hating becomes predominant, and is substituted for loving. He later ascribes the ego's capacity for mature, differentiated, interdependent relationships which are evenly matched in giving and taking, as the ideal picture (Fairbairn 1952: 145) and the source of good morale (Fairbairn 1952: 167).

Guntrip (1968: 406) focuses on the point that good supportive relationships are the foundations of a basic inner strength of ego development and enable a person to grow towards the ideal goal of being a mature and whole adult person.

Self psychology and the self ideal

Further impressive support for the significance of ideals (Eagle 1987: 72) is provided by Kohut who emphasises their psychological importance in reflecting and maintaining psychic health. In Kohut's (1979) view, the self is the core of personality and a child's healthy, or what he terms firm, self results from optimal interactions between the child and his self objects (usually parents). His conceptualisation of the self is important but not easy to explain. It is seen as bipolar in structure and embracing three major constituents. From one pole emanates the basic strivings for power and success; these include the child's earliest assertions to develop its skills and attain its ambitions and maturative goals. Parents can promote these strivings by their approval, admiration and confirmation of the child's worth. The other pole harbours idealised (in a maturative sense) goals which include the calmness, soothingness and strengths that the infant admires most about his parents. In due course these become the child's inner values and ideals and serve as a compass throughout life. An intermediate area of the self is made up of basic talents and skills that are activated by what is described as a tension between a person's ambitions and ideals.

In Kohut's view, there is a maturative form of idealisation between parent and child (in the form of mutual admiration) that develops the child's self-confidence and self-esteem (Kohut 1977). It is the internalisation of parents as self objects that forms in the child a store of self-support and approval and acts as a source for restoring his self-esteem. Self-disorders, defects, distortions and fragmentation of its structure in childhood and adulthood are considered to be due to a failure of self–self object relationships. When self–self object support is inadequate or missing in early life, the child's experience of parental withdrawal or rejection results in distortions and a weakening, not only in its assertiveness but also, in the development of its talents and skills and in a diminution, or distortion, of its guiding ideals. The failure leads to increasing grandiosity and exhibitionism in the child and also, in the absence of feelings of unity with an idealised object, to a disintegration anxiety and a self that is prone to fragmentation.

THE SELF/EGO IDEALS AND GROUP PHENOMENA

Freud (*SE* 18 and *SE* 21) extended the concept of ego ideal to the group in a way that he considered paralleled an individual's first family ties, stating that love relationships and emotional ties are the essence of the group mind, and that the leader embodies the ideals and perfections sought by an individual's own ego. A sense of group solidarity and pleasure arises when members feel that they share an important quality in common with each other, based on having the same ego ideal. The state of pleasure arises, in Freud's view, from obedience to the new authority in the group which can put the individual's former conscience out of action. Given this outcome it is difficult to know whether Freud is describing a defensively idealised form of supportive companionable patterns or not.

In describing the individual's relationship to the group, Sutherland (1971) views the personalities of the individual group members as being structured by an internal and dynamic bipolar self in object relational systems, as described by Fairbairn. In System A, the self is relating to its ideal objects, its function being to seek and maintain satisfying relationships in the group, while also attempting to come to terms with two additional closed systems. In the first, System B, the frustrated submissive self masochistically seeks the inner exciting and deserting parental object. The second, System C, is constituted by threatening and sadistic parental images which are projected on to the group leader or, if seemingly too dangerous, on to other group members. This means that during the course of the group life a new reality can be tested, and previously forbidden longings can be freely felt and expressed without fear or threat.

The realisation that the group can find their dominant fantasy, not necessarily in submission to an ideal admonitory father figure but, in the group itself, as an all-powerful mother with whom they can merge, is postulated by Chasseguet-Smirgal (1985). She also argues that groups may tend to choose for their leader the master illusionist and pseudo-idealist who conveys the belief that there are short cuts which obviate the need for human effort. Kohut provides the novel concept of a group self in terms that are analogous to his concept of an individual self, having similar skills, assertiveness, ambitions and a shared ego ideal. When the group's prestige and self-esteem is damaged or lost, manifestations of fragmentation may be seen, and reactions of rage and acts of vengeance evoked. He postulated a fusion between the self and its pole of ideals in messianic leaders who experienced themselves as displaying perfect probity, and a fusion with assertiveness in the charismatic leader who showed absolute certainty. Hence, the development of idolatry in which ideals become gods rather than guides and stifle creativeness. The D/S nature of these latter ideals is clear.

Hinshelwood (1987) grasps the nettle of the defensive idealisation of groups in his observations on people's attempts to engineer an ideal therapeutic community as a sort of magical agent which can be prescribed as a treatment to cure patients, with good results expected to flow automatically. He also writes of the problems posed to a therapeutic community when the community is idealised as a paradise by its members. The function of this idealisation allows everyone to feel good, and to deny and project the badness of the group (in terms of the distress and violence in it) into the world outside. Morale is also defensively increased by allowing the community to think itself and its approach, to be different and better than others.

A SHORT SUMMARY OF PSYCHOLOGISTS' PERCEPTIONS OF IDEALS OF CAREGIVING AND CARESEEKING

There is an interesting overlap between psychoanalytic and social psychological work on the concept of ego ideals, although social psychologists until recently appear to have been less influentially interested in this field. Some prove to be exceptions. McDougal's (1932) concept of a self-regarding sentiment as the central superordinate integrating force of the personality bears an important resemblance to the self/ego ideal. It imposes a motivating standard of behaviour which is consistent with an ideal image one has of oneself. His view is that instinctive tendencies or propensities, modified by learning and experience, and combined into sentiments e.g. to court and seek a mate, to protect the young, to be gregarious and to show loyalty, determine the major goals to which we strive. This view has broad resemblances to Bowlby's and our own view. Woodworth and Sheehan (1965) supported the view that ethological studies warrant taking McDougal's theory out of cold storage for reappraisal.

Maslow (1954) proposed an equivalent master drive towards health, which involved the actualising of human potentialities as they unfold in a benign environment. His concept of a planned hierarchy of ideals carries implications for careseeking in less satisfactory caregiving environments. Here the basic needs to do with survival, food, drink and safety have first priority, followed by the need for love, then the need for self-esteem and finally self-actualisation. These objects and activities are of value for their own sake as well as for the achievement of goals. The assumption is that human ideals have a corresponding aspirational hierarchy.

Klinger's (1977) incentive theory provides a cognitive-behavioural base and perspective for self/ego ideals which can lead to further integration. He maintains that man organises many aspects of his life in pursuit of and commitment to valued incentives which give meaning to life. The goals are valued because they are associated with potential sources of reinforcement or an avoidance of aversive outcomes, which when frustrated or lost lead to depression.

Finally, Roger's (1961) developmental thesis is that man's nature moves essentially towards socialising, maturity and a self which is personal and dynamic. The ideal is the self the individual would most like to possess, and on which he places the highest value for himself. Roger's emphasises the clinical significance of the discrepancy between a person's ideal self and actual self, considering that a modest discrepancy is appropriate, and acts as an incentive, fostering the motivation to acquire successive abilities and levels of skill. But the greater the discrepancy, the more the individual loses hope of reaching what is an unrealistic ideal and the more a sense of self-esteem and well-being is undermined.

We have all this information in mind when discussing the function of ideals and defensive idealisations in relation to caregiving in the next chapter.

Chapter 11

Values and ideals in promoting maturation and well-being

There has been considerable confusion among many clinicians about the significance of ideals. This is not surprising considering the confusions within the concept. For example: the terms self ideal and ego ideal stem from different theoretical approaches; some authors refer to the ideal as a goal (or to sub-goals on the way to it), while others refer to the ideal as the means or manner by which a goal is attained. The confusion is compounded by the use of the verb to idealise and the noun idealisation. Most clinicians refer to illusory defensive idealisations, but others write of parents idealising their children when admiring and affirming their achievements. It also seems that the assumptions on which theories of self/ego ideal have been explored are understandably weighted towards defensive and pathological idealisations rather than the development of maturative ideals.

Our impression is that to be useful to clinicians, the concept of self or ego ideals requires an empirically grounded taxonomy. In this chapter we continue a presentation of a preliminary attempt to do so. The foundations for it were presented in the unpublished paper given at a meeting celebrating Bowlby's eightieth birthday, an outline of which was given at a meeting of the Royal College of Psychiatrists (Lake 1989).

IDEALS AND MATURATION

The survey in Chapter 10 of the development of the concept of self/ego ideals shows that most theoreticians independently came to see self ideals as maturative or non-maturative, with the latter commonly seen as defensive. We are aware of the complexity inherent in defining the concept of maturative and non-maturative ideals. For example, one is attempting to describe: an individual's view of what they see to be 'the very best' for themselves; what the various groups they live in, conceive to be 'the very best' for that individual; and what people, who professionally claim to know about maturity and non-maturity, have described and defined. Furthermore we have to use an understanding of maturity and non-maturity that fits the functioning of the systems we have described. This has led us to view maturity as a state reached when each behavioural system is capable of functioning fully and effectively in a wide variety of contexts, with the propensity for using supportive companionable (SC) relating significantly outweighing dominating/submissive (D/S) relating. We use the term maturative to refer to movements towards the attainment of maturity.

Non-maturity describes states in which an individual's behavioural systems have failed to reach the stage at which age-appropriate functioning would be expected, and the propensity to use D/S relating is easily evoked. In the absence of genetic or organic disorders, immaturity can be regarded as primarily due to a dysfunction of the careseeking system brought about by failures of appropriate caregiving. This view of maturity and non-maturity leads to a description of maturative ideals as both developmental ideals that are potentially realisable and which take individuals from one stage of development to the next; and homeostatic or restorative ideals, which are realisable but have to be regularly reattained. In marked contrast, aspiring to reach what logically can be seen as non-maturative ideals we regard as defensive measures against disassuagement within close relationships. They are distorted, exaggerated and often illusory ways of attempting to attain either developmental or homeostatic ideals and we refer to them as non-maturative defensive idealisations. Their illusory nature means that they are frequently not attainable. Hence all non-maturative ideals can be thought of as defensive idealisations.

MATURATIVE DEVELOPMENTAL AND HOMEOSTATIC IDEALS

Human beings not only have the capacity to learn about the ordering of their homeostatic and developmental processes and those of other species, they are also able to communicate their observations. They can make judgements about whether homeostatic or developmental processes are on course or not. They can also agree or argue about the conclusions they come to. We regard an individual's capacity to have aspirations to reach the next stage of development to be an essential factor in the processes of physical and psychological development.

Developmental maturative ideals are envisagements of reaching realistic stages of further development with the help of caregivers (not always parents) who facilitate and take an interest in the individual's achievements. They are also envisagements of the support which provides opportunities for reflection and reassessment when ideals are not achieved. Maturative ideals can thus be seen as acting as standards for new levels of both physical and mental ability in each of an individual's interpersonal partnerships and the systems for intrapersonal self-management and exploration and also for such capacities as vigilance, resilience and endurance (which we consider are lower-order capacities) and prudence, discernment, hopefulness, insight, empathy and patience (high-order capacities). The latter play their part in extending, refining and transcending an individual's instinctive responses and their capacity to cope with frustration and loss. They help people to handle natural hazards and their own, and another's, D/S ways of relating.

Maturative homeostatic ideals are essentially the careseeking ideals of achieving (with the help of caregivers when necessary) self-reliant ways of satisfying hunger and thirst, requirements for shelter and rest, and of coping with one's own anxieties, all of which restore the capacity to be exploratory. From a clinician's perspective, careseekers value caregivers whose way of relating matches the descriptions of SC relating given in Chapter 3. This enables them to enjoy the experience of moving from one stage of maturational development to another, at a rate with which they feel comfortably stimulated. We consider that support for these views comes from factors that are now becoming established in relation to the quality of co-operative conversations (Kobak and Duemmler 1994); of caregiving (Kunce and Shaver 1994); and of negotiation through accommodation when parent/child goal-corrected systems are coupled (Marvin and Stewart 1990).

We regard the child who is rated secure in attachment terms as envisaging and achieving ideals which are maturative rather than non-maturative defensive idealisations. Cassidy (1988) showed that six-year-old children judged to be secure on the basis of reunion behaviour with their mothers tended to represent the self in a positive way, and most were also able to acknowledge less than perfect aspects of themselves.

Horney's (1946) classification of characteristic ways in which people behave is compatible with the attachment classification of secure and various kinds of insecure child and adult. We consider that Horney's wholehearted self has values that match the secure child or adult. As adults they assume responsibility for themselves, and show a readiness to recognise obligations towards those in whose values they believe. They relate to their own children, parents, peer colleagues, community or country in a way that shows respect for their rights, and a capacity for friendship which is free from sadistic domination or parasitic dependence.

Maturative defensive ideals

Maturative defensive ideals provide standards for defending oneself, when younger or older, from threats and attack using the knowledge that one has parents, and/or a network of other family members and friends who are prepared to offer protection and practical help when this is felt to be necessary. Standards of how one defends oneself and other people change as development and maturation proceed. In this way maturative defensive ideals are very different from non-maturative defensive idealisations.

We suggest that the criteria for discerning an individual's ability to achieve age-appropriate personal and social competencies (ego strength) or for assessing impairments of these abilities (ego weakness) are measures that put the individual's state of maturity into operational terms. This means that the balance an individual keeps between aspirations that relate to actual achievements and abilities and aspirations that palpably fail to do so is a measure of their maturity. A list of criteria that assess the possession of personal and social competence (i.e. ego strength or weakness) is summarised in Chapter 13.

NON-MATURATIVE DEFENSIVE ASPIRATIONS AND IDEALISATIONS

The concept of non-maturative ideals and defensive idealisations merits a discussion that is beyond the scope of this book. They arise from the activation of the system for intrapersonal defensive self-care and management. While maturative ideals carry the probability that they can be attained and then surpassed and, if not, that there is someone to give support and comfort while they are reviewed and/or changed, defensive idealisations carry no such surety. They are formed when caregivers are unavailable or ineffective and an individual feels on his own. They are envisagements of states of 'being someone' or 'doing something' whose achievement would bring a much desired sense of relief from feelings of disassuagement and loneliness, but with little or no thought of the consequences to oneself or others. Once standards to reach maturative developmental ideals are infiltrated and eroded by non-maturational standards to more than a critical degree, the individual is set on a course that, unless it is halted, ultimately leads to increasing abuse of the self and other(s).

States of defensive idealisation arise from experiences of rejection, abandonment or impingement, many of which are too painful to be kept in the individual's conscious mind (e.g. episodes of rejection, punishments or abuse, which made the recipient feel guilty, shameful, confused or bad). These are recorded in the appropriate IMER but are more, or less, segregated from conscious awareness. Such segregation corresponds to the Fairbairn, Guntrip and Sutherland conceptualisations of closed parent/child systems and include Guntrip's concept of a withdrawn self. Defensive strategies aided by perceptual distortions allow the individual to keep an image of himself and his parents as 'good' and worthy of being envisaged as an ideal. But the idealised relationship always depends upon the ability of the careseeker to maintain this defensive strategy. Defensive idealisation can be shown in exaggerated forms of self-responsibility and autonomy ('doing it my way' with an assumed superiority over others), or in a passive dependent over-valuing of a potential or actual protector (e.g. an individual, a group, institution or environment). There can also be a defensive idealisation of part-objects and things (e.g. breast, penis, fetish objects, drugs, money and personal possessions and environments) which individuals compulsively seek to obtain and experience, often as a defensive reaction to shame and criticism. A feature of these kinds of defensive idealisations is that they all involve major forms of exaggeration and distortion of what can realistically be expected of a child, adolescent or adult person. They are associated with defensive clinical syndromes such as alcoholism (Hewitt and Flett 1991) and are implied in the illusion of the gambler's winning game, or the criminal's perfect crime (Bollas 1987).

Non-maturative idealisations can be envisagements of states of 'being', without consideration of what might have to be done to achieve them (e.g. envisagements of having capacities for parenting or other personal abilities and skills that are beyond the competence or the talents of the individual). On the other hand, they may be envisagements and aspirations of getting relief by 'letting go', and 'giving up', without regard for the consequences. One of the functions of defensive idealisations is to compensate for a loss of well-being by substituting the promise of a better future state. The envisaged idealisation can induce an illusory hope and encouragement, and provide individuals with an incentive to continue which can temporarily restore their sense of self-esteem and well-being and act as a refuge from continuing disassuagement.

Once established, aspirations towards particular defensive idealisations can be evoked whenever, in any relationship (longstanding or new), there is a reminder of an earlier dysfunctional partnership with a primary or secondary caregiver. The forms they take are legion and a tribute to human ingenuity. They regularly become 'visible' in the transference/counter-transference relationship.

The most frequently described form of idealisation is set up when some aspects of a child's relationship with an ambivalent attachment figure are satisfying and enhancing, while in other situations the same attachment figure is critical, shaming and causes distress. The child unconsciously disclaims and represses the disassuaging aspects of the parental way of relating, 'remembering' only the satisfying aspects. They seek, often successfully (but at considerable cost to themselves), to evoke in the parent the desire to relate in a satisfying way. When in everyday life they experience reminders of the parental behaviour they have repressed, they tend to perceive the person (or other entity) that provides the reminder as if they were similar to the disassuaging aspects of the parental figure and feel, think and act accordingly.

Defensive idealisations and attachment

Three important empirical studies of internal working models: Main et al. (1985), Cassidy (1988) and Kobak and Sceery (1988) have findings which support the idea that insecurely attached children will envisage defensive idealisations rather than maturative ideals. Main found that parents of children earlier classified as insecure–avoidant dismissed and devalued attachment. They frequently claimed not to remember any incidents from childhood. Specific memories that emerged, despite this denial, were likely not to support the generalised (usually highly idealised) description of parents. Cassidy's study showed that subjects judged to be insecure–avoidant tended to depict the self as perfect, but without mentioning interpersonal relationships. In contrast most secure children were able to acknowledge less than perfect aspects of the self. Ambivalent children showed no clear pattern, and insecure and controlling subjects (linked to the disorganised classification in infancy) tended to make excessively negative statements about themselves. In Kobak and Sceery's (1988) study of young adults, they were surprised to find that the secure and dismissing (avoidant) groups resembled each other in terms of self-esteem and only the preoccupied (ambivalent) group had significantly lower scores. They explained this seemingly contradictory result in terms of defensive processes that may have led the avoidant group to deny personal imperfections.

Attachment types are also compatible with Horney's (1946) four kinds of predominating tendencies: the wholehearted, who correspond to the secure form of attachment; and the three insecure and defensive forms: the compliant, the aggressive and the detached. The compliant group manifest the traits that go with 'moving towards people'. They want to be liked and appreciated and show a compelling need for affection. Their special set of values lies in the direction of unselfishness, sympathy and humility, and they abhor (although they may secretly admire) the unscrupulous and wielders of power who represent strength. The predominant tendency and crucial need of the detached group is to be emotionally uninvolved, to be an onlooker and observer who is apparently self-sufficient, but who needs to feel superior. They value highly what they regard as freedom and independence. At times, they value generosity and self-effacing sacrifice, at other times callous self-interest. The aggressive group tends to assume that other people are hostile. They have a compulsive need to achieve success and prestige in a competitive society, to outsmart and make use of others, and to be good fighters. They are contemptuous of softness and place a high value on hardness, toughness and power. Motives for marriage are to enhance their own position and they are loath to admit fears. Horney emphasises that each of these three groups of people are equally estranged from others and from their own self, although the passionate need of the compliant type for closeness to others makes them desirous of believing that no gap between themselves and others exists. Each represses certain aspects of personality, and brings the opposite to the fore, which enables them to function but at considerable cost to themselves or to others.

Non-maturative idealisation in marital partnerships

The non-maturative defensive idealisations of husbands and wives are a frequent source of marital difficulties. They are demonstrated in one partner's quite unrealistic expectations of the other, and their injured and outraged feelings when they are not fulfilled, which usually surprise both partners by their intensity. Each partner anticipates a particular pattern of caregiving, of companionable interest-sharing or a particular way of having a sexual relationship. The failure of the partners to respond appropriately excites growing feelings of shock and betrayal, angry complaint, hate, fear of actual, violent behaviour or of hurt and cool withdrawal, or sometimes incoherent rage and dread. Each partner often feels a sense of total rightness and justification about their needs and values. Each expects and waits for the other to respond to what they feel to be their reasonable standard (e.g. all decent husbands or wives would behave in that way and failure to do so is unbearable). Defensive idealisations emerge from earlier experiences of a careseeking attachment to abandoning or rejective aspects of parents.

Taking into account the views expressed above and in Chapter 10, and the empirical evidence from attachment research, it appears that one way of denying the painfully despised self is to create a defensively idealised image and a way of behaving that matches this image. The individual presents himself in his relationships with others as superior and self-sufficient, as a shrewd operator and fighter, or as attractively compliant. They do so without showing any capacity that backs up the image with actions that others can take as evidence of effectiveness. Defensive idealisation can frequently exist side by side with maturative ideals and the individual can switch from one to the other depending on the associations and reminders evoked by whichever context they are in.

OPERATIONALISING MATURATIVE IDEALS AND DEFENSIVE IDEALISATIONS

A complication in recognising an individual's ideals is that they may not be referred to directly and can sometimes be held in a preconscious form until the process of achieving them is threatened.

Specific ideals (like being married, becoming an artist, an engineer, a parent) are made fully conscious when an individual has feelings of anxiety, fear, anger, grief or despair about the possible loss of a wished-for role, or of something felt to be an entitlement (e.g. that one would be protected by parents). The threat can lead either to a determination to achieve what is desired at all costs, to modify the desire so that it is more likely to be achieved, to postpone its attainment until another way of achieving it is found, or to give it up as unattainable and sometimes to devalue it. We have made the assumption that people's maturational ideals and defensive non-maturational idealisations are identifiable by observing what they most value, desire and seek to attain.

In relating an individual's maturative ideals or defensive idealisations to our understanding of working models we see them represented within all working models of the self and the world. These aspects of working models represent what an individual values most in terms of:

1 what they make or do when alone and the way it is best done;
2 what they do with others in relation to giving and seeking care, sharing interests with others, and in their sexual partnerships;
3 the ways for people to relate to them and they to others (i.e. covering the two patterns of relating (D/S and SC); and
4 defending themselves when attachment figures are too intrusive or unresponsive (i.e. covering the system for intrapersonal defence).

Aspirations to attain their envisaged maturational ideals and/or defensive idealisations of the future guide and shape a person's incentives and intentions. They also have the function of spanning the gaps between a person's past, present and future, that is to say between myself 'as I have been', 'as I am' and 'as I aspire to be'. Also they cover the gap between 'myself as I am' and 'as I would like to be' for family, friends and others in various contexts, and 'as I would like them to be for me'.

A person's maturational ideals and defensive idealisations can therefore be operationalised in terms of aspirations:

1 to do something that brings about a high level of satisfaction (e.g. fulfilling the role and function of an engineer, a parent, a cricketer) or to be someone (thinking of oneself as an engineer

or parent or as a sensitive, clever, friendly, sexy, tough or ruthless person);

2 to use the ways that are felt as the most effective to bring about the most highly valued roles or states of being.

What one values most can be achievable in either the short or long term. Long-term ideals and idealisations usually have subsets and sub-subsets that can be reached en route to attaining a longer-term ideal. These are comparable to the plan hierarchy described in Chapter 4.

Rudimentary ideals

Another difficulty is that maturational ideals and defensive non-maturative idealisations cannot come into play until the age is reached when a child can be aware of a future extending beyond life in the here and now. Before that age, we consider that a child can have rudimentary ideals and idealisations. These can be understood as experiences in particular contexts when a child recognises some-one or something as 'the best' and qualified as well worth repeating (e.g. a highly preferred caregiver, or having a game that provides the most enjoyment). Such experiences come to be represented in sym-bolic form, which convey the personal meanings and values a child gives to their experiences. One such symbol is the infant's transition-al object (Winnicott 1958: 232) in the form of a soft or hard toy. It is highly valued by the child, and is recognised as such by parents who forestall a predictable protest over its absence by carrying it around. This reasoning also applies to a child's or adult's personal supportive environment (e.g. the house, garden or life style which become highly valued transitional objects of attachment). The envisagement of this personal supportive environment resembles to some extent Parkes' (1971) description of an individual's assumptive world, which is made up of expectations which are mourned when they have to be given up.

The experience of reaching maturative ideals

Reaching a maturative ideal gives rise to:

1 a briefly maintained sense of uplift (a form of the eureka phe-nomenon) when a sense of 'fit' is experienced with little discrep-ancy between the envisaged form and its realistic attainment;

2 a sense of well-being following the affirmation and validation of the achievement in the form of companionable interaction to celebrate with those who share and approve it (e.g. family, and friends or colleagues at school, college, work or recreational settings) and its recognition by larger communities; and

3 a heightened form of well-being which is experienced when an ideal which has been planned and worked for with others is attained and each member of the group is attuning to the same affect.

IDEALS AND IDEALISATIONS OF ATTACHMENT EXPRESSED IN RELIGION

For those who work in the field of pastoral psychology the concept of God as an attachment figure will offer little surprise. Therapists with a minimal exposure to the Bible, the Koran, and prayer and hymn books will be reminded of a God who can be believed in and is sought as the ideal caregiver and a source of comfort, protection and guidance in a potentially threatening world.

Meissner (1984) examines the developmental perspective of religious manifestations and dispositions and the notion of an area of transitional phenomena as a middle ground, that is open to both subjective and objective input without being reduced to one or other. This conceptualisation opens up a new and challenging approach to religious phenomena.

We consider that the internal working models of any Deity and of self relating to that Deity are closely related to IMERs. How much an individual's or group's relationships with one or more Deity is influenced by the IMERs of self and parents or others is one issue. How much the working models of self and Deity may correspond to, compensate for or provide creative aspirations and ideals of caregiving, careseeking and companionable affiliative relating is another. Whether the internal model of self and Deity evokes maturative, non-maturative SC ideals or D/S idealisations is yet another. Kirkpatrick (1994) begins to address these issues in discussing religious functions, at least in part, as an attachment process. He raises the question whether individual differences in religious belief and experience parallel individual differences in attachment style.

THE TRANSMISSION OF PARENTAL IDEALS AND IDEALISATIONS

An implicit theme throughout this chapter has been that ideals and defensive idealisations are transmitted from parent to child. We now discuss explicitly some of the means by which maturative ideals and defensive idealisations may be transmitted, and how shared ideals and idealisations hold unrelated individuals within dyadic and triadic partnerships, groups, institutions and cultures. The processes by which ideals are transmitted from one person to another are still a matter for debate rather than certainty. They have variously been argued to be by identification, imitation, shaming and guilt evocation or other forms of coercion or seduction, with a role given to reinforcement as an augmenting factor. To this list can be added Stern's (1985) view that selective attunement is one of the most influential ways that a parent can shape the development of a child's subjective and interpersonal life; the sharing of subjective affective experience being a process through which an inter-generational template is created as part of everyday transactions.

There do appear to be differences between the ways in which maturative ideals are transmitted from parent to child and from peer to peer, and those through which defensive idealisations are transferred. There seem to be grounds for considering that the phenomenon of secure attachment renders children more susceptible to following a parental lead as a consequence of social referencing and attunement. Insecure attachment disturbs both of these functions, but appears to leave imitation intact. Coercive caregiving tends to lead some children to be subservient to a frightening caregiver and to other people, while other children are superficially subservient to the coercive caregiver but coercive and dismissive to those that they consider will become subservient. A third group are rebellious and counter-coercive to the caregiver and to others by copying how their coercive parental figures behave.

When parents have had the experience of finding satisfaction (overall) in their own parents' caregiving and also their own progress towards maturation, they are free to find satisfaction and pleasure in practising and developing their own caregiving skills and (later) in supporting their children to move from one maturational level to the next.

In these circumstances maturative ideals are promoted by the parent, while the child discovers the satisfaction and pleasure of being in a supportive, well regulated and exploratory environment which becomes a part of the child's own personal supportive environment. Such individuals are free to use SC patterns of relating most of the time. The episodes during which, through anxiety, they will be unresponsive and coercive will in the ordinary course of events be relatively few. Differences in opinion between such individuals and other people (including their own children) will inevitably arise. They will usually be settled by negotiation and the child will be prepared to listen to and reflect upon parental values. As that child grows and enters a peer culture, parental values will be modified (or sometimes fully accepted) through reasoning and experience rather than rebelled against.

Alternatively, when parents have suffered from anxious and coercive forms of caregiving, they have had little support for and little to value in their attempts to reach new levels of individual and social competence. They approach caregiving with an underlying anxiety, which may be masked by the excitement of becoming a parent. The fears they suffer require exploration by those they approach for help and cannot be guessed at. Nevertheless some principles pertain. Parents giving care from an insecure base are commonly fearful of either being inadequate or of the child restricting their freedom. Should the ordinary expectable attitudes and behaviour of careseeking infants and children remind insecure parents of disassuaging aspects of their own experiences of seeking care from their parents, they will tend to feel in the present as they did then. Their defensive ways of coping may either imitate or overcorrect what their disassuaging parental figures did. With these inter-generational influences, the ordinary careseeking behaviour of children can lead some parents to distance themselves from careseekers whom they believe they will never be able to influence. It may draw parents to indulge and admire some attitudes and behaviour of children, while rigorously controlling others. Commonly, the control is exerted by means of punishments, various forms of criticism which involve shaming or guilt making or seductive inducements, whose power parents know and value from their own experiences of being controlled.

The transmission and adoption of non-maturational ideals by evoking shame and guilt

The role of shame and guilt and its use by parents, families and communities to guide and control standards of behaviour has been increasingly emphasised (Wurmser 1981, Nathanson 1987, Gilbert 1992). We think of shame as an interpersonal phenomenon, the response to a non-verbal signal (backed by verbal embellishments) that devalues the person to whom the signal is sent. It is conveyed by looks, gestures and tone of voice. Guilt is experienced when an individual believes, or is led to believe, that they have injured or damaged a valued person or entity. Usually, the more valued the person or object, the greater the sense of guilt. Shame and guilt frequently coexist when the individual believes that he has failed to live up to the standards he or other(s) set for him. Using shame to influence a child to believe what a parent believes about them is frequently used by parents (and teachers) to control children's behaviour and to maintain standards which they (the adults) value highly. Stierlin (1977: 248–55) has described this transmission of beliefs as empowered by an 'inter-generational shame and guilt cycle' in which the child is shamed into fulfilling the parent's ideal and is made to feel guilty should it be resisted.

The disrespect that is shown for the worth and developmental aspirations of the child's (and adult's) developing self by shaming him can evoke two contrasting forms of response: either a sense of compliance when the shamer's message of the other's inadequacy or worthlessness is partially or totally believed; or a sense of outrage (often with feelings of hatred), accompanied by angry denial. The first of these responses can erode a child's maturational aspirations in the absence of any protection and support from another attachment figure. We think of shaming as an example of D/S patterns of relating rather than stemming from SC patterns.

There are many examples from the family therapy literature of parents leading children to comply with their values by coercing, coaxing, or otherwise inducing them to play particular roles or follow parental vocational aspirations. Many parents do this so that their children can fulfil aspirations of their parents which they themselves could not achieve. Parents can thus identify with and live vicariously on the child's success, thus reversing their role of caregiver to that of careseeker. Other examples include the parent who treats their spouse as a bad object and not infrequently seduces the child into the role of surrogate spouse and sometimes an idealised sexual partner. On other occasions, parents may collusively idealise each other as perfect parents, and treat the child as the source of their failures. Family therapists working with family scripts and myths (Byng-Hall 1995) develop and illustrate these themes.

The influence on the developing personality of parents who as children had to face unprotected the experience of repeated shame-inducing rejections from their own attachment figures provides an explanation for parental behaviour that is so often viewed as wicked and bad. We see this behaviour as the result of having to adopt defensive idealisations rather than maturative ideals in order to keep any sense of self-esteem and vitality.

An example of maturative ideals infiltrated by defensive idealisations

We use, as an example of the mixture of maturative ideals and defensive idealisation, Meissner's (1992) impressive study of the transmission and transformation of Ignatius Loyola's ideals at formative periods of his life. Meissner covers the shaping influence of Loyola's adolescence, his conversion experience, his student and pilgrim period and later life as Superior General of the Society of Jesus. This example shows the delicate balance that is often maintained between an individual's maturative ideals and their defensive idealisations and how the definition of each, and the difference between the two, is defined in the culture in which they were reared. It also shows the effect of a life-threatening event that affected Loyola's standing within his culture. The opportunity to reflect within an accepting, caregiving haven allowed a significant transformation of his ideals and idealisations. Hereafter in this account we use the word ideal to cover both maturative ideals and defensive idealisations.

It would appear that Loyola's early ideal as a chivalrous courtier and courageous soldier, and his later ideal as the knight of a spiritual order demanding sainthood and asceticism, were both accepted as maturative within his culture. The early ideal reflects an identification with his aristocratic, proud and authoritative father; with the latter reflecting aspects of a pious, self-sacrificing and self-effacing idealised mother. Each of these ideals was reinforced by the impact of romantic literature which conspired to shape his fantasies, and by the social expectations, norms and Catholic ideals of his time.

Meissner considers that it was after a life-threatening injury during the siege of Pamplona, which ended his secular political and military life, that a transformation of Loyola's ideals took place. Meissner postulates a regressive loosening and undermining of the grandiose and omnipotent aspects of Loyola's romantic and chivalrous ideals during his illness and convalescence, the sign of their dissolution being revealed in his capacity to fantasise and envisage a new system of values and the alternate role of sainthood and ascetic obedience to a new ruler. The ambivalent mixture of maturational and defensive egoistic ideals, which Meissner describes as Loyola's narcissistic potential, had emerged early in his life. It was shown in the identity of the dashing young hidalgo, which gave way to the ideal of glory as a promising statesman, and generous courageous soldier. The shattering of his leg and with it his egoistic ideals of glory, his awareness of shame over his bodily deformity and his dependence on the caring women who nursed and mothered him, induced a slow process of transformation. During this phase he moved, by identifying with stories about saints and notions of saintly deeds and glory, to a gradual awareness of the inadequacies of the guiding values of his earlier life. Meissner considers that Loyola developed a new ego ideal and identity which, despite the continuing blemishes of his old egoistic ideals (which showed in a continuing identification with his authoritarian father), slowly transformed his sense of identity. This was more fully realised as he became aware of a more realistic and more spiritual system of values.

THE FORMATION OF GROUPS THROUGH THE TRANSMISSION OF IDEALS

One of the most important features of the capacity to aspire to reach maturational ideals or defensive idealisations is the power they have to draw people together. Strangers tend to be attracted to each other on finding out that they share similar maturational ideals or defensive idealisations. The attraction can be the greater when there is also an attraction in the form of companionable and supportive relating. Alternatively people can be drawn to adopt ideals and idealisations through shaming and various kinds of threat, or through inducements of one kind or another, either from an individual or a group. This experience can lead to considerable inner conflict especially when either the shamer or the beguiler devalues the original ideals or idealisations of the individual.

Groups of people sharing similar aspirations are drawn to advance the purposes they have in common, whether it be to advance an interest they value or to register a protest over what they believe is being devalued. Groups formed on the basis of personally valued maturational ideals or idealisations, rather than the ideals or idealisations of others to which they have complied, are likely to be the more cohesive. In these circumstances a personal desire is motivating each member whether they are pursuing maturative ideals or defensive idealisations. Those motivated to reach defensive idealisations will be the less likely to negotiate or to endeavour to reach a mutually acceptable compromise and tend to be more intransigent and combative.

Living within a community whose aspirations are at variance with one's own often leads to conflictual relationships and feelings of isolation. These are more intense when individuals have to live with discrepancies between their own desires to reach maturative ideals and the desires of a group, institution or culture aspiring towards defensive idealisations. A more comfortable state may only be reached by leaving the group – if there is somewhere better to go. Most difficulties within groups can be seen either as clashes between those who are aspiring to reach maturative ideals and those pursuing defensive idealisations, or as conflicts between those who are pursuing different kinds of defensive idealisations. An example is given by Bion (1961) in his descriptions of the work group which is seen as maturative and the dependent, the pairing and the fight/flight groups which are seen as non-maturative. Psychotherapy can be defined as the art of helping people to exchange defensive idealisations for maturative ideals.

Part III

Principles of therapy guided by an attachment-based theory of caregiving

Theories used by therapists that implicitly or explicitly incorporate the caregiving aspects of attachment

When discussing therapy, Sutherland was known to comment 'There is nothing so practical as a good theory.' Once a therapist finds a theory useful in making sense of the client's predicaments he tends to become attached to it, although he may modify it. Attachment theory is relatively new, but many of its basic concepts are implicit or explicit within theories in common use. In this chapter we discuss the part the concept of caregiving plays in many of the major theoretical statements used by therapists in a variety of settings.

Since attachment concepts have been empirically substantiated to an increasing extent, many members of the classical Freudian and Kleinian schools are taking an interest in the attachment literature. Not much more than twenty years ago, Bowlby's work was still regarded with considerable suspicion. Even Guntrip, whose theory came nearest to an attachment view, was unaware of the similarities. Bowlby had approached him after his talk at the Tavistock Clinic on 'My analysis with Fairbairn and Winnicott' and had made the comment that he thought that their basic theories were, in many respects, quite similar. This had surprised him (personal communication) although on reflection he recognised its validity. Our impression is that Guntrip, whose major concern had been to develop a psychological and subjective theory of personal relationships and to avoid the confusions of the Freudian and Kleinian biologically based instinct theory, had tended, despite his recognition of innate patterns of behaviour, to overlook the significance of Bowlby's biologically based theory.

Guntrip's theory (Guntrip 1961, 1968, Hazell 1994: 9) began from the belief that the psychic reality of each patient, put in their own terms, was a challenge to the understanding of the therapist. It should not be seen as a battle between instincts and cultural pressures, as he considered Freud maintained, but rather about how the growth of human personality to full maturity can best be secured. Guntrip considered that therapists should be capable of giving a constructive form of love to their clients and have the vision to be able to say how that love could be enacted. In Guntrip's view (Hazell 1994: 402) it involved: taking clients seriously as people with difficulties; respecting and valuing them as individuals with their own nature; treating them as having a right to be understood, rather than blamed and moulded to suit other people's convenience; as well as showing them genuine interest, real sympathy, and believing in them, so that over time they can come to believe in themselves. He saw these as ingredients of true parental love (agape not Eros). We consider that Guntrip's description of how to relate therapeutically to a client matches, in large measure, our understanding of companionable supportive caregiving.

The extensive research associated with the development of attachment theory has become an indispensable component of a clinical bio-psycho-social theory of the human self. In the last few years the research findings of attachment theory appear to have had an increasing influence on the major schools of psychotherapy. These findings have begun to open new lines of communication between theorists of different schools, and between therapist and client. The clarity of the language in which they are presented has highlighted themes that were more or less implicit, and therefore underemphasised, in other theories.

Freud's ideas and vision proved to be the wellspring from which all later psychoanalytic and psychotherapeutic ideas have been influenced. Arising out of his work came the stance of psychoanalysts who, although seeking to maintain a neutral attitude, gave precedence to the analysis of sexual and aggressive themes. They tended to be minimally supportive despite Freud's later theory of object love. Klein's emphasis on the relational aspects of the infant ego, rather than the earlier Freudian view of it as an undifferentiated state, was a valuable advance. However, her theoretical concentration on fantasy, infantile sexuality, the death instinct and envy tended to divert attention from the effects of different kinds of caregiving relationships on the developing self, and from a view of anger as a response to frustration. It was in response, over thirty years ago, to these drive models, that we separately began to put our emphasis on the major revisions and extensions of aspects of

Freud's and Klein's work: notably by Suttie (1935, 1988), Fairbairn (1952), Balint (1968), Winnicott (1965, 1971), Guntrip (1961, 1968), Bowlby (1969: 1982, 1973, 1980), Kohut (1977), Dicks (1967) and Sutherland (1989).

The first influence, historically, came from Suttie (Suttie 1988: 252) who, in *Origins of Love and Hate*, had anticipated both Fairbairn's concept of object relations and Bowlby's theory of attachment by his early conceptualisation of a primal attachment to mother. It was also his view that aggression was not evoked by a death instinct but as a response to frustration. He also anticipated Kohut's conception of healthy narcissism and ideals by his conceptualisation of an infant communicating the germ of 'give and respond' from birth and his view of the mother's influence in the development of the child's ideals. Suttie prefigured our own conception of companionable interest-sharing relationships by his concept of 'interest relationships' with playfellows without the preliminary establishment of love between them. In his view, ideal parental qualities could be described as 'tolerance without weakness, equanimity without the indifference of self-isolation, firmness without punitiveness'. These provide a descriptive outline of supportive companionable caregiving. He observes that it is the assurance of security, of 'acceptability to the parent', the sureness of supplies of encouragement and of love, and the acceptance of forgiveness, that enables one to get on with the 'business of social living'.

Balint, who was influenced by Ferenczi, revised Freud's theory of primary narcissism, replacing it with a concept of primary relatedness and primary love – meaning the infant experiencing the mother as wishing to love and satisfy him. This runs in parallel with later attachment concepts. Balint discovered in his analytic work that a disruption of primary love in a pre-verbal period was experienced by some patients as a 'basic fault', something that was distorted or was lacking in the mind and needed to be put right (Balint 1968: 20–9). It was a feeling that patients described as someone having failed them. He observed that great anxiety surrounds this area, usually being expressed as a desperate demand that the analyst must not fail them, and that it was their due to receive what they needed. He was aware that this experience gives rise to a profound change of atmosphere in the analytic situation and it involved managing a patient's regression to an earlier stage of greater dependence. This dependence was greater than that experienced in the traditional focus of classical psychoanalysis on Oedipal conflicts. It was a crucial finding which echoed similar findings by Fairbairn, Winnicott, Guntrip and later analysts.

Balint's terms ocnophil and philobat structures are instances of these disturbances of primary love relationships: the ocnophil tends to cling to primary objects who are assumed to be supportive and experiences great anxiety when there are distances between them; the philobat tends to withdraw when the relationship is found to be too harsh and frustrating and the distance between them is felt as safe and friendly. This conceptualisation has similarities to Fairbairn's concept of the withdrawn schizoid and clinging hysteric, and Ainsworth's findings in the Strange Situation Test of the different behaviours of secure infants from those of withdrawn (avoidant) and clinging (resistant and preoccupied) children at one year of age.

Fairbairn's reconceptualisation of Freud's concept of libido as seeking for a relationship with an object (a person), and of a libidinal aim as the establishment of satisfactory relationships with objects, was a major theoretical achievement (Fairbairn 1952). His perceptions of what it means as an infant and child and later as an adult to be either valued or devalued by one's parents; to be accepted as good and/or rejected as bad; to make the transition from infantile dependence to mature interdependence on significant others; and the effect of all these experiences being internalised in representational forms in the mind on their subsequent feeling, thought and behaviour were supportive of Bowlby's later theory of attachment and loss and the internalisation of experiences with attachment figures in working models of relationships.

Fairbairn's open system of satisfactory infant–parent relationships is reflected in Bowlby's internal working models of the child's careseeking interactions with a sensitive and responsive maternal caregiver. His closed, sado-masochistic, internalised system of infant and parent interactions reminds one of Bowlby's later formulation of the defensive segregation of events that are too painful to be kept in consciousness. Fairbairn's clinical experience also led him to affirm that aggression in children and adults is activated by frustration. His revision of Freud's concept of libido into object seeking is equivalent to Bowlby's concept of an innate predisposition for careseeking. Freud's emphasis on libido as sexual drive was seen by Fairbairn as misplaced, as was Freud's and Klein's view of aggression and destructiveness as the emergence of a death instinct.

Winnicott's sensitive awareness of the subjective states of mind of mothers as caregivers, and of their significance for their infants and children, took analytical psychotherapy to a further stage of development. This included his conception of the mother's 'holding' of the child's anxieties, of the value of play and the function of the transitional object and its symbolic extension in culture (Winnicott 1971). It was this contribution by Winnicott to psychoanalytic theory, together with his concept of the facilitating maternal environment and his awareness that traditional psychoanalysis had yet to provide an answer to the question of what life is about, that led Guntrip to the view that structural theory must start not with an id but with an infant psyche capable of becoming a mature person given a facilitating environment (Guntrip 1968: 425).

Guntrip's appreciation and integration of Fairbairn's and Winnicott's work, and his own awareness of the significance of the self, led to his conceptualising a regressed and withdrawn ego, and to make explicit the fears and despairs of being either excessively used and emptied by intrusive exploitative parents, or of being abandoned or avoided by them. At their worst, he saw these as the child's and later the adult's ultimate terrors. The last and worst of these fears in Guntrip's view led to the feeling of being out of touch, in a vacuum, empty, and lost in a state of unreality (Guntrip 1968: 238). Guntrip added these states to Fairbairn's concept of an internalised, closed, sado-masochistic system which blocks the maturation of the ego or self.

In referring Guntrip's concept of the withdrawn ego to the sphere of attachment theory and research, these states of terror will be represented in working models of relationships (IMERs) and the behaviour of those children and parents who are defined as the most insecure in the Strange Situation Test and adult attachment interview. From a therapeutic perspective it led Guntrip to emphasise the need for the greatest empathy and sensitivity in responding to the patient's resistance against exposing this weakened and terrified aspect of the self to the therapist. Evidence of an increase of aggressive feelings and behaviour in therapy is seen as secondary to, and acts as a defence against, elementary fears and anxiety. Such individuals compel notice to be taken of their needs and views, and so to be recognised as notably bad rather than as weak non-entities (Guntrip 1968: 127).

A number of Kohut's formulations of a psychoanalytic theory of self, and recent modifications of them by members of that group, run parallel to many of our own, although the language in which the theory is embodied and some of the concepts are different. It is broadly similar to Guntrip's attempted redefinition of object relations theory in terms of the self. There are also similarities between Kohut's concept of self object which Bacal describes as the child's early caretakers (Bacal and Newman 1990: 42), and Bowlby's concept of an attachment between a careseeker and caregiving attachment figure. We consider that Kohut's concept of the functions of the self object is close to our concept of the internal supportive system.

Self psychology is concerned in therapy to renew the development of a patient's weakened and deficient self, and to re-establish the client's capacity to form a secure self object. This involves the therapist's empathic immersion in the experiences of the patient, and the formation of what are termed self object transferences which replicate the patient's early disruptions of self object relationships with parental figures. The process of therapy has basic similarities to Guntrip's (1968: 214–20) view of the therapist as providing empathic understanding and support for the client's weakened and disintegrated ego which is struggling for survival.

Kohut's emphasis on, and fresh conceptualisation of, ambitions and ideals was an important theoretical and therapeutic development that gave support to our views about the function of values and ideals.

RECENT THEORIES THAT FOCUS ON THE CAREGIVING ASPECTS OF ATTACHMENT

In her paper entitled 'From object relations to attachment theory' Heard (1978) provided the foundation for a later and more integrative formulation of attachment in adult life (Heard and Lake 1986). Heard noted that attachment theory is concerned with two goal-directed behavioural systems (caregiving and careseeking) and their relationship with systems subserving exploratory behaviour, fear/wariness and affiliative behaviour (Bretherton and Ainsworth 1974).

To describe the predictable movements between one system and another, she introduced the concept of an attachment dynamic, and saw that two important implications arose from this assumption. First, that there is some kind of organisation that ensures the smooth running of the whole organism and second, that in circumstances which elicit antithetical behaviours some systems will override others. She saw Winnicott's concept of a parent sustaining a child's state of playing by holding a situation as an example, taken from another paradigm, of the attachment dynamic. Parental holding of the child was seen as maintaining them in a state in which creative exploration and reality testing are possible. Holding requires empathy, which was described as the ability to take account of the goals and plans of other people. It was noted that an individual who feels worthless lacks this sort of parental support and the internal representations of it.

The function of the family is seen as both protective and educative. When functioning effectively the family acts as a system of relationships that sustains both homeostatic and developmental processes. The family system is held together by sharing continuing set goals aimed at an adequate termination of attachment behaviour. The goals, together with plans to reach them, are built into the representational models that each member carries in their brain. Family therapy from this perspective is therefore a process of examining and reappraising existing internal representations in order to incorporate new, more adaptive elements. Families could be categorised according to the degree and quality of unassuaged attachment behaviour, the self-regulating and defensive manoeuvres adopted to handle intensely aroused attachment behaviour, and the parental non-verbal and verbal behaviour shown by each member. These revealed information about each member's internal representations of the self in action, and the shared and idiosyncratic beliefs of their families, which defined the conditions under which supportive interaction is possible, approval is attained, disapproval dispensed and disaster predicted.

Of current theorists who relate therapeutic practice to attachment theory, we see ourselves as being nearest to the approach of Holmes (1993, 1989), Ryle (1990,1995), Hobson (1985), Bacal (Bacal and Newman 1990), Stevens (1982), Gilbert (1989, 1992), Klerman et al. (1984), and Lichtenberg (1989). Each is known for independence of thought, although their theoretical work appears to have been influenced by the attachment paradigm.

In his various writings on Bowlby and attachment theory, Holmes (1993, 1995) gives a lively and perceptive overview of Bowlby's work. He summarises his view of attachment theory and discusses its implications for psychoanalysis, the practice of psychotherapy, and for aspects of psychiatry and of society. In an earlier book (Holmes and Lindley 1989) he introduces the subject of values in psychotherapy and notes the problems for the psychotherapist in necessarily maintaining a balance between over-involvement or too much detachment in their relationship with the client. The ethical safeguards that are required to ensure responsible caregiving include their own personal training and supervision. His views on values and his exposition of attachment concepts, together with his integration of them with the work of other theorists – pointing out their significance for psychotherapy, psychiatry and for society – complements the model we have presented.

Ryle's (1990) impressive development of cognitive–analytic theory as a basis for therapy was originally derived, but with some differentiation, from object relations theories and attachment theory, supported by what was reliably known from observational studies. These latter were clinically valuable for an understanding of reciprocal role procedures. His conceptualisation of the roots of this concept is based on an infant's earliest post-natal experiences which are programmed to organise attachment behaviours that elicit and enmesh with the mother's caregiving behaviour. They are followed developmentally by increasingly complex reciprocal role procedures which inevitably bear some traces of the infant's particular experience and are accompanied by the development of a sense of self (Ryle 1990: 98). His concept of dilemmas in neurotic and personality disorders (e.g. that people act on the belief that if I care about someone, then I have to give in to them or that they have to give in to me) has similarities with our own view of dominant/submissive/compliant patterns of behaviour. Ryle (1995:13) also notes that recent attachment research points to the separate inter-generational transmission of mother's and father's working models as justifying the cognitive–analytic practice of identifying separately the reciprocal role patterns derived from each parent.

Hobson views the psychotherapist as both scientist and artist. His major formulation is the Conversational Model for psychotherapy (Hobson 1985). Important influences on his thinking came from Jung, from Suttie and from Bowlby's conceptualisation of bonding, separation, anxiety and loss. The synthesis of these influences enabled him to explore the artistry of the developing conversation between mother and child. His model deals with problems of intimate personal relationships, of love and with the empty silence and frozen isolation of loneliness. Written reports and tapes of therapeutic sessions demonstrate his therapeutic approach in action. He writes with particular effectiveness on symbols, feeling, imagination and vision, with examples derived from literature, religious imagery and philosophy. His conceptualisation with Meares of the persecutory therapist has been widely appreciated (Meares and Hobson 1977). Hobson's Conversational Model has been used for a number of years in clinical practice and research. The effectiveness of the model has been compared with prescriptive methods of therapy by Shapiro (1995) and his colleagues.

Bacal and Newman's (1990) integration of therapeutically useful object relational theories takes a view that the psychotherapeutic community was too quick to criticise Bowlby for not paying sufficient attention to intrapsychic issues. Bacal recognises that Bowlby's dislike of the term internal object was because it fails to emphasise the living reality of the attachment figure who feels and thinks and acts in highly significant ways. Bacal comments on the similarity of this figure to Kohut's concept of a self object to which one gravitates in need and that both theories point to the central importance of the attachment figure or self object for healthy development. Self psychology theory would in his view completely endorse Bowlby's stress on the importance for a child's development of the provision of a secure base and of encouraging them to explore from it, together with his contention that attachment needs are normal in adults when they are under stress. Self psychologists would also accept the view that attempting to contradict the patient's view is of no therapeutic value, and that sympathy and respect for the patient's frustrations and needs is of the greatest importance. We agree that Bacal's concept of the therapist's overall provision of responsiveness that is optimal for the client is of major significance for therapy.

We have become increasingly aware of the development of attachment theory as it applies to Jungian archetypal theory through Anthony Steven's (1982) understanding of archetypes. He observes that Bowlby quotes with approval Harlow's (1965) contention, based on experiments with rhesus monkeys, that five distinct affectional systems are called into function, and that broadly similar ontological steps occur in the maturation of human beings. These are the maternal and paternal systems, the infant–mother system, the peer system and heterosexual system. He relates these to Jung's biological concept of archetypes as an inherited mode of functioning and a pattern of behaviour. Steven's own research into the attachments formed between infants and their nurses in a home for unwanted children convinced him of the validity of attachment theory. He was struck by the correspondence between what he recognised from the behaviour of the infants as attachment and what the nurses described from their side of the relationship as love. His research findings allowed him to achieve a deeper understanding of his patients when he combined these insights with Jungian depth psychology.

Another stimulating clinician and researcher, Paul Gilbert (1984, 1989, 1992), combines evolutionary, ethological, attachment and cognitive behavioural theory in his conceptualisation of three biosocial systems and goals, those of attachment, alliance formation and ranking. He considers that internal processing modules in the brain organise information as to how far an individual's goals have been achieved, and what needs to be done to achieve them. The structure has the potential to create a core of meaning concerning the social interactions of caregiving and care eliciting, co-operating and competing. From an evolutionary perspective he sees these structures as increasing the likelihood of human beings acquiring resources and becoming successful. He emphasises the importance of peer-group support and that low-status evaluations lead to depression. Among his wide range of significant insights, the provision of care is regarded as the cornerstone of human culture and the development of peer-group support and friendship as crucial in inhibiting and modifying the more primitive processes of dominance and competitive fighting.

Lichtenberg (1989) has recently brought infant research, Kohutian self psychology and a conceptualisation of interactional motivational systems into an alternative to psychoanalytic drive theory. He marshals a wide range of research to support his theory of self and its expression in five interactive motivational systems. These are delineated as:

1 the regulation of physiological requirements
2 the attachment-affiliative system
3 the exploratory-assertive system
4 the aversive system and
5 the sensual-sexual system.

When the needs in each motivational system are met more often than not, an individual develops as a script rules of prediction that embody expectations of satisfactory regulation of physiological systems, the pleasure of intimacy in the attachment-affiliative system, the sense of efficacy and competence in the exploratory assertive system, the enjoyment of the sexual/sensual system and the instrumental power of the aversive system.

In a number of ways his approach has similarities with our 1986 and present view of instinctive systems. His conceptualisations differ in a number of ways from our own. One important difference lies in Lichtenberg's view that the distinction between attachment and affiliation is in the composition of the group rather than the kind of affective experience sought. He considers affiliation remains an extension of attachment within the group and its function and central goal is to gain pleasure in intimacy in the group rather than in a dyad. From our perspective, the focus of affiliative group play and work is on the interest each participant is sharing and is in advancing their standard of skill. Although we consider that mutual support is associated with interest-sharing, we regard each as a separate system with its own function and particular quality of intimacy. For example, if one participant is significantly distressed, the game or work in which each had a joint exploratory companionable interest would stop, having been overridden by this participant's need for comfort and support from peers or from a more experienced attachment figure. It can also be observed that a shared interest of a group of peers in a leisure activity frequently leads to two of them exploring and practising together new ways in which they can develop and increase their separate skills and competence. Our earlier differentiation appears to be supported by Hazan and Ziefman (1994: 164) who differentiate between parents and peers, for their interest and stimulation value, rather than security value.

Interpersonal Psychotherapy (IPT) is historically based on Mayer and Sullivan's bio-psycho-social approach including some of the conceptualisations of Fromm-Reichmann, Fromm and Horney (Klerman *et al.* 1984). It is widely used for the treatment of depression, and focuses mainly on the patient's current life situation and symptoms and their interpersonal context. Attachment theory and Bowlby's general approach to psychotherapy is recognised as an appropriate theoretical base for understanding the interpersonal context of depression and for developing strategies for modifying distortions arising from disorders of attachment in childhood.

Two important studies exemplify the value of the attachment paradigm in social work. Mattison and Sinclair (1979) described a social-work action-research project that gave a significant place to attachment theory in treating marital problems. The problems displayed were of the most despairing, dramatic and demanding kind. The authors integrated the theory of attachment and loss with Jung's vision of marriage as an emotional container, often used to ward off the conscious and unconscious attachment anxieties of each partner. The strategies they adopted in coping with these clients provide an example of the paradox caregivers experience in attempting to provide resources that match the careseekers' needs, or lowering expectations of what can be done for them. The caregiver's temptations are to blame the institution for not providing enough resources or to ignore the complications of the marital relationship. This dilemma was settled by offering a limited, reliable and defined contact, by avoiding the trap of becoming idealised by the clients, and by being aware of the ways in which both clients and social worker can defensively idealise their need for a perfect institution. Their final statement can be a warning to all caregiving attachment figures who undertake relational work with very disturbed clients – they should first set up the realistic preconditions for doing so.

We also note the significant contribution of attachment theory to the understanding of the many predicaments inherent in fostering (Downes 1992). Her work with adolescents and the foster parents who gave an adolescent sufficient security within their own secure base showed that the experience of time-limited fostering can provide adolescents with an experience that allows them to reappraise and renegotiate their significant relationships and gain confidence in the wider world.

Chapter 13

Assessment

Therapists of different schools have their own assessment procedures, which tend to focus on issues emphasised by their theoretical guidelines. The conclusions they reach will be their prediction as to whether the predicament presented by a potential client is likely to benefit from one of the many forms of counselling or psychotherapy or would have to include management of the individual's life style. Prospective clients, who come for assessment of their own volition, come with a complaint. In whatever way it is presented, a common factor underlies the complaints of those who are likely to benefit from a form of psychotherapy: the client knows he has lost a sense of well-being and feels anxious, angry or depressed about the fact that he is not coping effectively with some aspects of his life.

The procedure we describe in this chapter focuses on the assessment of a client's competence, or lack of it, to care for and manage their own lives and to form and sustain relationships that satisfy their affectional needs, maintain co-operative relationships at work and in the pursuit of leisure activities, and enable them to look after children. From this information a choice can be made about the kind of therapy that will be optimal for a prospective client. We do not discuss which kinds of therapy are related to each level of competence. Nor do we discuss the symptomatology and diagnosis of psychiatric illness, borderline states and other severe personality disorders. The information gathered in the course of this assessment will indicate whether a prospective client is capable of forming a therapeutic alliance, whether he is able to be helped by an exploratory form of therapy or require some degree of supportive therapy before this would be possible, or whether a further psychiatric or physical assessment is necessary.

The model of the self described in Part II is used as a frame of reference that helps the assessor organise the information given by the client, either spontaneously or after enquiry. It enables assessors to identify, as far as is possible:

1 the automatic mechanisms of defence that the client is using and the main defensive strategies that have been learned, which, while they diminish anxiety and disassuagement within the family circle, reduce personal and social competence;
2 the aspirations and strivings of the client that show how much he values shared or solitary activities, and which of the shared activities (caregiving and seeking, interest-sharing or sexual relationships) are given most attention;
3 the extent to which his aspirations match what he can actually achieve and which are held in fantasy; and
4 the use he makes of his high-order capacities (e.g. their general intelligence, capacity for metacognition (discussed later in this chapter) and empathy).

The assessment procedure we describe is primarily worked out for adults but is easily adapted for children.

The assessment made before therapy begins is based on what the prospective client feels safe to tell the assessor, which means that information about himself is likely to be incomplete and biased. An assessor is therefore making an approximation of the extent to which the client is, in each different area of his life, relatively secure, insecure and defensively compliant, controlling and aggressive, or avoidant and detached (see Chapter 11). The client's repertoire of defensive forms of relating will become more obvious whenever the assessor's behaviour provides the client with reminders of the earlier disturbing experience whose working model is more rather than less closed off. On the other hand, assessors can occasionally be affected by the client's behaviour to an extent that, despite their training, their own defensive strategies can emerge and affect their rapport with the client and the opinions to which they come. It hardly requires saying that the assessor needs to maintain a metacognitive stance in which they are able to appreciate how their behaviour is affecting the client, and at the same time be aware of the way in which client's behaviour is making them feel and possibly act.

This approach has many similarities to other psychotherapeutic assessments. The differences lie in the kind of information to which assessors give most attention, and the way in which theory is used as a support to their intuitive understanding of the client's predicaments and how they might best be helped. The model described in Part II represents our current understanding of how an individual's self functions. We match the client's functioning against this standard in order to reach an opinion about his capacity to form a therapeutic alliance and to use it to become more competent both personally and socially and to sustain his sense of well-being.

Before discussing the assessment procedure, we remind readers that throughout the session prospective clients are also making an assessment, not always consciously, of the assessor, and the extent to which it will be safe (let alone helpful) for them to reveal information about themselves and their background. The conclusions they come to in the course of the interview will be reflected in the way in which they treat the assessor, the amount of information they give and the clarity and coherence with which they give it. As a response to this ongoing assessment by the client, we rely on the wealth of clinical experience that demonstrates that assessors learn more about a client's anxieties and predicaments when they show a genuine interest in the client and an empathic, unanxious, non-judgemental respect for his views and values.

We have constructed a frame of reference in order to plot four different kinds of information which enable us to compare client against client and the same client against themselves at different phases of therapy. The initial assessment thus provides a baseline that later can show up changes that have taken place during therapy. The assessment is an opportunity to gather and reflect upon these four strands of information. They are embedded in the biographical information that constitutes the client's story about his complaint and the history of his life. The four strands are:

1 the manner in which the client treats and responds to the assessor, especially the psychological distance or closeness that he keeps at different phases of the session;
2 basic biographical information which the client presents as factual about the nature of his complaint and life history (e.g. the number of attachment, peer companionable, sexual and caregiving partnerships the client has now, had at earlier periods of life and would like in the future);
3 the extent to which this information is incomplete, in regard to particular issues (e.g. enquiries are met with 'I don't know' or 'I

have forgotten'), and the extent to which it is given in an unclear and incoherent manner; and

4 the degree to which the client's aspirations and intentions appear to be maturative or non-maturative defensive idealisations.

Biographical and other information is gathered in a way that seems haphazard, but is necessary to fit a conversational style of relating in which the assessor follows the client but returns to make considered enquiries about areas that have been left or require clarification. The order in which we now discuss each kind of information represents the frame of reference on to which the assessor fits items of information as and when they become available.

THE MANNER IN WHICH THE PROSPECTIVE CLIENT TREATS THE ASSESSOR

When client and assessor meet, the client is seeking help and can be seen as an adult careseeker, while the assessor will be seen by the client as a professional caregiver who will have views and opinions about him. These views will be based on the client's experience of people in authority, of various kinds of caregivers, and on the expectations aroused by the referrer, the client's friends and relations, or their view of what psychotherapy is all about. The client's views about the assessor and the interview are revealed in the ways in which he approaches and treats him. Looking at this phenomenon in attachment terms we think of clients as feeling safe or anxious about approaching the assessor for help.

The client's way of relating is likely to be a mixture between the way that would induce original caregivers to respond in a manner that satisfied at least some of his needs and the variants he has found to be safe (i.e. less anxiety provoking) when used with strangers in positions of authority. On this basis the assessor is treated in a manner which is, overall, either warm, friendly and trusting, or avoidant, controlling, aggressive, compliant or confusing, or with mixtures of these major ways of relating. The assessor monitors changes as the session progresses, noting how they vary according to the topic under discussion. The client's initial way of relating is usually a defensive manner which may become more relaxed or more obvious as the interview proceeds. Clients usually present in any of three ways. Some can urgently seek reassurance about their anxieties or their beliefs, and ask, plead or forthrightly demand that someone does X or Y (or just something) 'to make them better'. Others can maintain a controlled distance which can minimise their underlying needs. Or they can make demands and withdraw simultaneously, that is to say clients are overtly saying they want help, but is cagey about supplying information and their non-verbal behaviour is avoidant. Throughout the interview the assessor will stay aware of shifts in the degree of closeness and distance the client keeps, shown by his body language, for example how much eye contact is made, how responsive he is to what the assessor says, what tones of voice the client uses and how much these may vary. For example, does he use a warm, friendly and interested tone of voice and facial expression, or one that is coolly dismissive, or anxiously preoccupied with how the therapist is going to respond, and what level of consistency is maintained between information that is conveyed verbally and non-verbally.

The assessor monitors continuously the kind of person the client assumes he is relating to. Sometimes assessors are treated as though they were very special and a privilege to be with, sometimes as a person who has to be entertained (when painful if not tragic events are described in terms that make them into good stories), often as someone who is critical, keeps exacting standards and requires apologies for inadequacies and from people who cry. All these ways of behaving are clearly associated with insecurity. When the client is more secure about asking for help, which is less common, the assessor is treated as someone who is seen as wanting to be helpful and prepared to respond with understanding to signs of distress. Allowing oneself as an assessor to experience oneself as someone who is alien to the person one feels one is (without comment except when it is deemed helpful to the client) can often be unpleasant, despite a training to anticipate it.

THE BIOGRAPHICAL INFORMATION AN ASSESSOR SHOULD KNOW

The life history of the client is represented in a genogram and a life event time scale. Both can be constructed, should the assessor judge it helpful to do so, with the active co-operation of the client. The genogram represents the identity of the personnel that make up the family group with whom the client grew up. From the genogram the assessor can identify the hierarchy of primary and secondary attachment figures who have in the past and presently provide some form of care, and who have had, or still have, most to do with the client's problem and complaint, its duration, and the circumstances which aggravate or relieve it. On the genogram are plotted the ages and dates of death, occupations, educational status and other key features of siblings, parents and grandparents, together with an indication of the size of the groups of maternal and paternal aunts, uncles, great aunts and great uncles and the names of any of these, or other individuals, with whom the client either spent much of his time or took steps to avoid. It is also vital to include in the genogram the client's spouse or partner, the ages and general well-being of their children and the spouse's relatives who are seen to be significant figures in his or her life.

As the genogram is being constructed the assessor collects the information to construct a life event time scale, on which is plotted the age of the client when events took place that increased, or significantly decreased, the client's sense of well-being and often his competence (e.g. poor school reports or changes in employment). In summary these will be:

1 events at home that significantly changed the client's status in the family (e.g. the birth or death of a sibling and changes in the parents' life that altered the caregiving pattern of the parents);
2 events that changed the client's status in his community and friendship network (e.g. going to nursery school, primary school and other educational shifts including university, vocational and other kinds of training);
3 long-term separation from or the loss of attachment figures, and moves of domicile that involved losing touch with part of the attachment hierarchy or of peer companions with or without the opportunity to make new congenial friends and attachment figures (e.g. school teachers); and
4 illness that involved major physical and psychological discomfort, and/or the disruption of familiar routines (e.g. going to hospital or attending hospital outpatients regularly, wearing appliances for relatively long periods).

One of the purposes of the life event time scale is to chart patches of turbulence, in which several different kinds of change may have taken place over a relatively narrow time band, and to note the quality of well-being during periods of relative quiescence, between patches of turbulence. This kind of information often has to be collected indirectly by asking clients how they coped at school or at home or what they did in their time outside work or school hours. Descriptions of depressive periods can be used for carefully phrased and spoken enquires about suicidal ideation. For example, 'when you were feeling like this, did you ever feel that life was not worth living?' followed, if the answer is in the affirmative, by 'and how did you cope with the feeling?' In a similar manner enquiries about alcohol consumption and drug taking can be sought. Constructing the genogram also gives the assessor an opportunity to ask what were the client's earliest memories – and so discover the extent of childhood amnesia.

Another function of the scale is to relate the timing of significant changes to the developmental status of the client, for example whether these happened before or during the ages of three to six years, between six years and puberty, during adolescence or in adult life. Significant indication of turbulence on the scale, or one signifi- cant event before the age of three years that massively changes an individual's most important attachment relationships, points to traumata likely to give rise to a basic fault (see Balint in Chapter 12). In contrast the later the trauma the more the client can have a better understanding of himself as a person.

We have regularly found that the representation of an individ- ual's history in these two visual forms can draw attention to events that prospective clients have seldom thought of or seen as a whole unfolding picture. If the information is painful, the client can feel angry or upset. Therefore when the assessor is unlikely to be the therapist or if a further assessment may be thought to be necessary, it is better to collect the information and not to involve the client in the actual construction of the time event scale.

THE COMPLETENESS OF THE BIOGRAPHICAL INFORMATION

We listen with care for the readiness with which biographical infor- mation is given. Sometimes information is given with apparent readiness suggesting that it is complete, but later in the session the client makes a comment about a relative who was not named as a member of the family. Or sometimes a person mentioned as impor- tant by the referrer is omitted from the history given by the client. Certain methods are used, either consciously or unconsciously, to evade giving information. One is to bypass a query. For example an enquiry is made about how the client felt about a certain issue and the answer is on the lines of 'Yes, that is interesting, I always think . . .' and thoughts continue to be given on the subject but feelings are omitted. Less subtle forms of evasion lie in changing the subject, or describing a relationship as 'all right'. Or when relationships with key figures are described in black and white terms with no reference to feeling other than pleasure or disgust. When information is 'forgotten', or confusion shown, a sympathetic enquiry about whether the client 'ever finds that he goes blank and it is difficult to think of anything' can bring to light the not uncommon and distressing phenomenon that we refer to as 'panic thinking' and consider to be associated with disorganising experiences.

Obvious gaps in biographical information and significant degrees of childhood amnesia can represent the experience of painful disassuaging information that has been more or less segregated from conscious recall and closed off in one or more IMER. Assessors who inadvertently provide reminders of these experiences can sometimes evoke sudden avoidant responses in the client. Alternatively clients can have been put in touch with disassuaging information before coming for assessment. When distressing memories are described as having returned in a particularly vivid form, it is likely that an experience involving extreme fear, horror or revulsion, often involving unmourned loss, has been tapped. Such information is noted with care but no detail is sought by the assessor other than that volunteered by the client. The decision to do so lies in the province of the therapist.

THE CLARITY AND COHESION OF THE CLIENT'S INFORMATION

One of Main's strokes of genius was to look beyond the informational content of the adult attachment interview (see Appendix B), which focuses on the adult's early attachment experiences and relationships, to the way in which the information was presented, and to use the degree to which information is coherent as a variable (Main and Goldwyn 1989). In so doing, she related the degree to which information is coherent to the person's capacity for metacognition, mentioned in Chapter 7 as a high-order capacity. Its presence or absence points to the ability of the client to benefit from a form of exploratory therapy and represents a measure of psychological mindedness.

Assessment and metacognition

The term metacognition refers to the consideration of a person's cognitive processes as being objects of thought and reflection. The ability to think in this way is acquired by children between three and six years of age (Main 1991). It refers, for example, to the capacity to reflect about relationships and put into words feelings and attitudes that have been implicit at a younger age. It is knowledge about cognition, and represents the ability to make a remark such as 'I am a person who thinks I am an unworthy person, rather frequently'. Main tackles this issue by noting the differences between representational artefacts (e.g. drawings or interview transcripts) and the internal processes they are presumed to represent. She moves to ask what form or forms are taken by internal representations, and is it valid to presume that thinking unfailingly follows the rules of formal logic. The answers to both these questions are still unknown. Main accepts the views of Johnson-Laird (1983), which are similar to Craik's (1967) ideas of working models, and concludes that although reasoning does take place through formal logic, it can also happen without logic by using mental models and coming directly to conclusions. This process can give rise to incompatible conclusions from similar premises. As we understand Main's argument, this can happen with respect to attachment working models. She links this reasoning to Bowlby's concept that models which carry incompatible and/or contradictory information (when both cannot be true at the same time) give rise to multiple models, and draws support for this kind of thinking from Harter and Budden's (1987) findings that the majority of four-year-old children used all-or-none thinking in regard to emotions. They were unable to integrate sets of positive and negative emotions, these emotions being viewed as conceptually distinct and therefore incompatible.

When discussing the capacity of the self for metacognitive monitoring and standards of coherence in the adult attachment interview, Main and Goldwyn (1989) viewed the capacity of the self for high standards of metacognition to be exemplified in Grice's (1975) formulation of the general principle of coherent conversation (called the Co-operative Principle) in which he used the four maxims of:

1 Quality – be truthful and have evidence for what you say.
2 Quantity – be succinct, and yet complete.
3 Relation – be relevant.
4 Manner – be clear and orderly.

Main and Goldwyn incorporated these maxims in their provision for specifications for rating the 'coherence of transcript' in the adult attachment interview. Their findings showed that the 'coherence' of the resulting narrative strongly predicted security of attachment (the Strange Situation Test was used as an external criterion) in the children of these adults, and 'incoherence' predicted insecurity of infant attachment. In another of their studies, judges observed that parents of secure infants were highly coherent during the adult attachment interview. They had an easy access to childhood memories, were coherent in describing, discussing and evaluating the effects of their experiences, and no contradictory evidence within the transcript was found. In contrast, parents of insecure infants showed evidence in their transcript of relative incoherence, in the form of inability to focus on interview questions, the presence of logical and factual contradictions, inability to stay with the interview topic, anomalous changes in wording or intrusions that are inappropriate to the topic, metaphors or rhetoric inappropriate to the topic, and difficulties in obtaining access to attachment related information. In other words, she found that the strongest correlation of infant security of attachment to a given parent was the overall 'coherence' of the parent's presentation of his or her own attachment history.

Later findings appeared to be more specific for parents of avoidant and ambivalent infants. Parents who were dismissing of attachment behaviour and have avoidant children violated 'the maxim of quality' (have evidence for what you say). Such parents idealised their own parents in ways that contradicted their autobiographical memories. Their transcripts also frequently violated the 'maxim of quantity' exhibited by their excessively succinct and thus incomplete responses.

Preoccupied parents of ambivalent infants violated the maxims of quality, quantity, relevance and manner by rapid and unexplained oscillations of viewpoint, failure to be succinct, irrelevant responses and entangled, run-on sentences. Parents of disorganised/disoriented children were not infrequently moderately coherent in terms of collaboration and co-reference, but made highly implausible statements regarding the causes or consequences of traumatic attachment and related events such as loss, indicating belief in 'magical causality surrounding a death or trauma'.

Main's findings, relating a mother's incoherent narrative about her own childhood to the security and insecurity of her infant, have been taken a stage further by Fonagy, Steele and Steele (1991). They showed that the findings from a mother's adult attachment interview during pregnancy could predict the security status of her child at one year of age. All the findings from the adult attachment interview suggest that individuals who show temporary loss of the capacity for metacognition when speaking of their childhood relationships with attachment figures had or have (if they are still in close contact with that person) an insecure relationship with them. Furthermore the pattern of insecurity they now show in the way they treat other people is a pointer to the kind of relating they once experienced.

It must be noted that some of Main's criteria for coherence include incomplete information. This form of incoherence can be associated with the phenomenon of 'going blank' and can come and go in relation to what the client is recalling and to how the client is assessing the assessor. During the therapy that follows assessment, we have noted that panic thinking is associated with past interactions with one or more terrifying attachment figures or with terrifying consequences following the loss of a protective attachment figure. We do not suggest that the assessor tries to rate incoherence but notes shifts in coherence, the presence or relative absence of panic thinking as well as the capacity for metacognition relating to the topic under discussion at the time.

The clarity, cohesion and completeness with which the client tells their story, and the incidents associated with lack of clarity, incoherence and omissions, alert the assessor to the kind and amount of disassuaging information that is being defensively kept from review. In general terms the more avoidant, incoherent and 'forgetful' the client is, the more supportive the therapy needs to be.

ASSESSING THE BIAS TOWARDS MATURATIVE IDEALS AND DEFENSIVE IDEALISATIONS ASSOCIATED WITH EACH OF THE BEHAVIOURAL SYSTEMS AND THE POTENTIATING CAPACITIES

The final strand of information is the assessment of the abilities the client values most, and those that he appears to devalue, that are associated with each of his behavioural systems and the potentiating capacities. In assessing whether a client values a particular ability or competence, the statement that he values something is not enough, especially when given as the verbal response to an enquiry.

The non-verbal signals, the emotion and degree of quiet seriousness or enthusiasm shown each time the ability is talked about is more affirmative of its value.

A case has been made by Lake (1985) for the translation of ego strength, for long considered an important indicator of outcome of psychotherapy, into terms which are descriptive of personal and social competence and can provide clearer guidelines for the assessment of a patient for an optimal psychotherapy. Lake used the definition of competence as ability (to do, for a task); suggested synonyms include proficiency and skill (*Concise Oxford Dictionary*). Thus personal and social competence (ego strength) demonstrate an effective and creative management of the self, its systems and capacities. The greater the degree of personal and social competence in a wide variety of contexts, the better the therapeutic prognosis. Poor prognosis is associated with low levels of personal and social competence exemplified in those with severely impaired self-concept, identity diffusion, intense self-depreciation, excessive guilt feelings oscillating with grandiose forms of self-identification, and poor impulse control combined with antisocial behaviour. Lake's translation enables assessor and client to talk about the client's strengths and weaknesses, complaints and problems in a language that each can understand. It is not intended to provide answers to a complex construct, but to emphasise that in any assessment of psychological health or disorder, personal adequacy and inadequacy are measured not only against the norm of the average man (which is a major criterion of assessment for psychotherapy in the National Health Service), but also against the norm of a cultural definition of the ideal man.

In Chapter 11 we discussed maturative ideals as envisagements of something that the individual has the ability to achieve and which mark a further stage of their development. In contrast, defensive idealisations guide and shape the individual towards standards and aims which lead to an illusory sense of competence and well-being (ego weakness). To assess the bias between aspiring to reach maturative ideals and defensive idealisations associated with each system, we use the list of abilities that operationalise the differences between ego strength and weakness.

The contrast between aspirations to reach maturative ideals or defensive idealisations associated with each of the behavioural systems

We assess the client's aspirations to reach maturative ideals, or defensive idealisations, in regard to each of the behavioural systems (see Chapter 7), by noting the presence or absence of a list of abilities closely derived from those used as items for assessing ego strength or weakness. We have listed the abilities and aspirations related to each system, followed by a statement of the associated maturative aspirations and defensive idealisations.

Abilities and aspirations associated with interdependent and defensive independent self-care and management

These are:

1 The ability to look after essential needs for food and shelter and to be self-supporting with a capacity for work, associated with maturative aspirations to provide adaptive ways to attain basic needs, to look after personal health and manage money appropriately. They are a measure of self-management. In contrast, aspirations and abilities to be self-supporting can be limited or absent and aspirations focus on dependency or withdrawal.

2 The capacity to establish and maintain mutually helpful and supportive relationships, at home, at work and at leisure. These abilities are associated with maturative aspirations for a sharing relationship, with the ability to give and receive affection; a capacity to show interest and respect for others and oneself; a willingness to sacrifice part of oneself for another person, sharing a degree of altruism and not viewing the world only as a source of individual gratification. One sustained or reliable relationship in the patient client's life suggests a basis for a treatment alliance (Brown and Pedder 1979). In contrast, defensive idealisations can be associated with enjoying irresponsible and unreliable attitudes, maintaining inflexible moral values (Dewald 1969), and extreme self-centredness.

3 The ability to cope adaptively with change, loss, and uncertainty (loss of family member, friends, jobs, money, change of routine, illness). These abilities are associated with aspirations to be maturely interdependent and self-reliant; to cope compassionately with one's own and another's loss and grief, aspirations to

behave with dignity and courage. By contrast, defensive idealisations distort one's own and others' suffering by showing shallow or aggressively ascetic idealisations of suffering which deprive the experience of its meaning and the sufferer of his dignity.

4 The ability to cope with relationships and experiences that are for the most part difficult, upsetting and involve suffering, at home, at work or at leisure. These abilities are closely associated with maturative aspirations to be companionably caregiving with a realistic and compassionate acceptance of one's own and others' conflicts and suffering; aspirations to relieve or if necessary bear with or withstand them; aspirations to attain the capacity to show respect, empathy, tact, flexibility, humour, tolerance, firmness and resourcefulness in such situations. There are desires for parenthood and family life notwithstanding their demands, frustrations and restrictions. In contrast, defensive idealisations and aspirations are increasingly based on receiving care from others rather than caregiving; or on the denial or rejection of one's own or another's unhappiness and suffering; defensive idealisations are associated with unempathic, coercive, and dominating attitudes, moral extremism, fanatical obsession with an idea or principle of caregiving, or the idealisation of a self-centred contentment with one's own standard of giving care.

The abilities and aspirations associated with supportive companionable caregiving

The abilities include maintaining a home which careseekers experience as a safe base and have already been described under the headings of self-care and management. Such caregiving abilities are associated with maturative aspirations to maintain a home which is organised so that useful routines, hygiene and nutrition are consistently maintained with some enthusiasm and pleasure but without excessive displays of emotion. There is appreciation of aesthetic values in the form and disposition of belongings and the value given to education, shown by the topics discussed with careseekers and the interests pursued by caregivers. By contrast, defensive idealisations are concerned with excessively demanding perfectionist levels of one or more aspects of homemaking with overprotection and idealisation of their children. Alternatively caregivers who have come to devalue caregiving usually idealise whatever provides them with relief from their own unassuaged careseeking and from the demands of their legitimate careseekers (e.g. other activities including excessive work, entertainment, sexual activity, or alcohol and other drugs).

The abilities and aspirations associated with interest-sharing

The abilities associated with the interest-sharing system are those required to establish and maintain interesting, stimulating and enjoyable relationships at home, at work and at leisure.

These abilities are associated with maturative aspirations to explore and share aims and interests with peer companions in dyads and in groups, and to engage in joint plans to achieve them; to communicate effectively, to co-operate with and adjust to others' appropriate aims, to feel satisfaction in and enjoyment at what each other is doing, and to attain confidence and self-esteem in the ability to achieve short- and long-term aims. By contrast, defensive idealisations are concerned with solitary pursuits or with controlling competitive engagement in work and recreations.

The abilities and aspirations associated with intrapersonal exploration

The abilities associated with intrapersonal exploration are those required to derive interest and satisfaction from the individual performance of skills at work and leisure.

These abilities are associated with maturative aspirations relating to the person's desires: to express his own talents and creative skills in work and recreation; to derive interest and enjoyment from his own performance and achievement; and to value the expression of his own talents and their overt significance to others. In contrast defensive idealisations are concerned with an overvaluation of one's own or another's talents and skills and/or living on promises rather than realistic commitments to reaching declared aims.

The abilities and aspirations associated with the sexual system

The ability associated with the expression of sexuality within a mutually enjoyed and established relationship is associated with maturative aspirations to 'be in love' in which the longing for and attainment of mutual sexual enjoyment, with tenderness and generosity, is experienced as the fulfilment of the sexual relationship, and a deep commitment to the relationship. In contrast defensive idealisations are concerned with fantasies or ideas of using others possessively and/or aggressively as objects for sexual satisfaction, or of being used in such a way by others.

This fourth strand of information is collected in the course of constructing the genogram and life events time scale.

THE LAST STAGE OF ASSESSMENT

In the last stage of the assessment assessors communicate to the client the opinion they have come to about his predicament, and their suggestions and advice. This could be that further investigation is required, that the client would be better helped in another way or that a particular therapy is recommended. In this model the assessor gives the client opportunities to discuss whichever alternative has been suggested and its implications, including the cost in terms of money and time. We consider it important that the client's questions are answered, especially about issues of confidentiality and what therapy is likely to entail, and that clients come to their own decision about whether they feel able to make a commitment to a course of therapy. During this phase the assessor will find out how the client treats him once he has turned from being an empathic listener into someone who has opinions of what might be best for the client.

COMPUTING THE INFORMATION USED TO ARRIVE AT AN OPINION

The end of the assessment process consists of the assessor using their mental model of this frame of reference to organise all the information they have collected in order to write a report. The use of the frame of reference as a tool begins by first setting out demographic information and the nature of the complaint and then rating answers to questions grouped under the headings:

1 How did the client relate to the assessor?
2 How did the client present his story?
3 Who makes up the client's attachment hierarchy and hierarchy of supportive companions? How much are each of these people valued?
4 How many traumatic events did the client report? What was the severity of these events and at what ages did they occur?

5 To what degree are the client's aspirations maturative or non-maturative idealisations in regard to his self-care and management, caregiving, interest-sharing and sexual relationships.

The answers to these questions are found in memory, aided by notes made during the assessment and by using the questionnaire in Appendix D. This questionnaire organises the information gathered during the assessment, and helps the assessor come to a decision about the client's degree of maturity (or ego strength) and his motivation for therapy.

Factors that are generally regarded as leading to the client benefiting from a more exploratory rather than a more supportive form of therapy are: an attachment hierarchy that is overall more mutually satisfying than frustrating, in which the people at the top are secondary attachment figures rather than primary; a capacity to communicate coherently; a bias towards maturative aspirations rather than defensive idealisations; and the presence of a high level of motivation to reach maturational ideals.

Chapter 14

The therapeutic alliance and the creation of a safe base for personal development

Undertaking psychotherapy gives therapists an intense awareness of the range and depth of human suffering and the infinite varieties of being badly hurt. The fact that there are well over a hundred named types of psychotherapy, and practitioners who identify themselves with each type, suggests that different forms of psychotherapy will continue to be required to meet the needs of all psychological sufferers and the necessity to specialise in particular types of psychotherapy will remain. However the expansion of the demand for therapy and economic considerations of how it can be provided have meant that many of the training programmes have broadened the range of psychotherapeutic skills and research to meet the growing demand. This recognition of the value and limits of each particular approach has meant that psychotherapists have steadily come to be more appreciative of each other's contribution and less critical of each other's limits. There also seems to be an increasing recognition of core elements or so-called non-specific factors (Frank 1971, 1979, Strupp 1979) in each therapy which need to be understood and practised if the skills of each special therapy are to be fully developed. We continue to hold the hypothesis that how therapists relate to and look after their clients is the issue that covers all these common factors, and that the key to understanding them lies in understanding the processes underlying caregiving and its development.

The model developed in this book of a dynamic, systemic, social self shows the place of caregiving in a supraordinate system for self-care and management. The model is outlined in Part II and shows how without the adequate development of this system, individuals are unable to cope constructively enough with the vicissitudes of everyday life. Their caregiving system is insufficiently developed to rear a new generation and they require therapeutic help in order to shift on to a more constructive developmental pathway. Therapy need not focus on the client's caregiving or even the lack of it, but the therapist must be aware of what he might do that blocks the maturative development of the client's system for self-care and management. We see the therapist taking the role of a professional caregiver, and the therapeutic alliance as the vehicle that allows the client to move from their present developmental pathway on to one that is more maturative. Clients in our experience are rarely on a single pathway. There are areas in their lives in which certain behavioural systems function more effectively than in others. The role of the therapist is to recognise the more maturative aspects of the client while identifying those aspects whose maturation has been impeded and helping the client to accept, understand and cope with them

The psychoanalytically oriented approach to therapy that we use can help a broad range of clients in a wide range of circumstances. Although practitioners from different schools would phrase the main aims of their practice somewhat differently, it is a recognisably shared interpersonal approach and takes, to a greater or lesser extent, supportive elements of caregiving into account. We differ from some by giving an attachment-based slant to a Fairbairn-Guntrip conceptualisation of object relations theory. This leads us to see the aim of the therapist as that of shifting between a more supportive and a more exploratory interpretative form of relating, to match the cognitive affective state of the client. In some circumstances, clients have needed a considerable measure of empathic support before they felt safe enough to look at explanations about themselves and other people, and arrive at a level of understanding that allows them to try to resolve their major conflicts and uncertainties. Other clients, while requiring a supportive framework, welcome an exploratory interpretative approach from the beginning. We work from the assumption that clients require a relationship with a therapist of sufficient security before they can explore and express their doubts, deceptive denials and despairs, and develop the hope that their lives might become less stressful, more enriching and more enjoyable.

DIFFICULTIES IN ILLUSTRATING THERAPEUTIC PRACTICE AND THEIR RESOLUTION

This chapter and the next showing how we use this theory of care-giving in the practice of psychotherapy have been difficult to write. First, our style of referring to the authors as 'we' makes it sound as though therapy was undertaken by two clones, who felt, thought and acted in the same way, which is far from true. Second, we had found it straightforward to argue out points of theory to reach an agreed position after giving each other sufficient evidence for the point under discussion to become clear. Then the word 'we' had a validity that was felt to be fitting. It was quite a different story when we began to put into words what a therapist actually did, which we each separately considered was therapeutic, and to find examples to illustrate our practice. We knew from working together with marital couples that we tend to rank-order rather differently the disassuaging events that take place between couples. We feel this difference has been helpful in conjoint therapy. It enables one of us to make an understanding comment that make a disassuagement explicit sooner than it would otherwise have been made.

There is of course more to it. When we began to write about therapy, we realised the different slants we placed on an event, or on a client's reactions to it, led to elaborations of the picture which always introduced a greater complexity of relationship than can be dealt with in this book. We also realised that many of our more recent clients were trainee psychotherapists having a personal therapeutic experience or were figures well enough known to be difficult to disguise. Finally we were aware that an account of a piece of therapeutic work shows the particular blend of attachment styles and defences adopted by a client of a particular temperament with a particular history of attachment relationships. Therefore every case history and the story of every client's therapy is unique. The accounts do not readily illustrate principles of how to act in a therapeutic way that can be used with many clients. We therefore came to the decision that in these two last chapters we would attempt to put into words what we consider a therapist has to do and be before clients with different attachment experiences and defences can feel secure enough to change well-established restrictive ways of relating to other people and of expressing their talents. We have chosen to put into words and into operational terms how we use the concept of a secure base from which to explore the world in therapy and, as an extension, how we see the practice of therapy to be based on the concept of constructing and maintaining a safe-enough therapeutic frame for the client to be able to explore their predicaments.

THE USE OF THE CONCEPT OF A SAFE BASE FOR EXPLORATION IN THERAPY

The metaphor of a safe base from which to explore the world requires very little elaboration for most people to use it as a means of communication. Its power is threefold: it is felt by people to make sense of their experiences in everyday life; it can be used by therapists and clients as a way of talking to each other about complex issues associated with achieving or losing what they most value; and it can be used by scientists as a concept with explanatory power. None the less, clients in therapy seldom give the impression that their security for exploration rests only on people who are external to them, although their availability to the therapist seems to be essential. They also seem to be searching for, or trying to preserve, safe places and beliefs that will enable them to live with less anxiety. We therefore see the global concept of a secure base for exploration as having three interdependent components which consist of safe people, safe places and safe beliefs.

To provide a rationale for thinking about a secure base in this way we restate the essential aspects of the model described in Part II. These are:

1 that human beings are innately programmed to need a small hierarchy of reliable people who can support them in moving from one developmental stage to another;
2 that the human brain is structured so that an infrastructure of homeostatic programmes enables linear developmental processes to be carried forward to limits that are dictated by the genetic endowment of the individual, which includes their temperament;
3 that each individual is innately programmed to attempt to survive and to this end is endowed with self-correcting factors that maintain their physical and psychological homeostasis;
4 that parents have an innate expectation that they will maintain an environment that is secure enough to sustain their own developmental processes and those of their offspring. Offspring require caregiving attention a great deal when they are infants and young

children but to a decreasing degree as childhood progresses and their capacity for self-care and management develops.

We begin by describing what clients seem to need when the issue of losing their safe people, places or beliefs arises. Our experience has been that every client asking for therapy is in a state of insecurity that involves his attachment hierarchy, and is thrown back on to relying, for the security he feel he needs, on his personal supportive environment (safe places) and the beliefs, however illusory, that lead him to do things that feel safe.

By and large, safe places are those in which individuals can feel a sense of privacy (i.e. freedom from interruption), as well as a comfortable nearness to and distance from those on whom they have to rely although feeling them to be demanding, critical, upsetting or actually dangerous. Safe places seem to serve three purposes for human beings: they are places (and they come in many varieties) in which individuals are able to be alone with themselves, engaging in their own interests and reflections; they are places in which individuals can be with one safe person, to enjoy a caregiving/careseeking (CG/CS), interest-sharing (IS/IS) or a sexual partnership; and places in which they can have CG/CS or IS/IS partnerships with two, or a small group of, safe and congenial people.

Safe beliefs are those from which individuals can make reliable (i.e. trustworthy) predictions about how they will be treated by those on whom they ultimately depend for their well-being and about how to act within other relationships and towards things and events, without feeling that it is endangering themselves. We consider these beliefs are expressions of their IMERs and other working models and embody rules about reaching the goals of each system. They are an important element of the internal supportive system (see Chapter 5) and are taken into account when planning how to cope with any situation. The internal supportive system consists of both secure and insecure (good and bad) internalised representations of all experiences in relationships with each attachment figure in the hierarchy. Some of these will be associated with SC relating, others with defensive D/S relating. They have some equivalence to Fairbairn's concept of a libidinal and antilibidinal ego and Freud's concept of the super-ego. Beliefs associated with the internalised recording of secure relationships with attachment figures are based on interactions with empathic, maturely supportive, companionable and far-sighted attachment figures. These beliefs, which include beliefs about the individual's worth and competence, constitute the most secure aspects of an individual's internalised safe base. Those representations that record insecure relationships with attachment figures are based on painful interactions with avoidant or intrusive, domineering or subservient, or deceiving seductive attachment figures. They give rise to defensive behaviour and associated beliefs in which the individual may either grossly undervalue or grossly overvalue himself. For example, individuals feel undervalued when seeking, or competing, unsuccessfully for caregiving resources. The balance achieved between beliefs that enable SC relating and those that promote D/S relating, at any time and stage of development, represents the overall degree of security provided by the internal supportive system. The balance will depend to a large extent upon how individuals construe themselves at each stage of their development, when interacting with people and in the world at large.

So far, we have written about clients needing a safe base from which to explore their fears and anxieties. It is equally the case that a therapist also needs a safe base from which to undertake the task of helping other people explore their fears and despairs, some of which may act as reminders of the therapist's own fears. The therapist's safe base will include: congenial working arrangements; time to reflect, to take stock and update his own beliefs; and trustworthy professional caregivers with whom he can discuss aspects of a client's responses to therapy that are confusing, disassuaging or indicate that no progress is being made.

The personal beliefs that are relevant to our professional work with clients include the belief that there are limits to what it is possible to predict and thus uncertainty cannot be banished. A second belief is in the power of supportive companionable (SC) relating to promote the developmental processes of careseekers, when it is used by caregivers consistently enough over a long enough period. A third belief concerns the validity of any theory and is one we share with Craik (see Chapter 8). If one sees a theory as a working model of some process, then the term model should be considered as an analogy which is bound to break down at some point. This is reached when the model points to properties not found in the process it imitates, and when the model fails to point out properties in the process it is supposed to imitate, that it does not itself possess. The third belief applies to our therapeutic work. The theory we propose may not fit all people. It certainly fits some of those clients who have the capacity to maintain a therapeutic alliance, whose beliefs can ultimately be expressed in words and be reflected on by the client. But what about the people who cannot make a therapeutic alliance, whose beliefs cannot be so fully shared or explored? And all the others who do not feel the need for a therapist? The majority seem to be those who can manage life using the relationships available to them (the secure enough group), but others appear to have difficulties in maintaining close relationships and do not seem to feel upset about the loss of them as most people do. In economic terms, this last group can often be successful, but not infrequently create a trail of hurt people. We can explain what they seem to be doing by using the theoretical working model we have described, but we can feel no certainty we are correct until more definitive research emerges.

THE CONCEPT OF THE WITHDRAWN SELF AS IT APPEARS IN THERAPY

It was a central feature of the theories of both Guntrip and Bowlby, although they each expressed it differently, that intensely painful disassuaged aspects of the self are, through defensive measures, closed off from recall and review. Guntrip referred to aspects of the self associated with certain of these experiences as the withdrawn self. From this perspective, both considered that the task of the therapist is to create a partnership in which the client feels safe enough to bring into the relationship withdrawn aspects of themselves that they feel are not acceptable to others or to themselves.

In attachment terms these withdrawn aspects of people's selves, sheltering behind a desire to survive, are associated with intensely painful feelings of inadequacy, incompetence and low self-worth, the absence of relationships in which they can feel accepted, the loss of places in which they can feel safe, and the lack of belief about their ability to manage themselves and their relationships with others. These unappreciated aspects of the individual lurk in the IMERs, completely or partially withdrawn from the process of maturative development. In this light, therapy is a process in which the client and therapist build a relationship which, after repeated testing, the client experiences as sufficiently reliable and trustworthy for him to explore and put into words: first his understanding of what he had done, or not done, that had been considered intolerable, and then how he had lived with this unacceptable part of himself. In this way the client begins a process of updating, integrating and reorganising his IMERs and in so doing alters his attitudes and beliefs.

We understand the phrase 'putting into words' to be a task for both therapist and client, in that the therapist picks up from the client (or suggests as a possibility) metaphors about his feelings, thoughts and beliefs, which the client experiences as 'right' and which match what he feels has been done to him and what he did (or wanted to do) in return. These metaphors then become part of the therapeutic discourse. For example, one client began to talk about feeling shut up in a bell jar from which she dare not emerge. This was a part of her that wanted to do things and it became a central topic in therapy to explore what might happen should she try to emerge, what she wanted to do once outside, and what sent her back into the bell jar. Another client, when asked to take on responsibilities she was well qualified to assume, felt as if she shut herself safely in a cupboard in her house of origin (in real life, she actually withdrew a lively very interesting vital part of herself and had intense difficulties in leaving home). The explorations that were undertaken fitted her metaphor of running back into the cupboard when frightened. What made her so frightened was also a subject for exploration.

We do not try to explain what actually happens between client and therapist when a metaphor that feels 'right' to a client is found, beyond saying that one senses something important and freeing for both has taken place. It is as though the client is, paradoxically, much closer and at the same time freer to come and go.

Just as we found that the global concept of a safe base from which to explore the world requires some unpacking before it can be used to the full with clients, so also does the concept of the withdrawn self. Using the description of the self introduced in Chapter 7, we see clients who come for therapy as people whose attachment system is aroused and who consider they have no suitably responsive person within their attachment hierarchy to whom they can reliably turn for understanding, appropriate comfort or other aspects of caregiving. They are likely to be people whose attachment system has been rendered to a greater or lesser extent dysfunctional by the repeated experience of failure to reach the interpersonal goal of careseeking – to the point of regularly being exposed to disassuagement. Hence their system for defensive self-management will also have been aroused. This means that defensive strategies (and the psychological mechanisms of defence outlined by Bowlby) that had been found in the past to be effective in forestalling the impact of disassuaging responses will play their part in how these clients relate to the therapist. The function of all defences is to reduce distress, maintain survival and restore some sense of self-esteem and potential for competence. Effective defences against disassuagement in CG/CS partnerships are those by means of which a careseeker can influence a caregiver to cease being disassuaging or at least minimise his suffering.

We showed in Chapter 13 how defensive thoughts, feelings and behaviour may be assessed, and have discussed in Chapters 8–11 how they can arise. In this chapter we do not try to discuss further the processes by means of which individuals relate to themselves and to others in various partnerships, through the perception of representations in the IMERs. Aspects of these processes are currently being re-explored and reformulated by Fonagy and Target (Fonagy and Target 1996, Target and Fonagy 1996) from a psychoanalytic perspective. In this chapter we focus on how clients defensively attempt to influence the therapist's feelings, actions and attitudes. And we also keep in the picture how clients can, through processes associated with attunement, become aware of the feeling states of the therapist and vice versa. These processes allow client and therapist alike to become aware of feelings about which (through the processes of defensive segregation of information) either party may be currently unaware. Moreover, by the same processes, intrapersonal conflicts of which an individual is either unaware or can defensively 'put out of mind' and 'forget' may be revealed. We consider that processes allied to attunement can explain many aspects of the phenomenon of projection and of projective identification in which a second party finds himself identifying with and feeling the feelings of another, to which he had attuned without being initially aware of having done so.

FORMS OF DEFENSIVE RELATING BY CLIENTS WITH WHICH THERAPISTS COMMONLY HAVE TO INTERACT

In recent years parent/child interactions have been increasingly examined from the point of view of the defensive behaviour employed by the child. Examples are given in the volume edited by Greenberg *et al.* (1990) and patterns of defence have been described by a number of analysts including Fairbairn (1952). We have mentioned elsewhere that the range of defensive strategies that have been described is legion and that a description of them is beyond the scope of this book. In this chapter we outline some common defensive patterns which therapists frequently encounter.

We describe defences in terms of D/S patterns of relating. What we have said earlier in relation to SC and D/S ways of relating means that individuals whose internal supportive systems are derived from interactions with attachment figures in which SC relating is predominant will tend to deal with painful aspects of caregiving interactions differently from a second group of careseekers whose internal supportive systems are derived from interactions with caregivers in which domineering, coercive or alternatively subservient ways of relating are predominant. The first group have internal supportive systems in which SC patterns of relating predominate while the second group have internal supportive systems in which D/S relating predominates and emerges in contexts in which anxiety and fear have been evoked. The more that D/S patterns are present in representations within the internal supportive system the more difficult it is to make an effective therapeutic alliance and to reach withdrawn aspects of the self. In contrast clients in the first group, who would be classed as securely attached, are able to make a therapeutic alliance more rapidly, discuss their predicaments more freely and coherently, and they are more psychologically minded and motivated.

Careseekers with internal supportive systems representing interaction with anxious caregivers who offer SC relating alternating with D/S relating, respond defensively to such caregivers in the contexts in which they have been disassuaging. Such caregivers have most commonly been dominating, and have either kept careseekers at a distance (psychologically and/or physically) or forced a distressing degree of closeness. Both of these caregiver commands are enforced through verbal and non-verbal shaming (with guilt induction), punitive threats or acts of punishment.

Anxious caregivers who alternate between SC and D/S parental relating characterise one form of ambivalent CG/CS partnership. Another form is demonstrated by caregivers alternating between behaving in a dominating way and being subservient to forceful demands from the careseeker. A third form describes an incomplete SC relating. It is illustrated in the first vignette described below. Anxious caregiving can affect any of the interpersonal or intrapersonal systems described in Chapter 7. This brief outline of a way to conceptualise the essential differences between secure and defensive modes of relating draws attention to the contribution of D/S patterns of relating to the emergence of psychopathology. Five vignettes serve as illustrations principally of dyadic relationships. Triadic relationships and interactions in which two or more care-seekers are attempting to reach their careseeking goals from over-stretched caregivers or from those who for their own defensive reasons give preference to some careseekers more than others are not discussed. The following three vignettes illustrate how hard children work to restore some form of SC relating with their attachment figures. The last two episodes illustrate relationships in which careseekers cannot influence caregivers to provide SC relating.

Vignette 1: The entertainer

In our experience it is not uncommon to meet clients who have discovered early in life that they can induce parental figures to be more lively and as supportive and companionable as possible. An example is the child who can evoke acceptance and admiration by being amusing and engendering a sense of vitality in other people prone to feeling rather dull or depressed. This end is attained at some expense. Attempts to share painful experiences and fears are met with distractive ploys or otherwise bypassed. These children (and later when they are adults) work hard for a living. They do not feel hurt or depressed so long as they can maintain a cheerful front and are successful in influencing others to change from being withdrawn, complaining or rejective into being accepting.

The SC relating offered by such parental figures is incomplete. It lacks a quality that enables parental figures to reach out to care-seekers experiencing deep distress, but not to be so affected by the experience that they become devitalised and unable to offer empathic and constructive tuning (see Chapter 3). It is replaced by a form of purposeful misattunement that in effect becomes what Stern (1985: 213) terms 'emotional theft'. It would appear from working in therapy with adults, who have experienced this as a child, that they have found this experience to be confusing and deeply hurtful and followed the emotional lead of the caregiver. Frustration and a sense of incompetence at not being able to influence attachment figures to listen to their experiences of disassuagement are momentarily dispelled and with it the upsurge of intentionality to act associated with anger. Some of these children, who at heart are insecure, can grow up to be popular guests (who can make the party go), a few others may become successful professional entertainers, but all of them have to be successful as entertainers to avoid feeling incompetent and unconsoled. They can be recognised by a tendency to cheer people up, an inability to be quietly comforting over a sustained period, and a tendency to withdraw or to exhort, coax, or use straight coercion when people do not respond.

Vignette 2: The rebellious dare-devil

An example of SC relating very closely related to D/S patterns is given by parents who came complaining about the outrageous and often dangerous behaviour of their seven-year-old son. But their descriptions of 'a proper little devil who was not going to take no for an answer' were couched in tones of glowing admiration, although the little devil could only go so far. When his assertions and apparently exploratory attempts to do things some adults did alarmed his parents, they resorted to punitively coercive methods which they described despairingly as being 'no use' in stopping their son's frightening activities. These parents showed affection and a desire to be supportive and companionable, but they were unaware that in many contexts their non-verbal messages showed that they approved and admired the kind of behaviour they otherwise endeavoured to stop.

It became apparent later that the parents had their own defensive reasons to support their son being rebelliously assertive, that the child felt his punishments were 'unfair' and that he was very frightened by his parents when they were in a punishing mood. In these circumstances it appeared that he could not stop doing the kind of things that so often brought approval.

If these parents had not shown an ability to be fully supportively companionable in some contexts, their son might have adopted domineering forms of behaviour towards everyone whom he considered would submit. In so doing he would have behaved like many bullies who have been treated by D/S relating parental figures who scorn natural careseeking behaviour and expressions of tenderness and consider them weak and babyish. As a consequence the expression of tenderness becomes taboo as noted by Suttie (1935 and 1988), the behaviour of parental figures is copied and their attitudes and beliefs are adopted as being the only way to escape disapproval, shaming and/or more straightforward punishment. Individuals who are defended in this way usually have confidence in their ability to dominate either by force or by deception. They can therefore feel powerful and safe. However, the sense of security engendered by their beliefs about themselves is threatened when they find themselves confronted by someone who proves to be as relentlessly dominating or wise to their deceptions. At this point some of these individuals can find good reasons to withdraw from the relationship. If withdrawal brings loss of vital resources (e.g. a job or a relationship with sufficiently satisfying elements) these individuals begin to suffer fear and depression. The introduction of negotiation about the conflictual issues can for some be seen as an invitation to submit which is in its turn seen as the relinquishment of any hope of being seen as a person worthy of respect. Rather than suffer this fate they can continue to act in a coercive aggressive way which can lead to seriously antisocial acts. Many marital conflicts and conflicts between parents and teenage children are of this type.

Vignette 3: The confused precocious caregiver

This example is of a child who turned out to be an angry, confused and precocious caregiver. The parents came with their eleven-year-old daughter because she was doing badly at school and could not respond to parental coaching. Her parents considered her to be stupid and feared that she was retarded. It turned out that anyone who had not made it to Oxbridge was considered by both parents to be 'dim'. Her mother had not done so (although she was deemed fit to sit an entrance examination) and so considered herself 'dim', and she thought her daughter even more stupid than she was. Psychological assessment showed that the child was performing at a level just above average and not near the level required to achieve a university place. She had above average dexterity and artistic ability and her parents described admiringly how thoughtful and helpful she was at home. 'She always knows when I need a cup of tea.' The child turned out to be depressed about her 'stupidity' and that the things she was good at doing, which were admired by her parents, were ranked as not important. However producing cups of tea (and undertaking other caregiving acts) did something to stem the flow of complaints and criticisms about her stupidity. What might happen to the development of a child's capacity to caregive, after a precocious defensive spur to its development, cannot in our experience always be predicted. The girl described above showed that as well as being confused about her level of ability, she was angry about having to do domestic chores from which her brothers were excused. This girl had found that by being in sympathy with her distressed mother and doing what she sensed her mother wanted, she could gain approval and feel that she could influence her mother temporarily not to be critical. But she felt there was too little supportive and companionable relating to maintain even a submissive role. Defensive precocious caregivers in childhood can become compulsive adult caregivers who can be highly effective and can feel rightly confident in this capacity, but only if careseekers respond to the kind of care the compulsive caregiver finds it necessary to give. Otherwise the caregiving becomes coercive and empathy is lost.

Responses to relentless coercion by a caregiver

In the examples given above, SC relating was either incomplete or was complete in some contexts and confusing in others. The last two vignettes are examples of caregiving responses that are so much interfered with by the defensive needs of the caregiver that the suffering of the careseeker is entirely overlooked. The sufferer is unable to influence the actions of the caregiver and a relentlessly abusive relationship can ensue. There are variants of this pattern where caregivers can have an apparently affectionate relationship with particular careseekers, but when they are in contexts in which their sense of well-being and power is threatened will attempt to reaffirm it by abusing a careseeker who is unable to retaliate or escape. The caregiver can plausibly deny the abuse to an extent that it seems as though the internal representations of both kinds of relating are kept on parallel tracks and communication between the representations is entirely shut off. These variants describe but do not explain the phenomenon of denial used by abusing parental figures.

The combinations of these major patterns of defensive relating can be complicated by the fact that a child can know about and enjoy a fair degree of SC relating from one parent while experiencing the other as an insecure figure who, in the eyes of the child, is liable to show D/S relating all too easily. Life can be less anxious if the situations in which D/S behaviour is shown are predictable. It is more disturbing when a child is unable to make reliable predictions, and especially if the predominantly SC parent is frequently not available. A proper comparison of these issues opens a discussion that is beyond the scope of this book.

Vignette 4: Time-limited events which are deeply disassuaging

Vignette 4 describes events repeated over a limited time span in which individuals, usually as infants or young children, had been unable to influence an attachment figure to protect or relieve them of their intense distress. They had survived, and the incidents had been put beyond recall with the help of their psychological mechanisms of defence, but these individuals remained ready to be alerted to danger by any reminder of the situation. Sometimes such a traumatic event has not been segregated so completely and can flood back in dreams or after reminders which before therapy are usually unrecognised. The trauma, although beyond recall, can manifest itself in daily life by an unexplained dislike and avoidance, to the level of phobia, of certain situations and people who act in particular ways. The therapeutic exploration of such events requires experience and training. It is always difficult and is not attempted in this book.

Vignette 5: The repeated experience of deeply disassuaging events

A second variety of event that can lead to subservience in all relationships with parental type figures and also marked avoidance is that of regularly repeated, painful and deeply disassuaging interpersonal events in situations in which individuals could not influence the disassuaging figures to cease being so, or find others to act in a protective way. When they cannot influence the disassuaging person, the sufferer tends to use passive and fatalistic defences which can limit or appear to dissociate them from pain (they sometimes watch it happening to someone else). When children are old enough to make plans, they endure the suffering and can then, or later, play through various imaginative scenarios of being aggressive (not uncommonly to the point of murder). Such people in ordinary life are unassertive and often solitary but the imaginative scenarios are active especially whenever they feel put down. On occasions the urge to put aggressive plans into action takes over.

SETTING UP A SAFE PLACE FOR THERAPY

From what has been said earlier about the components of a secure base, the setting up of a therapeutic alliance will begin with creating a setting in which both therapist and client will feel sufficiently secure. There is a long tradition that supports the kind of setting we describe. The room should have comfortable seating, and be arranged, furnished and kept at a temperature experienced as pleasing. It is usually kept without much change and becomes familiar and enduring – both features of great importance for the very insecure client.

There are a number of straightforward rules accepted by most therapists that help to make the parameters in which therapy will take place a safe place for client and therapist. These are spelt out and agreed by the client before therapy begins. They make explicit the temporal and economic basis of the setting. They concern timekeeping, length of session, expectable holiday gaps, duration of therapy, financial transactions, issues of confidentiality and some statement about the tasks client and therapist will do together. These issues are sometimes described as the frame in which the process of therapy takes place. The frame has to be acceptable to both client and therapist, but before it is acceptable to the client, the therapist has to be seen to be safe enough.

Before discussing in Chapter 15 the setting up, maintainence and, when necessary, adaptation of a therapeutic frame, we describe our conception of how a therapist will need to think, feel and behave in order to be seen as a sufficiently secure person by a client. It is widely recognised that in order to be therapeutic, therapists need to be accepting, non-judgemental, reliable, and show respect for the client. If we add to that list those capacities that attachment concepts suggest, then the therapist also has to be sufficiently available, empathic, protective, comforting and knowledgeable for a client to experience adequate support in handling his painful problems and difficulties, and to entertain some hope that any developmental achievements he makes will be validated. Before discussing how we approach a client who is secure enough to admit to himself that help is necessary and to keep the contract that defines the therapeutic frame to which he has agreed, we give an example of how a safe base was provided for a very insecure client who when first seen was unable to make a therapeutic alliance. Although what was done is common practice in many circles, the act of introducing the metaphor of the creation of a safe base to all the various workers involved in the care of this client, helped a social worker illustrate in practical action, the principle that not only careseekers but also caregivers require a safe base in order to give effective treatment and support.

EXAMPLE OF PROVIDING A SAFE THERAPEUTIC FRAME FOR AN INSECURE CLIENT AND ALSO FOR THE DISPARATE PROFESSIONAL CAREGIVERS HE APPROACHED

This example of providing a safe enough therapeutic frame for an extremely insecure client and for the various professional caregivers with whom this client was entangled is taken from Burns (1992). We use it as an illustration of the way in which the therapeutic frame needs to be envisaged when it cannot be maintained within one therapeutic relationship, but has to extend to include all the people most actively involved in giving care to a client.

Mr T was referred for social assessment. He had a long history of regularly seeking out social work support, and then refusing it. On two occasions in the previous year he had been admitted into hospital for depression and on discharge discontinued all medication. Later he burnt his hand and was admitted to hospital for treatment. It was noted that he was prone to giving an inaccurate and confusing history and there were undertones of a suicide attempt. When discharged for outpatient treatment he refused to co-operate with the physiotherapist. He would regularly arrive at her department, refuse to exercise, leave after twenty minutes and then present at casualty. His diagnoses over time had included personality disorder, possible alcoholic dementia, symptoms of irritable bowel syndrome, anxiety states, hypochondria and a prognosis as 'a hopeless case'.

At a first meeting with his social worker, Mr T complained of abdominal pain, believing he was going to die. Over time, he was offered and refused a day centre place and meals on wheels. In noting his counter-transference the social worker had a sense of his efforts being actively frustrated and made useless and was aware that Mr T had evoked similar feelings in other workers who expressed views of not knowing what to do with him.

In view of Mr T's regular requests for help, and then refusing it, the social worker realised that he was not in a position to offer the level of support Mr T appeared to require. He therefore negotiated with the home help service who provided a daily ten-minute call. Remembering Mr T's sorry history of giving inaccurate information to different agencies, the social worker saw it as essential that, in order to avoid the confusion and duplicating of services and the reinforcement of Mr T's inappropriate behaviour (e.g. presenting at casualty), future communications between all the people involved with Mr T should be clear.

A clue as to how to handle Mr T's difficult behaviour came when the social worker became more aware during his home visits of the way in which Mr T was expressing his distress. He would retire to bed but was then in and out of it, pacing the room. This reminded the social worker of attachment concepts and distressed searching behaviour seen following loss. He therefore developed a pattern whereby he was able to calm Mr T down by acknowledging the severity of his distress. When this was done Mr T was more able to respond and eventually began to confide at length his feelings of isolation, fear of abandonment at home, and fears that he was going to die. These were the only times Mr T was able to engage at a verbal level. Mr T's behaviour then became increasingly destructive, cuts appeared on his wrists and he began to talk about his feelings of hopelessness and despair. As a result home help services were prepared to increase their input to provide, as they saw it, 'some motivation to encourage Mr T to help himself'. The social worker offered to support the home help service in finding how best to respond to Mr T's complaints. Together they were able to develop a common approach which helped empower the home help who was beginning to have results where many professionals had failed in the past. The approach included discussing with Mr T what the home help was prepared to offer. The social worker also continued to visit Mr T and made clear to the home help service that he would respond whenever they contacted him. The social worker made contact with and shared information with both hospital and community-based workers with the aim of supporting the home help services in their task. He described his main aim as creating and servicing a 'secure base' for Mr T with the following objectives: to facilitate communication among agencies; to obtain a cooker for Mr T; to offer unstructured counselling and support; and to encourage Mr T to seek treatment for his depression. Gradually Mr T's presentations at casualty decreased, he started to keep his medical appointments and was considering going to a luncheon club with the support of home help. When asked, Mr T stated that he 'felt not too bad', which was the first time that any positive reaction had been witnessed.

In the next and final chapter we outline the development, maintenance and adaptation of a therapeutic frame in order to give clients, who can maintain a therapeutic alliance, the experience of a relationship with enough experience of empathic understanding to be maturatively mutative. This kind of relationship helps to keep the client from breaking the therapeutic frame unilaterally and also makes ending it a natural process of moving on to another stage of development.

Chapter 15

Separation anxiety, impingement and the therapeutic frame

Therapy, in our view, begins after client and therapist have set up a therapeutic frame which spells out where they will meet, the length of the session, its frequency, the approximate duration of the therapy, in broad terms what they will discuss and any necessary financial arrangements. We are using the term 'frame' to refer to all aspects of the contract that is made, more or less explicitly, between client and therapist. It covers what the client thinks of as 'my therapy' and the developmental aspirations they hope it will unlock. The therapist will have their own conception. In broad terms it covers the relationship they need to keep with the client, and the work that has to be done before the client can manage their life more effectively. We see the frame as the ambience in which the client (and therapist too) keeps or breaks different aspects of the contract and in that way expresses their hopes and fears about core issues associated with disassuagement.

MAINTAINING AND ADAPTING THE THERAPEUTIC FRAME SO THAT IT REMAINS A SECURE STRUCTURE FOR THE CLIENT

The therapeutic frame which is made on the suggestions and advice of the therapist usually involves some negotiation with the client over times of meeting and payment. Clients who have a possibility of meeting their therapist outside a therapy session should be informed that, for the maximum benefit to be gained, it is advised that, if they happen coincidentally to meet, there should be no mention or discussion of therapy; and that any role they formerly shared should be held in abeyance until therapy has been completed. This constraint is advised, partly to maintain confidentiality and partly to maintain the topic of discussion agreed in the therapeutic contract, and to avoid confusing the role of client and therapist with any other relationship. This means that therapists should not consider undertaking therapy with a friend or a colleague with whom they work on a regular basis. This contract is accepted by the client either willingly or with reservations before they have had an opportunity to test the implications and the safety of the enterprise into which they are entering. Entering therapy is thus for many an act which evokes anxiety. Their past experiences have led them to feel that talking about their anxieties and fears is unacceptable and fruitless. The therapeutic frame is therefore the relational structure and atmosphere which the client will continually be testing to see whether the therapist will respect and understand their feelings and conflicts and will be able to bring them some relief – a task which no currently available person has managed to do sufficiently well.

Many clients have missed out on a close and caring experience because attachment figures had not been sufficiently able to respond to their non-verbal or verbal expressions of needs and feelings. Either their attachment figures were not readily available when needed, or when physically present often showed disinterest and/or dislike. Or, in contrast, caregiving has been insensitively close and intrusive and in this way rejective of their need to develop some independence and autonomy. This leads clients to feel in some measure either unwanted or excessively needed and their physical and mental autonomy devalued or denied. Furthermore, having to interact with either of these kinds of attachment figures has given them little help in regulating their feelings in any comfortable way. They will have been periodically overexcited, made anxious and depressed, having been forced to pay attention to, for example, their parents protesting, dismissive or possessive ways of relating, which they could do little to change or relieve. Both the avoidant and the impinging attachment figures are likely to have become frighteningly angry in their attempts to influence their child, either to keep his distance or alternatively to satisfy his impinging demands. In some way most will have been coerced into a role in which they were expected to enact their parents' idealised conception of how a good child would behave and are likely, unconsciously, to re-enact their responses to and feelings about their parents in the parental type relationship they build up with their therapist.

Thus in order to keep the therapeutic frame safe enough for the client to use, therapists need to be alert to the client's feelings of being forced into a position in which he felt either abandoned or impinged upon. They will also need to be sensitive to the feelings they themselves may be non-verbally communicating to the client, which they may consider 'normal', but which the client may regard as being either too close or too withdrawn. Although some clients make clear exactly what they feel the therapist is doing, many are unable to put into words the feelings that primary attachment figures have ignored, and will express them in the way in which they perceive and use the therapeutic frame (e.g. coming late or having to leave early, being careless with the furniture, complaining about the temperature, or alternatively being unnaturally quiet and unobtrusive).

The therapist's primary task is therefore twofold. First to be able to understand and communicate about feelings conveyed non-verbally and to enable the client to translate into words their painful and hidden unshared experiences. The second is gradually to bring the painful intensities of the client's affective experiences to more comfortable levels, which enables their psychological capacities to function more effectively. We describe this latter process using Stern's concept of tuning. In practical terms, this involves being able to attune to the client's affective state, showing a degree of arousal (largely by tone of voice and rate of speech), that is at a level that is estimated to be slightly above what is expressed by a client who is depressed and slightly below that expressed by a client who is overexcited. Many therapists do this quite naturally without think-ing about it, others may stay at too high or too low a level for a par-ticular client, without realising that they are impeding the client's experience of comfortable psychological closeness. Therapists are also prone to be caught out when the client's disassaugement reminds them of disassuagements of their own. If the therapist is unaware that this has happened, he can respond to the client with a lack of empathy, shown either by a defensive withdrawal, or an approach, both of which come across to the client as a disconcert-ing misattunement – a phenomenon we regard as covered by the concept of projective identification.

The therapist is therefore assessing how active or passive they need be to keep a degree of psychological closeness or distance that is optimal for the client, that is to say at a level that feels comfort-able for the client and therefore feels safe. If the therapist is felt as impinging, or too distant and especially if he is experienced as dis-interested, clients will defensively withdraw or protest and usually feel as impotent as they had in the past, when they had failed to influence people they had expected would listen and relieve them of their feelings of distress. Therefore in order to maintain, as far as possible, a high degree of rapport and comfortable psychological closeness with the client, the therapist's capacity to regulate his own non-verbal and verbal communication and suggested explanations (interpretations) will have a considerable influence on how his clients keep and use the therapeutic frame. All this means that it is important for therapists to stay in a state in which their empathic metacognitive self is functional. The experience of interactions with a therapist, who can observe the effect his communications are having on the client, and maintain consistently a good enough level of communication of the observations they make about their interactions with the client, enables the client in turn to observe himself in his interaction with others. In this way he begins to understand how others can feel, and is better able to achieve with others the supportive and companionable interactions he values having had with the therapist.

With these considerations about the therapeutic frame in mind we see the frame as a potentially safe base in which the client's non-verbal forms of communication about fears of separation or impingement can be understood and then put into words. Putting never previously verbalised experiences into words begins the process of freeing clients from earlier conditions in which fears could not be discussed and mutually understood. The therapist can help this process by asking clients about their feelings in relation to the experiences they have just talked about, adding if necessary his own empathic remarks and explanatory suggestions. The phrasing of such comments (which are sometimes of a transferential nature) in the form of possibilities is important. In our experience, a number of clients, who have been told what they feel and what to believe by parental figures, react unfavourably to any comment other than a suggestion phrased as an exploratory possibility. They treat them as though they were critical edicts. This whole way of relating provides a means for the client to gain an understanding of the significance of experiences that antedate words. Thus the therapeutic relationship and frame in which it is enacted enable fears not only to be expressed verbally but to emerge in the client's positive or negative ways of relating to the therapist (the transference) and the therapist's possible counter-transference to the client.

It is the continual evaluation and assessment made by the client over repeated sessions of the therapist's capacity to be accepting and respecting in his empathic responses, that allows the client to modify the predictions he makes on the basis of his earlier experiences with caregivers. It also enables clients to re-test the therapist's responses each time earlier frightening experiences of painful, hostile or rejective events are evoked. If clients remain unconvinced about the understanding and reliability of the therapist, there is ample reason for them to hold on to earlier beliefs.

The therapist's knowledge of attachment research will inform him that the client's capacity for exploration, especially when it involves moving into areas where the risks of disassuagement are considerable, will be highly dependent on the therapist's ability to support and sustain the client, or in Winnicott's phrase to 'hold' him or her. The same knowledge will also lead therapists to expect defensive measures to be awakened and shown by the client in behaviour that is often described as resistant and will help the therapist to tolerate the repeated testing of his or her sensitivity and empathy.

The way the client uses the therapeutic frame and first construes the therapist seems to us to be indicative of the attachment classifications shown by his parents, which may well be different for each. Avoidant attachment figures are biased towards keeping themselves too distanced and withdrawn for the child's careseeking needs to be adequately met. Ambivalent resistant figures will alternate between being too close and intrusive or too distant and awaken a sense of uncomfortable and potentially disassuaging closeness and distance. Therapists will also have some awareness of the client's own attachment classification from the assessment. They will have some notion of whether clients are more, or less, insecure in their attachments, and whether they fall within the range of being more, or less, avoidant and distancing, whether they also have some ambivalent (too close alternating with too distant) or disorganised (a more intense experience of the latter) tendencies. A knowledge of all this information gives therapists an indication of the ways in which the client is likely to relate to them, and the relational and interactional stresses and patterns of transference they are likely to experience.

ADAPTATION OF THE THERAPEUTIC FRAME

Working in the north of England where psychoanalytical psychotherapists are relatively few and far between in comparison with London and the South, we have made some adaptations to the usual psychoanalytic contract in order to meet the logistical and psychological needs of clients, especially those who have to travel long distances. We aim to see clients once or twice a week rather than three to five times a week, and usually see them face to face rather than on the couch, although we use the couch when there appear to be indications that it would be helpful. Our usual timing of the session is sixty rather than the more usual fifty minutes. In our experience the extra ten minutes gives time for an issue which has taken some time to emerge, to be at least noted and partially understood before the client has to deal with it on his own for some days. Using the ten minutes in this way helps clients to emerge from their inner preoccupations and move into a state in which they can attend to their current responsibilities.

Most of our work is in long-term therapy. In our view this form of therapy goes on for as long as it is needed and other reality-based circumstances allow. At the end of most periods of therapy (longer or shorter) we usually build in the concept that, should unpredictable vicissitudes in the future cause anxieties to surface that have not been addressed, a further set of sessions could be arranged with some notice.

Adapting the frequency and cost of the session

The clients we see are usually coping with their family life and/or work in conditions of considerable stress and often have to cope with added stress in the form of illness or death of people important to them, threats to employment and other events, particularly those that separate them from friends or the possibility of a life style that they would like to enjoy. We work on the assumption that conflicts and anxieties are worked through more effectively when the client feels he is empathically 'held' by the therapist's appreciation of the pain they are suffering.

To act in a therapeutic manner towards such clients, we consider it is necessary to use a form of therapy that is optimally responsive rather than one which increases frustration. Therefore at each session we assess whether clients are in a state in which they can effectively use their metacognitive capacities for insight, or whether they are too anxious, depressed or excited to do so. We regard this latter state as the client's expression of wordless feelings of confusion, mistrust, hostility or despair, associated with an equally wordless wish to draw from the therapist an understanding of his total state.

In this instance we use a more supportive approach for a time with the aim of providing sufficient understanding to give enough relief from the suffering to reinstate some capacity for metacognition.

At times of crisis, such as those indicated above, and particularly when repressed memory of disassuaging experiences is coming to light, we discuss whether it would be helpful to have extra sessions during this time. If the offer is accepted we arrange for the client to have them over the period of the crisis. These are often taken on the telephone at an agreed time for a period of thirty to forty-five minutes, When the client is able to cope with the added stress, the sessions revert to their usual frequency. We have regularly found that when a client knows that an extra session is available, he becomes better able to cope with emerging anxieties without requesting extra help, and we have not met with any abuse of this adaptation of the therapeutic frame. We keep two to three emergency ad hoc hours per week for this purpose.

All adaptations to the contract, whether in the short or longer term are made on the therapist's assessment of what will be to the long-term benefit of the client. Any adaptation is made after discussion of the reasons for the change and what in the therapist's view might be the consequences of adapting or not adapting the frame.

Clients often wish to talk about topics other than their own concerns which can frequently centre on a curiosity about the life and concerns of the therapist which at first sight appear to be unrelated to their own predicaments. Here the original contract is maintained, with reasons given why this should be. To use a dictum from Guntrip, the therapist does not give the client 'sweeties', that is to say a form of relating that in the short term might seem helpful but in the long term would not lead the client to make any maturative moves. There are different ways in which this frequently encountered situation is handled by therapists. Our own view is that it is necessary to find a way to help the client understand their need to find out more about the therapist without reinforcing the feeling that the therapist is deliberately and unfeelingly keeping him in the dark. This persistent attention to the lifestyle and personal concerns of the therapist is frequently found in clients with particular forms of dysfunctional CG/CS systems and partnerships. One example is the client who is a defensively compulsive caregiver. He is acting on the belief that there is little chance of him ever receiving care unless he first shows concern for the other. Other examples relate to clients with ambivalent caregivers who have a compelling need to know enough about the caregiver (therapist) to predict how he or she will respond to particular aspects of the careseeker's (client's) behaviour. Some are helped by recognising the meaning and significance of their behaviour. Others seem in a state in which anything other than a direct answer to their queries is felt, and responded to, as a hurtful rejection. We cannot here open a discussion on this complex issue which includes how much therapists should reveal about themselves other than showing that one understands the client's frustration at the limits the therapist has set for the therapeutic relationship and also how to help the client discover his own solution to the problem.

THE COMMUNICATIVE ASPECTS OF DREAMS IN THERAPY

Dreams have a highly significant function as a form of communication between client and therapist. Many dreams slip back into oblivion for every one that by being remembered, remains in consciousness. We can only speak of dreams that are brought to therapy. In our experience the dream can act as a reminder to the client of conflictual experiences and as a scenic and symbolic expression of past or present inner conflicts and dilemmas of which the client is often largely unaware. Therefore for some clients the dream can be used as a major form of communication about their predicaments as they are represented in their IMERs and other internal models and are subjectively experienced.

By and large, it has been our experience that dreams fall into two groups. Some are primarily concerned with the dreamer's preoccupation with inner conflicts and doubts concerning homeostatic issues. They give indications of dependence on attachment figures for basic nurture in the form of food, drink, shelter, comfort and protection. They are often concerned with inner conflicts and dilemmas about issues of dominance and rage, compliance and weakness, shame and guilt.

Other dreams are more focused on developmental processes, as in the dream cited below. They highlight conflictual situations associated with the dreamer's aspirations to reach maturative ideals. These dreams are also concerned with issues of strength and weakness, guilt and shame, obstacles and achievements and with the recognition of lost, repressed aspects of oneself and their reunion with the rest of the self.

THE EFFECTS AND MANAGEMENT OF DIFFERENT
TYPES OF SEPARATION, LOSS AND REUNION

Most of the work that goes on in therapy deals with the day-by-day problems and traumata of the week between sessions. Our therapy is essentially the same in nature and aim as that of Fairbairn and Guntrip. It includes examining the client's fears and strains at home and work. These often reverberate earlier experiences of separation and loss involving primary attachment figures which continue to be experienced and contained in the more closed aspects of the IMERs within the client's internal supportive system. Once the client begins to trust the therapist, the therapist is used increasingly as an empathic and reliable person to whom the client can turn, who will accept and try to understand his difficulties in a non-judgemental way. At this point clients come to recognise that there are meaningful, often transferential explanations for their symptoms of anxiety and depression. Many clients find that their dream and fantasy life becomes more active and often points to deeper intrapsychic conflicts, and sometimes previously disturbing and repressed states of mind begin to emerge. The therapist is thus given some notice of the client's further needs and demands, and the possibility of some need for adaptation to the therapeutic frame in order to make it more secure for the client.

A frequent but not usually serious period of stress can be the ten or five minutes before ending the session. The client's wish to continue the session, when it takes place only once a week, is considerable, despite the rules of the therapeutic alliance. For this reason it is sometimes necessary to give a warning when the end of the session is approaching and ask the client how he is feeling. We find this intervention helps clients make a bridge between one session and the next and find how they can come to terms with their desires.

Another period of frequent and occasionally of intense stress can develop before the therapist's vacations. The threat of being left for any period that is longer than the interval between the regular sessions can bring up reminders of earlier periods of excessive strain, when attachment figures were unable to be in touch and fears and experiences of desertion or abandonment arose. These anxieties usually occur two or three weeks before vacation time when the therapist observes the client not being his usual self, often showing symptoms of being either more anxious or withdrawn, sometimes with complaints of aches or pains, or else talking of someone else's distress. Dreams with the theme of separation or loss may also be brought, usefully discussed and interpreted. Speaking of any feelings that refer directly to the vacation gap is relatively rare. Occasionally clients will act out their feelings and break the frame by missing a session which usually expresses their protest and despair over the anticipated 'desertion' by taking control and deserting the therapist first. With all clients in this state we explore whether the client has any explanations for their malaise. It often turns out that the client is suffering a form of separation anxiety and we discuss his understanding of the break and means of coping with it.

One client experienced a severe panic reaction to taking a vacation with her family abroad, which she felt had to be honoured. A major reason for this was considered to be her perfectionist ideal of parenthood and duty which her anxious, dominating and essentially rejective mother and ambivalent father (both needy and careseeking parents) had encouraged in a reversal of roles. She had also experienced in childhood periods of separation from her father on occasions when he had periods of work away from home. There had been no opportunity for sharing how she felt when the father she primarily relied on was not available. It had never occurred to her that a discussion of these very distressing events might be possible. Transferring this belief to the present situation of separation from the therapist, it had not crossed her mind that it might be possible to share her feelings and to discuss how she might be supported during this period of separation. When the similarities between the present situation and the past had been explored the client became aware of the difference between the two. After discussing and negotiating how some of her anxiety and distress might be alleviated, it was agreed that the therapeutic frame could be adapted to enable her to have two shortened sessions by telephone, should she feel this necessary. It was an adaptation which sufficiently reduced the client's anxiety and enabled her to travel. But despite using the telephone sessions, she nevertheless experienced for two days severe suffering from fibrositis of the neck, back and arms, which kept her relatively immobile in bed and required medical attention. On her return she was aware and able to express some of her feelings of loss, of distress which had previously been either unnoticed or rejected, and of rage over her parents' neglect of her. She also expressed her distress and anger over the therapist's unwillingness to give her more time. On later vacations she was able to make plans and enjoy holidays without suffering any undue anxiety or needing extra sessions. This client later moved to a stage where she was able to see the therapist as sufficiently understanding and trustworthy to feel that the work they had done within the therapeutic frame had in certain ways strengthened her internal supportive system. She was much less dependent and submissive, was increasingly able to make accurate interpretations about her states of mind and body in different contexts and was increasingly effective in coping with her family and work.

Reunion experiences, particularly those following the therapist's vacation, are not infrequently accompanied by some coolness and withdrawal by the client. Some admit to having felt hurt and resentful at having been deserted. Others may be late and occasionally forget to turn up for the first session after the gap. Sharing feelings about what the gap meant to the client and seeing it as a natural response to earlier experiences of unavailability of attachment figures reduce their feelings of shame at what had been felt as a pathetic weakness.

The termination of a well-established therapy before it comes to its natural conclusion is frequently a serious stressor of the therapeutic frame. It arises most commonly from illness or change of residence of either therapist or client. When the therapist is making the break and the question of termination arises, there can occasionally be a return of symptoms and commonly feelings of anger or hopelessness over what is felt to be the therapist's rejection and desertion, despite the client's ability to cope effectively without similar feelings and symptoms when holiday gaps had occurred. Termination appears to be seen as a separation without the possibility of reunion and sometimes acts as a reminder of the untimely death of the parental figure.

When premature termination comes about at the instigation of the client the picture can be different. Sometimes a major dream may occur in which some previously withdrawn aspect of the self is recognised. One client, some months before having to end therapy prematurely for her own logistical reasons, dreamt of walking in a wood on an unused path and coming to an old and neglected shed in which she found a moribund baby lying in a decrepit pram almost entirely covered by a dirty blanket. She thought the baby might be dead, but recognised a minimal sign of life and decided to pick it up, not knowing what should be done with it. A vague figure appeared in the hut and the client handed the baby over. The figure accepted the baby and held it. In discussing the relevance of the dream, the client was partially aware of the baby representing a part of herself, but could not go any further. After some mutual exploration of the possible message of the dream, and whether the accepting figure was also part of herself or someone else, the client seemed to favour the interpretative suggestion that she did not wish to leave without bringing this deeply withdrawn and apparently moribund part of herself to be held and cared for in co-operation with the therapist, until she felt more able and knowledgeable about how she might take over the caring role herself with more assurance. This client was aware of a growing capacity to take more care of herself and felt sufficiently able to accept and take more responsibility for the withdrawn and deprived aspect of herself.

HOW SHOULD THERAPY BEST BE ENDED?

Therapists using psychoanalytically oriented therapies for short-term work, or longer-term therapies of one or two sessions a weeks, often suggest a three- or four-month review following termination to test the level of security felt by the client after what has effectively become a three-month separation following termination. Some provide an occasion for a second review if required later. Others build in the recommendation that, if necessary, a further period of therapy could be sought. However, many therapists using the three or more sessions per week consider this arrangement as undermining the client and the therapist's psychotherapeutic frame and the therapist's capacity to recognise when the client is able to be autonomous. We belong to the former group, and think that the difference of view is likely to be a function of the severity of the deprivation the client has experienced and the number and frequency of sessions the clients have had. In our experience there seems to be something entirely natural about wanting to leave therapy when therapist and client have worked within the psychotherapeutic frame sufficiently for it to have become a secure enough base within the client's internal supportive system.

EPILOGUE

This outline of therapy guided by caregiving concepts provides the reader with some indications of the way in which a relationship with a caregiving person can be internalised to become a permanent feature in an individual's system for self-care and management. As a result of effective therapy, painful experiences of caregiving, which cause hatred and conflict, can be shared, understood, accepted and often forgiven. The processes whereby observation of self and others takes place can be continued after therapy with a deeper understanding of caregiving and careseeking interactions as they take place between two or more individuals, between individuals and their domestic pets, and between individuals and their God or Gods. We doubt if this process of growth can ever be complete.

We have integrated an inter-generational theory of caregiving and attachment into a personal and object relations theory of the self. This integration, which has the potential to be empirically investigated, suggests that deficits of caregiving lead to damaging styles of human careseeking and self-care that in their turn lead to a further failure to support and promote the development of the innate human caregiving capacity. We do not see parents who cannot help their children as bad. Rather we see them as people who have been unable to develop their potential for caregiving as the result of having failed to receive sufficient maturative caregiving from their own families and friends, their communities and broader cultural environment.

Attachment research and theory focus on the basic issues of human individual, interpersonal and social development in every culture. They integrate the objective empirical aspects of human careseeking and caregiving and the subjective perceptions, feelings and values that are associated with them. As such they have immense significance for understanding human psychological and physical health and well-being and some grounds for providing a reality-based approach to future generations of careseekers and caregivers.

The Strange Situation Test

The Strange Situation Test (Ainsworth *et al.* 1978) is a laboratory-based observation of infant response at one year old to separations from their primary caregiver in an unfamiliar setting. There are eight episodes, each except the first taking three minutes. During the first episode parent and baby are introduced to a comfortable room with toys in it, the parent and baby are then left together giving the baby the opportunity to explore the toys. A stranger then enters, speaks with the parent and attempts to join the baby in play. The parent then leaves the baby with the stranger and returns in the fifth episode to greet the baby, the stranger unobtrusively leaving the room. The baby is then left alone, the stranger returns and finally the parent returns; for the final reunion. During each parental reunion the parent is advised to pause at the door, greet the child and to allow the child to respond. In the final episode, the parent is instructed to pick the child up.

Each episode of separation and reunion were observed and rated from videotapes. Classification is based on the infant's and not the parent's behaviour. Ainsworth's group of research workers identified, from the behaviour of the infant on reunion with mother at the end of episodes 5 and 8, three different overall patterns of behaviour.

Secure (type B)

The baby shows sign of missing the parent, but is readily comforted by a responsive parent and rapidly returns to play. He may explore the environment and play with toys during the separation episodes.

Insecure–avoidant (type A)

On both reunions the baby immediately looks and turns away from the parent and remains neutral when picked up. The baby usually continues to explore the toys and appears competent but affectless.

Insecure–ambivalent (type C)

On reunion the baby focuses insistently upon the parent, seeking proximity and contact actively or passively, and then actively or passively resisting it. These babies are difficult to comfort and are often still crying at the end of the reunion episode.

Interjudge agreement on the three classifications are high (Ainsworth *et al.* 1978, Main and Weston 1981). Ainsworth considered the psychological significance of the three reunion patterns of attachment behaviour rests first on their close association with the mother–infant interaction at home and second on their persistence over time. In samples of North American middle-class families, approximately two-thirds of infants are classified as secure, a fifth to a third avoidant and a small minority insecure–ambivalent. Further experience showed that each of the three original categories could be subdivided (e.g. B3 describes the very secure, A1 the most avoidant, while C1 describes the actively angry, insecure, ambivalent infant, and C2 describes a passive infant too distressed to approach. It has also regularly been shown that an infant can be secure with one parent and insecure with the other (Main and Weston 1981).

Disorganised/disoriented (type D) pattern of attachment

Some years after the identification of the three categories, Main and her colleagues identified a fourth (Main 1995) by examining unclassifiable video tapes many of which were drawn from high-risk samples. These describe disorganised/disorientated behaviour of the infant on reunion with the parent in the Strange Situation Test. These infants seem to have no behavioural strategy for dealing with reunion with the mother. Main (1995) distinguished seven items of which the following were prominent. The infants may freeze on moving towards the parent, show a dazed or confused expression, and display contradictory disorganised behaviour that suggests conflict.

Appendix B

The adult attachment interview

In a number of studies Main (1991:141) describes a structured, fifteen-question, semi-clinical interview focusing largely on the individual's early attachment experiences and their effects and influences. The subject is asked to choose five adjectives which best describe the relationship with each parent during childhood, and then asked to illustrate from memories each of these choices of adjective. Later the subject is asked what they did when upset during childhood; to which parent they felt closer and why; whether they ever felt rejected or later threatened by their parents; why parents may have behaved as they did; how the relationship may have changed; and how these earlier experiences (including experiences of major loss up to the present time) may have affected their adult functioning and personality.

A single classification for overall state of mind with respect to attachment can be reliably assigned to each verbatim interview transcript (Main and Goldwyn 1989). Judgements (made blind) are made on the basis of an assessment of the coherence of the transcript and other aspects of present state of mind. Four central classifications have been distinguished: secure/autonomous (F) when the presentation and evaluation of attachment experiences are coherent and internally consistent; dismissing (D) when the importance of attachment experiences are minimised and the individual appears co-operative but contradictions render them apparently untruthful; preoccupied and entangled (E) when interviews show either an angry or passive and confused preoccupation with the attachment figure in attachment-related events; unresolved/disorganised (U) when the interview shows evidence of lapses in the monitoring of reasoning of their discourse when discussing potentially traumatic events (e.g. loss of important persons through death or physical or sexual abuse).

These four classifications predict a corresponding pattern of infant response to the parent in the Strange Situation Test. Parents described as F have secure infants; those described as D tend to have avoidant infants; those classified as E tend to have resistant infants whilst those described as U tend to have disorganised/disorientated infants.

An outline of the emergence of the study of attachment style in adults

Griffen and Bartholomew (1994) discuss the complexities inherent in finding measures that are valid for assessing attachment style and its nature, noting the rapid expansion of this field of study following Hazan and Shaver's (1987) discovery that Ainsworth's infant classification system could be used to assess attachment style in adults. They make the point that there is no common methodology for defining and measuring attachment style and that new assessment instruments have been derived empirically usually through factor analysis. In their discussion of the metaphysics of measurement, they give an overview of the range of methods currently used. This topic is also discussed by Crittenden (in press). They join with Hazan and Shaver (in press) for a renewed focus on the theoretical tenets of attachment theory and for researchers in adult attachment to take theory not measures as their starting point. Thus methods of measurement should be chosen on the basis of theory, which itself is acknowledged and tested. They raise three fundamental questions. Can attachment style be seen as a set of categories which define different types of people? Can style be described in terms of combinations of continuous dimensions along which people vary? Or is it better described in prototypical terms by showing how far an individual has the features that are common to a particular category? They regard it as premature to choose a winner from among the different approaches that are currently used to measure the complexities of attachment.

Ainsworth and also Main have chosen to focus on systems of classification rather than on continuous scoring. They are each of the opinion that classification constitutes a first step in the organisation of complex behavioural data (Main 1995: 415). Griffen and Bartholomew (1994: 23–4) suggest that a combination of prototypi-

cal and categorical approaches is especially appropriate for attachment research. It enables an assessment to be made of how well
individuals fit the prototype of selected categories on any occasion
and how the fit varies over time. This kind of thinking led to the
development of a complex four-category attachment model
(Bartholomew and Horowitz 1991) in which it is recognised that
most individuals exhibit elements of more than one of the four
recognised attachment categories. Questions selected differentiate
the four attachment categories and rate the degree of positivity
about the self and positivity about the other in particular relationships. The ratings depend upon the answers to a relationship questionnaire (RQ) and a relationships scales questionnaire (RSQ). The
RQ is a general orientation to the secure, fearful, preoccupied and
dismissing attachment patterns. Subjects are asked to rate on a
seven-point scale how much 'like me' or 'not like me' are statements
such as 'it is easy for me to become emotionally close to others' and
'It is very important to me to feel independent and self sufficient'.
These statements can be related to specific other people and reword-
ed in the third person to rate the subject's view of other people. The
RSQ has thirty questions (also scored on 'like me', 'not like me' ratings) that have been shown to be related to one or other of the four
categories mentioned above. Positive self models have been shown
to be held by secure and dismissing individuals while negative self
models are held by preoccupied and fearful individuals. High anxiety has been shown to be related to low positivity about the self.
This model can be used in a semistructured interview and also
adapted for subjects to rate from a written questionnaire.

ROMANTIC LOVE AS AN ATTACHMENT PROCESS

An interest in moving the exploration and explanation of attachment processes from infancy to a later stage of life led Hazan and
Shaver (1987) to explore the possibility that adult romantic love is
an attachment process, and that the key components to explain
attachment processes in infants, the three major styles of attachment (secure, avoidant and anxious/ambivalent) could be translated
into terms appropriate to romantic love. The notion was that a person's attachment style is largely determined by childhood relationships with parents and the continuity of an attachment style is due
to internal mental models of self and social relationships. Hazan
and Shaver developed two questionnaire studies, the first a 'love

quiz' printed in a local paper. A love-experience questionnaire was based on previous adult-love measures and extrapolations from infant-caregiving attachment literature. A single-item measure of the three attachment styles was designed by translating Ainsworth's (1978) descriptions of infants into terms appropriate to adult love.

To many people the results seemed remarkable. Of the first 620 of over 1,200 replies (205 from men, 415 from women, age range from fourteen to eighty-two) just over half, 56 per cent, classified themselves as secure, 25 per cent and 19 per cent as avoidant and anxious/ambivalent respectively. The secure group described their most important love experience as being especially happy, friendly and trusting: they were able to accept and support the partner despite their faults and their feelings waxed and waned and returned at times to the former level. The avoidant subjects characterised themselves as having fears of intimacy, emotional highs and lows and jealousy. They thought romantic love did not last and head-over-heels love didn't exist in real life. The anxious/ambivalent lovers experienced love as involving obsession, emotional highs and lows, desire for reciprocation and extreme sexual attraction and jealousy. They thought it easy to fall in love, that it waxes and wanes, and often partially happens, and that finding real love was rare. Differences in attachment history which included how each parent had generally behaved towards them during childhood (responsive, caring, critical, intrusive), and the parents' relationship with each other (affectionate, unhappy, argumentative) showed that the best predictor of adult attachment type was the respondent's perceptions of the quality of their relationship with each parent and of the parents' relationship with each other.

A second study, making up for possible limitations of bias in the first, was based on the data from 108 undergraduates (thirty-eight men and seventy women, 75 per cent of whom were eighteen years old). The results were highly similar to the first study: 56 per cent were secure, 23 per cent avoidant and 20 per cent were anxious/ambivalent. Similar characterisations of love experiences were found in each group.

LOVE AND WORK: AN ATTACHMENT-THEORY PERSPECTIVE

In a second paper, Hazan and Shaver (1990) extended their research on adult attachment to include exploration, in order to explain some of the links between love and work and demonstrate the integrative and explanatory power of attachment theory. Two questionnaire studies indicated that the relations between adult attachment type and work orientation are similar to attachment/exploration dynamics in infancy and early childhood. The summarised results showed that secure attachment seems to support the most satisfying and healthiest approach to work. There was a high level of work satisfaction and subjects were confident that co-workers evaluated them highly. Work left time for friends and leisure activities, and relationships were valued more highly than work. Avoidant subjects preferred to work alone and used it to avoid having friends or a social life. They failed to take enjoyable vacations. Anxious/ambivalent subjects worried about their work performance, felt unappreciated and feared rejection for poor performance but nevertheless preferred to work closely with others. They were easily distracted and had trouble over completing projects, unless work was seen as an opportunity both to work closely with others and gain love and respect. They had difficulty in focusing on tasks and continuing to work after receiving praise.

CAREGIVING, ATTACHMENT AND SEXUAL BEHAVIOUR WITHIN ADULT ROMANTIC RELATIONSHIPS

Kunce and Shaver (1994) propose that adult romantic relationships can be conceptualised as involving attachment, caregiving and sexual behaviour. Their concern is to assess more accurately the determinants that affect the activation and expression of a person's caregiving behavioural system. In seeking to develop a reliable and valid self-report measure of caregiving in adult romantic relationships, they found that caregiving dimensions could be reasonably reduced to four: proximity versus distance; sensitivity versus insensitivity; co-operation versus control; and a dimension defined in terms of the degree of compulsive caregiving. Scales covering each dimension were constructed and their validity demonstrated in a preliminary way. Sensitivity to partner's cues and the provision of proximity emerged as two major caregiving dimensions, with co-operative interaction and compulsive caregiving as two other caregiving factors. Some limitations to these conclusions are discussed. For example, because the current studies are correlative in nature, their results cannot be used to draw conclusions about causal effects of attachment style on caregiving, although infant research shows that attachment emerges before caregiving. However, once established, a child's attachment style might exert further shaping on his caregiving behaviour. For example, anxious attachment may encourage a person to become an anxious intrusive caregiver. Secondly the design of the studies does not allow any conclusions about whether adult-to-adult caregiving style is based on caregiving received from parents.

Questionnaire about a prospective client for assessors to complete after assessment: to be used in association with the assessment procedure described in Chapter 13

How did the client relate to the assessor?

1 How avoidant was he? (information strands 1 and 3)
How much did this lessen/decrease or remain unchanged in the course of the session?
2 How much does the client approach the assessor in terms of the body language used and degree of initiative taken to converse? (information strands 1 and 3)
How much did this vary in the course of the session?
3 How mixed were the two styles and was one or other linked to any particular topic?
4 What levels of emotion were shown, what kind of emotion and about what topic or circumstance? (information strands 1 and 3)
5 In what manner did the client relate to the assessor – warmly, defensively, on guard or compliantly?

How did the client present their story?

1 How intelligent did the client appear to be?
2 How incomplete was the information given by the client and what was his earliest memories? (information strand 3)
3 How coherent and how organised was the presentation of information? If there was incoherence, how closely was this linked to a particular topic? (information strand 3)
4 How much evidence did the client give of being able to think of themselves and others using metacognitive skills?

The number and quality of the client's relationships

1 Who are the most supportive people within the client's attachment hierarchy?
2 Who ranks the highest and is it a primary or secondary attachment figure?
3 Who are the most frustrating people within the client's attachment hierarchy and are they primary or secondary attachment figures?
4 How many people pursue interests with the client, and what are the interests? Was the situation better or worse when a child or teenager?
5 Has the client got a satisfying sexual partnership, a frustrating one or mixed or none?
6 To what degree is the client monogamous or promiscuous?
7 To how many people is the client currently a caregiver? What are their ages?

The number and kind of traumatic life events and their spacing

1 Overall how traumatic has the client's past life been?
2 Did the client suffer serious traumata before the age of 3 years?
3 Were there patches of turbulence, and at what ages?
4 What quality of care did the client receive during turbulent periods and between them?

The balance kept between maturative aspirations and defensive idealisations and the quality of both

1 What degree of balance is kept between maturative aspirations and non-maturative idealisations in regard to self-care and management?
1b What form do the maturative aspirations take?
1c What form do the defensive idealisations take?
2 What degree of balance is kept between maturative aspirations and non-maturative idealisations in regard to caregiving?
2b What form do the maturative aspirations take?
2c What form do the defensive idealisations take?
3 What degree of balance is kept between maturative aspirations and non-maturative idealisations in regard to interest-sharing?
3b What form do the maturative aspirations take?

3c What form do the defensive idealisations take?

4 What degree of balance is kept between maturative aspirations
   and non-maturative idealisations in regard to intrapersonal activities (work and hobbies)?

4b What form do the maturative aspirations take?

4c What form do the defensive idealisations take?

5 What degree of balance is kept between maturative aspirations
   and non-maturative idealisations in regard to sexual relationships?

5b What form do the maturative aspirations take?

5c What form do the defensive idealisations take?

Bibliography

Ainsworth, M., Blehar, M., Waters, E. and Wall, S. (1978) *Patterns of Attachment: Assessed in the Strange Situation and at Home*, Hillsdale, New Jersey: Erlbaum.

Ainsworth, M. and Eichberg, C. (1991) 'Effects on infant–mother attachment of mother's unresolved loss of an attachment figure or other traumatic experience', in C. M. Parkes, J. Stevenson-Hinde and P. Marris (eds) *Attachment Across the Life Cycle*, London: Routledge.

Ansbacher, H. L. and R. R. (eds) (1964) *The Individual Psychology of Alfred Adler*, New York: Harper Row.

Arnold, M. B. (1960) *Emotion and Personality*, Vol. I and Vol. II, New York: Columbia University Press; London: Cassell 1961.

Astington, J. W., Harris, P. L. and Olson, D. R. (eds) (1988) *Developing Theories of Mind*, New York: Cambridge University Press.

Bacal, H. A. and Newman, K. M. (1990) *Theories of Object Relations: Bridges to Self Psychology*, New York: Columbia University Press.

Bailey, K. (1987) *Human Paleopsychology*, London: Lawrence Erlbaum Associates.

Balint, M. (1968) *The Basic Fault*, London: Tavistock.

Barach, P. M. M. (1991) 'Multiple personality disorder as an attachment disorder', *Dissociation*, 4: 117–23.

Bartholomew, K. and Horowitz, L. M. (1991) 'Attachment styles among young adults: a test of a four category model', *Journal of Personality and Social Psychology*, 61: 226–44.

Bartlett, F. (1932) *Remembering: A Study in Experimental and Social Psychology*, London: Cambridge University Press.

Bateson, G. (1968) 'Information and codification: a philosophical approach', in J. Ruesch and G. Bateson (eds) *Communication: the Social Matrix of Psychiatry*, New York: W. W. Norton (first published in 1951).

—— (1973) *Steps to an Ecology of Mind*, Paladin Books, especially pp.423–40.

Bibring, G. (1964) 'Some considerations regarding the Ego Ideal in the psychoanalytic process', *Journal of the American Psychoanalytic Association*, 12: 517–23.

Bion, W. R. (1961) *Experiences in Groups and other Papers*, London: Tavistock.

Birtchnell, J. (1993) *How Humans Relate: A New Interpersonal Theory*, Westpoint USA: Praeger.

Blos, P. (1962) *On Adolescence*, New York: The Free Press of Glencoe.

—— (1970)*The Young Adolescent: Clinical Studies*, New York: Free Press.

—— (1979) *The Adolescent Passage*, New York: International Universities Press.

Bollas, C. (1987) *The Shadow of the Object: Psychoanalysis of the Untaught Known*, London: Free Association Books.

Boniface, D. and Graham, P. (1979) 'The three year old and his attachment to a special soft object', *Journal of Child Psychology and Psychiatry*, 20: 217–24.

Bowlby, J. (1982) *Attachment and Loss*, vol. 1: *Attachment*, New York: Basic Books and London: Hogarth, first published in 1969.

—— (1973) *Attachment and Loss*, vol. 2: *Separation: Anxiety and Anger*, New York· Basic Books and London: Hogarth.

—— (1980) *Attachment and Loss*, vol. 3: *Loss: Sadness and Depression*, New York: Basic Books and London: Hogarth.

—— (1988) *A Secure Base*, London: Routledge especially Chapter 6, 'On knowing what you are not supposed to know and feeling what you are not supposed to feel', pp.99–118

Bretherton, I. and Ainsworth, M. D. S. (1974) 'Responses of one-year-olds to a stranger in a strange situation', in M. Lewis and L. A. Rosenblum (eds) *The Origin of Fear*, New York: Wiley.

Brown, D. and Pedder, J. (1979) *Introduction to Psychotherapy*, London: Tavistock.

Brown, G. W. and Harris, T. (1978) *Social Origins of Depression: A Study of Psychiatric Disorder in Women*, London: Tavistock Press.

Burns, G. J. (1992) 'Attachment theory: a useful conceptual framework in social work for clients who display challenging behaviour or personality disorders', unpublished MSW Thesis, University of York.

Byng-Hall, J. (1995) *Rewriting Family Scripts*, London: Guilford Press.

Cantril, H. (1950) *The Why of Man's Experience*, New York: MacMillan.

Cassidy, J. (1988) 'Child–mother attachment and the self at age six', *Child Development*, 57: 331–7.

—— (1990) 'Theoretical and methodological considerations in the study of attachment and self in young children', in M. T. Greenburg, D. Cicchetti and E. M. Cummings (eds) *Attachment in the Pre-school Years*, Chicago University Press.

Chance, M. R. A. (ed.) (1988) *Social Fabrics of the Mind*, Hove: Lawrence Erlbaum Associates.

Chasseguet-Smirgal, J. (1985) *The Ego Ideal*, London: Free Association Books.

Cicchetti, D. (ed.) (1989) *The Emergence of a Discipline*, Hillsdale New Jersey: Lawrence Erlbaum Associates.

Collins, N. L. and Read, S. J. (1994) 'Cognitive representations of attachment: the structure and function of working models', in K. Bartholomew and D. Perlman (eds) *Attachment Processes in Adulthood*, London: Jessica Kingsley Publishers.

Craik, K. (1967) *The Nature of Explanation*, Cambridge: Cambridge University Press.

Crittenden, P. M. (1990) 'Internal representational models of attachment relationships', *Infant Mental Health Journal*, 11: 259–77.

—— (1994) 'Attachment and psychopathology' in S. Goldberg, R. Muir and J. Kerr *Attachment Theory: Social Developmental and Clinical Perspectives*, Hillsdale, New Jersey: The Analytic Press.

—— (in press) 'The effect of early relationship experiences on relationships in adulthood', in S. Duck (ed.) *Handbook of Personal Relationships* 2nd edn, Chichester: Wiley.

Cummings, E. M. and Davies, P. T. (1994) 'Maternal depression and child development', *Journal of Child Psychology and Psychiatry*, 35: 73–112.

Decourcy, K. R. and Jenssen, T. A. (1994) 'Structure and use of male territorial headbob signals by the lizard *Anolis carolinensis*', *Animal Behaviour*, 47: 251–62.

Dewald, P. A. (1969) *Psychotherapy: A Dynamic Approach*, Oxford: Blackwell.

Dicks, H. V. (1967) *Marital Tensions*, London: Routledge and Kegan Paul.

Dixon, N. F. (1971) *Subliminal Perception: The Nature of a Controversy*, London: McGraw-Hill.

Downes, C. (1992) *Separation Revisited*, Aldershot: Ashgate.

Eagle, M. N. (1987) *Developments in Psychoanalysis. A Critical Evaluation*, Cambridge, Mass.: Harvard University Press.

Emde, R. N. (1988a) 'Development terminable and interminable I. Innate and motivational factors from infancy', *International Journal of Psycho-Analysis*, 69: 41–63.

—— (1988b) 'Development terminable and interminable II. Recent psychoanalytic theory and therapeutic considerations', *International Journal of Psycho-Analysis*, 69: 283–96

Emde, R. N., Biringen, Z., Clyman, R. B. and Oppenheim, D. (1991) 'The moral self of infancy: affective core and procedural knowledge', *Developmental Review*, 11: 251–70.

Erdelyi, M. H. (1974) 'A new look at the new look: perceptual defence and vigilance', *Psychological Review*, 81: 1–85.

Erikson, E. H. (1965) *Childhood and Society*, Harmondsworth: Penguin Books.

Fairbairn, R. (1952) *Psychoanalytic Studies of the Personality*, London: Tavistock.

Fernald, A. (1985) 'Four-month-old infants prefer to listen to motherese', *Infant Behaviour and Development*, 8: 181–95.

Flavell, J. H. (1963) *The Developmental Psychology of Jean Piaget*, Princeton, New Jersey: Van Nostrand.

Fonagy, P., Steele, H. and Steele, M. (1991) 'Maternal representations of attachment during pregnancy predict the organisation of infant–mother attachment at one year of age', *Child Development*, 62: 891–905.

Fonagy, P. and Target, M. (1996) 'Playing with reality: I', *International Journal of Psycho-Analysis*, 217–33.

Frank, J. D. (1971) 'Therapeutic factors in psychotherapy', *American Journal of Psychotherapy*, 25: 350–61.

—— (1979) 'What is psychotherapy?', in S. Bloch, (ed.) *An Introduction to the Psychotherapies*, Oxford University Press
Freud, S. (1914) 'On narcissism: an introduction', *Standard Edition of the Complete Psychological Works of Sigmund Freud*, SE 14, London: Hogarth.
—— (1915) 'Instincts and their vicissitudes', *SE* 14.
—— (1920) 'Beyond the pleasure principle', *SE* 18.
—— (1921) 'Group psychology and the analysis of the ego', *SE* 18.
—— (1925a) 'An autobiographical study', *SE* 20.
—— (1925b) 'Inhibitions, symptoms and anxiety', *SE* 20.
—— (1930) 'Civilisation and its discontents', *SE* 21.
Gilbert, P. (1984) *Depression: from Psychology to Brain State*, London: Lawrence Erlbaum Associates.
—— (1989) *Human Nature and Suffering*, Hove: Lawrence Erlbaum Associates.
—— 1992) *Depression: The Evolution of Powerlessness*, Hove: Lawrence Erlbaum Associates.
Goodman, A. (1991) 'Organic unity theory: The mind–body problem revisited', *American Journal of Psychiatry*, 148: 553–63.
Greenberg, M. T., Cicchetti, D. and Cummings, E. M. (1990) (eds) *Attachment in the Preschool Years*, Chicago: University of Chicago Press.
Grice, H. P. (1975) 'Logic and conversation', in P. Cole and J. L. Moran (eds) *Syntax and Semantics III: Speech Acts*, New York: Academic Press, pp. 41–58.
Griffen, D. W. and Bartholomew, K. (1994) 'The metaphysics of measurement: a case of adult attachment', in K. Bartholomew and D. Perlman (eds) *Attachment Processes in Adulthood*, London: Jessica Kingsley Publishers.
Guntrip, H. (1961) *Personality Structure and Human Interaction*, London: Hogarth.
—— (1968) *Schizoid Phenomena, Object Relations and the Self*, London: Hogarth.
—— (1975) 'My experience of analysis with Fairbairn and Winnicott', *International Review of Psycho-Analysis*, 2: 145–56.
Hadley, J. (1989) 'The neurobiology of motivational systems' a contribution in J. D. Lichtenberg *Psychoanalysis and Motivation*, New Jersey: The Analytic Press.
Hamilton, V. (1985) 'John Bowlby: an ethological basis for psychoanalysis', in J. Reppen (ed.) *Beyond Freud: A Study of Modern Psychoanalytic Theorists*, New York: Analytic Press.
Harlow, H. F. and Harlow, M. K. (1965) 'The affectional systems', in A. M. Schrier, Harlow, H. F. and Stollnitz, F. (eds) *Behaviour of Nonhuman Primates*, London: Academic Press.
Harris, P. L. (1994) 'The child's understanding of emotion: developmental change and the family environment', *Journal of Child Psychology and Psychiatry*, 35: 3–28.
Harter, S. and Budden, B. J. (1987) 'Children's understanding of the

simultaneity of two emotions: a five-stage developmental acquisition sequence', *Developmental Pathology*, 23: 288–99.

Hazan, C. and Shaver, P. (1987) 'Romantic love conceptualised as an attachment process', *Journal of Personality and Social Psychology*, 52: 511–24.

—— (1990) 'Love and work: an attachment-theoretical perspective', *Journal of Personality and Social Psychology*, 59: 270–80.

—— (in press) 'Attachment as an organisational framework for research on closer relationships', *Psychological Enquiry.*

Hazan, C. and Ziefman, D. (1994) 'Sex and the psychological tether', in K. Bartholomew and D. Perlman (eds) *Attachment Processes in Adulthood*, London: Jessica Kingsley Publishers.

Hazell, J. (ed.) (1994) *Personal Relations Therapy: the Collected Papers of H. J. S. Guntrip*, New Jersey and London: Aronson

Heard, D. H. (1978) 'From object relations to attachment theory', *British Journal of Medical Psychology*, 51: 67–76.

—— (1982) 'Family systems and the attachment dynamic', *Journal of Family Therapy*, 4: 99–116.

Heard, D. H. and Barrett, M. C. (1982) 'Attachment and the family relationships of children with specific reading disability', in C. M. Parkes and J. Stevenson-Hinde (eds) *The Place of Attachment in Human Behaviour*, London: Tavistock Publications.

Heard, D. H. and Lake, B. (1986) 'The attachment dynamic in adult life', *British Journal of Psychiatry*, 149: 430–9.

Henderson, S., Byrne, D. G. and Duncan-Jones, P. (1981) *Neurosis and the Social Environment*, Sydney: Academic Press.

Hewitt, P. L. and Flett, G. L. (1991) 'Perfectionism in the self and social contexts: conceptualisation, assessment, and association with psychopathology', *Journal of Personality and Social Psychology*, 60: 456–70.

Hinde, R. A. (1979) *Towards Understanding Relationships*, London: Academic Press.

Hinde, R. A. and Stevenson-Hinde, J. (1986) 'Relating childhood relationships to individual characteristics', in W. W. Hartup and Z. Rubin (eds) *Relationships and Development*, New Jersey: Lawrence Erlbaum Associates.

Hinshelwood, R. D. (1987) *What Happens in Groups*, London: Free Association Books.

Hobson, R. F. (1985) *Forms of Feeling*, London: Tavistock Publications.

Hofer, M. A. (1987) 'Early social relationships: a psychobiologist's view', *Child Development*, 58: 633–47.

Holmes, J. (1993) *John Bowlby and Attachment Theory*, London: Routledge.

Holmes, J. and Lindley, R. (1989) *The Values of Psychotherapy*, Oxford: Oxford University Press.

Horney, K. (1946) *Our Inner Conflicts*, London: Routledge and Kegan Paul.

Hutt, C. (1966) 'Exploration and play in children', *Symposium of the Zoological Society of London*, 18: 61–81.

Izard, C. E. (1993) 'Four systems for emotion activation: cognitive and noncognitive processes', *Psychological Review*, 100: 68–90.

Jacobson, E. (1954) 'The self and the object world', *Psychoanalytic Study of the Child*, 9: 75–127.

Johnson-Laird, P. N. (1983) *Mental Models: Towards a Cognitive Science of Language, Inference and Consciousness*, Cambridge, Mass.: Harvard University Press.

Jones, S. (1993) *The Language of the Genes*, London: Harper Collins.

Jung, C. G. (1953) 'Two essays on analytical psychology', *The Collected Works of C. G. Jung*, Vol. 7, Bollinger Series, New York: Pantheon Books.

—— (1954) 'The development of personality', *The Collected Works of C. G. Jung* Vol. 17.

Kagan, J. (1994) *Galen's Prophecy*, London: Free Association Books.

Kelly, G. A. (1955) *The Psychology of Personal Constructs*, Vols 1 and 2, New York: Norton.

Kernberg, O. (1980) *External World and External Reality*, New York: Aronson.

Kirkpatrick, L. A. (1994) 'The role of attachment in religious belief and behaviour', in K. Bartholomew and D. Perlman (eds) *Attachment Processes in Adults*, London: Jessica Kingsley Publishers.

Klerman, G. L., Weissman, M. M., Roundsaville, B. J. and Chevron. E. S. (1984) *Interpersonal Psychotherapy of Depression*, New York: Basic Books.

Klinger, E. (1977) *Meaning and Void*, Minneapolis: University of Minnesota Press.

Kobak, R. and Duemmler, S. (1994) 'Attachment and conversation: towards a discourse analysis of adolescent and adult security', in K. Bartholomew and D. Perlman (eds) *Attachment Processes in Adulthood*, London: Jessica Kingsley Publishers.

Kobak, R. and Sceery, A. (1988) 'Attachment in later adolescence: working models, affect regulation, and perception of self and others', *Child Development*, 59: 135–46.

Kohut, H. (1977) *The Restoration of the Self*, New York: International Universities Press.

Kohut, H. (1979) 'Four basic definitions of self psychology', paper presented to the workshop of Self Psychology, Chicago.

Kunce, L. J. and Shaver, P. R. (1994) 'An attachment-theoretical approach to caregiving in romantic relationships', in K. Bartholomew and D. Perlman (eds) *Attachment Processes in Adulthood*, London: Jessica Kingsley Publishers.

Lake, B. (1985) 'Concept of ego strength in psychotherapy', *British Journal of Psychiatry*, 147: 471–78.

——(1989) 'Psychological health and ego ideals', *Psychiatric Bulletin*, Abstracts Supplement, 2: 54.

Langer, S. (1967) *Mind: An Essay on Human Feeling*, Baltimore, Maryland: John Hopkins Press.

LeDoux, J. E. (1994) 'Emotion, memory and the brain', *Scientific American*, 6: 32–9.

Lewin, K. (1952) *Field Theory in Social Science*, London: Tavistock.
Lichtenberg, J. D. (1989) *Psychoanalysis and Motivation*, New Jersey: Analytic Press.
Liotti, G. (1992) 'Disorganised/disoriented attachment in the etiology of dissociative disorders', *Dissociation*, 5: 196–204.
McDougal, W. (1932) *The Energies of Men: A Study of the Fundamentals of Dynamic Psychology*, London: Methuen.
MacLean, P. D. (1990) *The Triune Brain in Evolution*, New York: Plenum Press.
Main, M. (1991) 'Metacognitive knowledge, metacognitive monitoring, and singular (coherent) vs. multiple (incoherent) model of attachment: findings and directions for future research', in C. M. Parkes, J. Stevenson-Hinde and P. Marris (eds) *Attachment across the Life Span*, London: Routledge.
—— (1995) 'Recent studies in attachment', in S. Goldberg, R. Muir and J. Kerr *Attachment Theory. Social Developmental and Clinical Perspectives*, Hillsdale, New Jersey: The Analytic Press.
Main, M. and Hesse, E. (1990) 'Parents' unresolved traumatic experiences are related to infant disorganised status: Is frightened and/or frightening parental behaviour the linking mechanism?', in M. T. Greenberg, D. Cicchetti and E. M. Cummings (eds) *Attachment in the Pre-school Years*, Chicago: The University of Chicago Press.
Main, M. and Goldwyn, R. (1989) 'Adult attachment rating and classification system', unpublished scoring manual, Department of Psychology, University of California: Berkeley.
Main, M. and Weston, D. (1981) 'The quality of the toddler's relationship to mother and to father: related to conflict behaviour and the readiness to establish new relationships', *Child Development*, 52: 932–40.
Main, M., Kaplan, N. and Cassidy, J. (1985) 'Security in infancy, childhood and adulthood: a move to the level of representation'. in I. Bretherton and E. Waters (eds) *Growing Points of Attachment Theory and Research*. Monographs of the Society for Research in Child Development 50 (1–2, Serial No. 209), 66–104.
Marvin, R. S. and Stewart, R. B. (1990) 'A family systems framework for the study of attachment', in M. T. Greenberg, D. Cicchetti and E. M. Cummings (ed.) *Attachment in the Pre-school Years*, University of Chicago Press.
Maslow, A. H. (1954) *Motivation and Personality*, New York: Harper Row.
Mattison, J. and Sinclair, I. (1979) *Mate and Stalemate*, Oxford: Blackwell.
Meares, R. and Hobson, R. (1977) 'The persecutory therapist', *British Journal of Medical Psychology*, 50: 349–39.
Meissner, W. W. (1984) *Psychoanalysis and Religious Experience*, New Haven: Yale University Press.
—— (1992) *The Psychology of a Saint Ignatius of Loyola*, London: Yale University Press.
Miller, G. A., Galanter, E. H. and Pribram, K. H. (1960) *Plans and the Structure of Behaviour*, New York: Holt, Rinehart and Winston.
Murray, L. (1992) 'The impact of postnatal depression on infant development', *Journal of Child Psychology and Psychiatry*, 33: 543–61.

Murray, L. and Trevarthen, C. (1985) 'Emotional regulation of interactions between two month olds and their mothers', in T. M. Field and N. A. Fox (eds) *Social Perception in Infants*, Hillsdale, New Jersey: Norwood.

Murray, L., Kempton, C., Woolgar, M. and Hooper, R. (1993) 'Depressed mother's speech to their infants and its relation to infant gender and cognitive development', *Journal of Child Psychology and Psychiatry*, 34: 1,083–101.

Muslin, H. L. (1985) 'Heinz Kohut: beyond the pleasure principle, contributions to psychoanalysis', in J. Reppen (ed.) *Beyond Freud*, New Jersey: The Analytic Press.

Nathanson, D. L. (1987) *The Many Faces of Shame*, London: Guilford Press.

Norman, D. A. (1976) *Memory and Attention: Introduction to Human Information Processing*, 2nd edn, New York: John Wiley.

Nunberg, H. (1932) *Principles of Psychoanalysis*, New York International Universities Press.

Ortony, A. and Turner, T. J. (1990) 'The primitive building blocks of other non-basic emotions', *Psychological Review*, 97: 315–31.

Ortony, A., Clore, G. L. and Collins, A. (1988) *The Cognitive Structure of Emotions*, Cambridge: Cambridge University Press.

Parkes, C. M. (1971) 'Psycho-social transitions: a field for study', *Social Science and Medicine*, 5: 101–115.

—— (1986) *Bereavement: Studies in Grief in Adult Life*, 2nd edn, London: Tavistock Press.

Parkes, C. M., Stevenson-Hinde, J. and Marris, P. (eds) (1991) *Attachment Across the Life Cycle*, London: Routledge.

Piaget, J. and Inhelder, B. (1948) *The Child's Conception of Space* (translated 1956), London: Routledge and Kegan Paul.

Piers, G. and Singer, M. (1953) *Shame and Guilt. A Psychoanalytic and Cultural Study*, Springfield, Illinois: Charles C. Thomas.

Price, J. S., Gardner, R., Gilbert, P. and Rohde, P. (1994) 'The social competition hypothesis of depression', *British Journal of Psychiatry*, 164: 309–35.

Reich, A. (1954) 'Early identification of archaic elements in the superego', *Journal of the American Psychoanalytic Association*, 2: 218–33.

Reite, M. and Field, T. (1985) *The Psychobiology of Attachment and Separation*, New York: Academic Press.

Rogers, C. R. (1961) *On Becoming a Person: A Therapist's view of Psychotherapy*, Boston: Houghton Mifflin

Rutter, M. and Rutter, M. (1992) *Developing Minds*, London: Penguin Books.

Ryle, A. (1990) *Cognitive–Analytic Therapy: Active Participation in Change*, Chichester: Wiley and Sons.

—— (1995) *Cognitive Analytic Therapy: Developments in Theory and Practice*, Chichester: Wiley and Son.

Sandler, J., Holder, A. and Meers, D. (1963) 'The ego ideal and the ideal self', *The Psychoanalytic Study of the Child*, 18: 139–58.

Sands, S. H. (1994) 'What is dissociated?', *Dissociation*, 7:145–52.

Schank, R. C. (1982) *Dynamic Memory*, Cambridge: Cambridge University Press.

Schneider, N. (1988) 'Primary envy and the creation of the ego ideal', *International Review of Psychoanalysis*, 15: 319–29.

Schore, A. N. (1994) *Affect Regulation and the Origin of the Self*, Hillsdale, New Jersey: Lawrence Erlbaum Associates.

Shapiro, D. (1995) 'Finding out how psychotherapists help people change', *Psychotherapy Research*, 5: 1–21.

Sorce, J. F., Emde, R. N. Campos, J. J. and Klinnert, M. D. (1985) 'Maternal emotional signalling and its effect on the visual cliff behaviour of one-year-olds', *Developmental Psychology*, 21: 195–200.

Sperry, R. W. (1987) 'Consciousness and causality', in R. L. Gregory (ed.) *The Oxford Companion to the Mind*, Oxford: Oxford University Press.

—— (1990) 'Forebrain commissurotomy and conscious awareness', in C. Trevarthen (ed.) *Brain Circuits and Functions of the Mind*, Cambridge: Cambridge University Press.

Steele, H. and Steele, M. (1994) 'Inter-generational patterns of attachment', in K. Bartholomew and D. Perlman (eds) *Attachment Processes in Adulthood*, London: Jessica Kingsley Publishers.

Steklis, H. D. and Kling. A. (1985) 'Neurobiology of affiliative behaviour in nonhuman primates', in M. Reite and T. Field (eds) *The Psychobiology of Attachment and Separation*, New York: Academic Press.

Stern, D. (1985) *The Interpersonal World of the Infant*, New York: Basic Books.

Stevens, A. (1982) *Archetype: The Natural History of the Self*, London: Routledge.

Stierlin, H. (1977) *Psychoanalysis and Family Therapy*, New York: Aronson.

Stratton, P., Heard, D., Hanks, H. G. I., Munton, A. G., Brewin, C. R. and Davidson, C. (1986) 'Coding causal beliefs in natural discourse', *British Journal of Social Psychology*, 25: 299–313.

Strupp, H. (1979) 'Specific vs nonspecific factors in psychotherapy', *Archives of General Psychiatry*, 36: 1,125–36.

Sutherland, J. D. (1971) 'The individual's relationships in the group', in H. Walton (ed.) *Small Group Psychotherapy*, Harmondsworth: Penguin Books.

——(1989) *Fairbairn's Journey into the Interior*, London: Free Association Books.

Suttie, I. D. (1935) *The Origins of Love and Hate*, London: Kegan Paul, Trench, Trubner and Co.

—— (1988) *The Origins of Love and Hate*, London: Free Association Books.

Target, M. and Fonagy, P. (1996) 'Playing with reality: II' *International Journal of Psycho-Analysis*, 77: 459–79.

Trevarthen, C. (1979) 'Communication and co-operation in early infancy: a description of primary subjectivity', in M. Bullova (ed.) *Before Speech: The Beginning of Interpersonal Communication*, New York: Cambridge University Press.

—— (1990) 'Editor's preface', 'Growth and education of the hemispheres', in C. Trevarthen (ed.) *Brain Circuits and Functions of the Mind*, Cambridge: Cambridge University Press.

Tulving, E. (1985) 'How many memory systems are there?', *American Psychologist*, 40: 385–395.

Turner, T. J. and Ortony, A. (1992) 'Basic emotions: can conflicting criteria converge', *Psychological Review*, 99: 566–71.

Vaux, A. (1988) *Social Support: Theory, Research and Intervention*, New York: Praeger.

von Bertalanffy, L. (1968) 'General systems theory – a critical review', in W. Buckley (ed.) *Modern System Research for the Behavioural Scientist*, Chicago: Aldine.

Vygotsky, L. S. (1978) *Mind in Society*, M. Cole, V. John-Steiner, S. Scribner and E. Souberman (eds), Cambridge, Mass.: Harvard University Press, especially pp.79–91.

Waddington, C. H. (1957) *The Strategy of the Genes*, London: Allen and Unwin.

Weiss, R. S. (1974) 'The provisions of social relationships', in Z. Rubin (ed.) *Doing unto Others*, New Jersey: Prentice-Hall.

—— (1986) 'Continuities and transformations in social relationships from childhood to adulthood', in W. W. Hartup and Z. Rubin (eds) *Relationships and Development*, New Jersey: Lawrence Erlbaum.

Winnicott, D. W. (1958) *Collected Papers through Paediatrics to Psychoanalysis*, London: Tavistock.

—— (1965) *The Maturational Processes and the Facilitating Environment*, London: Hogarth.

—— (1971) *Playing and Reality*, London: Tavistock.

Woodworth, R. S. and Sheehan, M. S. (1965) *Contemporary Schools of Psychology*, London: Methuen.

Wurmser, L. (1981) *The Mask of Shame*, Baltimore: John Hopkins University Press.

Young, J. Z. (1964) *A Model of the Brain*, London: Oxford University Press.

Author index

Subject index